"十四五"职业教育国家规划教材

经全国职业教育教材审定委员会审定

旅行社经营与管理实务（第三版）

Handbook of the Operations and Management of Travel Agencies

主　编　梁　峰　叶设玲
副主编　叶　业　刘一览　吴　胜
主　审　杨　进

南京大学出版社

图书在版编目(CIP)数据

旅行社经营与管理实务 / 梁峰,叶设玲主编.
3版. — 南京:南京大学出版社,2025.3. — ISBN 978-7-305-29183-8

Ⅰ.F590.63

中国国家版本馆CIP数据核字第2025NW2936号

出版发行	南京大学出版社		
社　　址	南京市汉口路22号	邮　编	210093

书　　名　**旅行社经营与管理实务**
　　　　　LÜXINGSHE JINGYING YU GUANLI SHIWU
主　　编　梁　峰　叶设玲
责任编辑　裴维维　　　　　　　　编辑热线　025-83592123

照　　排　南京南琳图文制作有限公司
印　　刷　南京玉河印刷厂
开　　本　787 mm×1092 mm　1/16开　印张11.75　字数299千
版　　次　2025年3月第3版
印　　次　2025年3月第1次印刷
ISBN 978-7-305-29183-8
定　　价　45.00元

网址:http://www.njupco.com
官方微博:http://weibo.com/njupco
微信服务号:njuyuexue
销售咨询热线:(025) 83594756

* 版权所有,侵权必究
* 凡购买南大版图书,如有印装质量问题,请与所购
　图书销售部门联系调换

前　言

旅游业是"一带一路"经济带建设的战略性先导产业,具有强大的动力产业功能和广泛的联动效应,为构建人类命运共同体提供了新支点。随着越来越多的国家和地区拥护和践行"一带一路"倡议,旅游潜力必将得到更大的释放,旅行社的健康发展必将对区域旅游业的繁荣发挥更大的作用。在此背景下,旅游院校理应担负起旅游人才培养的责任。作为知识和思想的载体,以及来自实践又能指导实践的理论概括类教材,其既具有基础性又具有前瞻性的特点,使得它成为高质量人才培养的首要保证。

我国历史上第一家旅行社诞生于20世纪20年代,在百年的发展历程中,旅行社业进入了由数量增长到质量提升的转型升级新阶段。在此过程中,我国旅行社业的分工体系也发生了一些新的变化,逐渐将垂直分工体系的流程再造理念植入到旅行社业的发展过程,并形成了中国特色的基于混合分工体系的现代旅行社业务流程。

正是基于这样的认识,我们编写了本教材。教材以国家职业标准和行业标准为依据,在内容体系构建上进行了大胆的探索,针对旅行社主要业务模块和业务流程,优化重组知识结构和能力框架,将教材内容划分为旅行社概述、旅行社客源市场细分、旅行社产品研发与设计、旅行社计调与采购管理、旅行社分销渠道管理、旅行社促销管理、旅行社接待业务管理、旅行社服务质量和财务管理等九个模块,强化学生对旅行社岗位能力的系统认知,使学生掌握作为一名合格的旅行社服务和管理人员必须具备的各种实务知识和综合实践能力。

教材根据新时代学生的特点,理论阐述简明扼要,操作流程条理清晰,便于读者借鉴。建议分别从了解、熟悉、掌握三个能力层次对本书内容予以把握。

——了解,要求对旅行社行业相关知识能够准确再认、再现,即知道"是什么";

——熟悉,在了解的基础上,能够深刻领会旅行社行业的运作流程,即明白"为什么";

——掌握,要求能够灵活运用相关知识和方法,综合分析、解决旅行社运营与管理过程中的理论和实际问题,即清楚"怎么办"。

为引导学生学思用贯通、知信行统一,把党的二十大精神落实到旅行社经营管理业务全流程和全过程,教材每一章首页都增加了党的二十大报告原文重要语句的摘录;每一章拓展教学资源都增加了旅行社相关领域或行业学习、贯彻、落实党的二十大精神的工作思路、具体举措和基层案例,致力于更快更好更准确地推动党的二十大精神落地见效。

  本书可作为国内旅游管理类及相关专业教材,也可作为企事业单位相关从业人员业务素质提升的拓展培训用书,更是"一带一路"国家和地区国际留学生不可多得的双语参考教材。为方便广大师生教学和读者自学,教材附送电子课件和实训指导书(电子稿),作为对本书内容的补充和延伸。由于编者学识有限,书中难免存在错漏之处,恳请各位专家、同行和广大读者批评指正,以臻完善!

编 者

2025年3月于无锡大学城

目 录

第一章　旅行社概述 …………………………………………………………… 001
第一节　旅行社的基本业务与分工体系 …………………………………… 002
第二节　旅行社的设立 ……………………………………………………… 009
实训项目 01　旅行社设立申请书制作 …………………………………… 017

第二章　旅游市场细分、选择与定位 ………………………………………… 019
第一节　旅游市场细分 ……………………………………………………… 020
第二节　旅游目标市场选择 ………………………………………………… 024
第三节　旅游市场定位 ……………………………………………………… 027
实训项目 02　旅行社产品目标市场分析报告 …………………………… 031

第三章　旅行社产品研发与设计 ……………………………………………… 033
第一节　旅行社产品的含义与类型 ………………………………………… 034
第二节　旅行社产品的开发流程 …………………………………………… 039
第三节　旅行社产品的评价与筛选 ………………………………………… 048
实训项目 03　旅行社产品设计与开发 …………………………………… 055

第四章　旅行社计调与采购管理 ……………………………………………… 057
第一节　旅行社计调业务概述 ……………………………………………… 058
第二节　旅行社产品要素采购及供应链管理 ……………………………… 063
第三节　旅游服务采购的内容 ……………………………………………… 069
第四节　旅游产品定价 ……………………………………………………… 072
实训项目 04　旅行社计调工作方案设计 ………………………………… 079

第五章　旅行社分销渠道管理 ………………………………………………… 081
第一节　旅游中间商的类型 ………………………………………………… 082
第二节　分销渠道的概念及类型 …………………………………………… 086
第三节　销售渠道的选择 …………………………………………………… 091
第四节　分销渠道的发展趋势 ……………………………………………… 097

实训项目 05　旅行社分销渠道设计 …………………………………………… 103

第六章　旅行社促销管理 ……………………………………………………………… 105
第一节　旅行社促销概述 …………………………………………………………… 106
第二节　旅行社产品促销运作流程 ………………………………………………… 109
第三节　促销效果的评估 …………………………………………………………… 116
　　实训项目 06　旅行社促销方案设计 …………………………………………… 121

第七章　旅行社接待业务管理 ………………………………………………………… 123
第一节　旅行社接待概述 …………………………………………………………… 124
第二节　团队旅游接待业务 ………………………………………………………… 127
第三节　散客及特殊旅游接待 ……………………………………………………… 132
第四节　旅行社同业批发业务管理 ………………………………………………… 137
　　实训项目 07　旅行社接待计划的制订 ………………………………………… 141

第八章　旅行社服务质量管理 ………………………………………………………… 143
第一节　旅行社服务质量概述 ……………………………………………………… 144
第二节　旅行社服务质量的评估 …………………………………………………… 148
第三节　旅行社服务质量的控制与改进 …………………………………………… 152
　　实训项目 08　旅行社服务质量方案 …………………………………………… 155

第九章　旅行社财务管理 ……………………………………………………………… 157
第一节　旅行社资产管理 …………………………………………………………… 158
第二节　成本费用管理 ……………………………………………………………… 163
第三节　营业收入与利润的管理 …………………………………………………… 167
第四节　旅行社的财务分析 ………………………………………………………… 174
　　实训项目 09　旅行社财务报表分析 …………………………………………… 178

参考文献 ………………………………………………………………………………… 180

Contents

Chapter One   An Overview of Travel Agencies ················ 001
   Section One   The Basic Business Structure and Division System of Travel
                 Agencies ·· 002
   Section Two   The Establishment of Travel Agencies ·············· 009
   Project 1   Submit an Application to Establish a Travel Agency ········ 017

Chapter Two   Segmentation, Targeting and Positioning in Tourism Market ········ 019
   Section One   Segmentation of the Tourism Market ················· 020
   Section Two   Tourism Market Targeting ·························· 024
   Section Three   Tourism Market Positioning ······················ 027
   Project 2   Conduct a Target Market Analysis Report for Travel Agnecy
           Products ·· 031

Chapter Three   Research and Design for Travel Agency Products ············· 033
   Section One   Definition and Types of Travel Agency Products ········ 034
   Section Two   The Development Process of Travel Agency Products ···· 039
   Section Three   Evaluation and Screening of Travel Agency Products ······ 048
   Project 3   Prepare a Presentation on the Design and Development of Travel
           Agency Products ··· 055

Chapter Four   The Operations and Procurement of Travel Agencies ·············· 057
   Section One   An Overview of the Operations of Travel Agencies ········ 058
   Section Two   The Procurement of Travel Agency Products and Supply Chain
                Management ······································· 063
   Section Three   The Components of Tourism Service Procurement ········ 069
   Section Four   Pricing Strategies for Tourism Products ················· 072
   Project 4   Design a Work Programme for the Operators in Travel Agencies
           ·· 079

Chapter Five   Distribution Channel Management in Travel Agencies ············· 081
   Section One   Types of Tourism Intermediaries ····················· 082

Section Two　Definition and Types of Distribution Channels ………… 086

　　Section Three　Selection of Sales Channels ……………………………… 091

　　Section Four　Development Trends of Distribution Channels …………… 097

　　Project 5　Design Distribution Channels for Travel Agencies …………… 103

Chapter Six　Promotion Management for Travel Agencies ……………… 105

　　Section One　An Overview of Travel Agency Promotion ………………… 106

　　Section Two　The Procedure of Product Promotion in Travel Agencies …… 109

　　Section Three　Evaluation of the Promotion Effect ……………………… 116

　　Project 6　Design a Promotion Mix for Travel Agencies ………………… 121

Chapter Seven　Management of Reception in Travel Agencies …………… 123

　　Section One　An Overview of Travel Agency Reception ………………… 124

　　Section Two　Reception of Group Tour …………………………………… 127

　　Section Three　Reception Services for Individual and Special Tourists …… 132

　　Section Four　Management of Inter-industry Wholesale Business in Travel
　　　　　　　　　Agencies …………………………………………………… 137

　　Project 7　Make a Reception Plan for Travel Agencies …………………… 141

Chapter Eight　Service Quality Management in Travel Agencies ………… 143

　　Section One　An Overview of Service Quality in Travel Agencies ……… 144

　　Section Two　Evaluation of Service Quality in Travel Agencies ………… 148

　　Section Three　Strategies for Controlling and Improving Service Quality in Travel
　　　　　　　　　Agencies …………………………………………………… 152

　　Project 8　Design a Service Quality Scheme for Travel Agencies ………… 155

Chapter Nine　Financial Management in Travel Agencies ………………… 157

　　Section One　Asset Management in Travel Agencies …………………… 158

　　Section Two　Management of Costs and Expenses ……………………… 163

　　Section Three　Revenue and Profits Management ……………………… 167

　　Section Four　Financial Analysis of Travel Agencies …………………… 174

　　Project 9　Conduct a Financial Performance Analysis for Travel Agencies … 178

References …………………………………………………………………… 180

第一章　旅行社概述
Chapter One　An Overview of Travel Agencies

> 【学习目标】　Learning Objectives
>
> 1. 理解旅行社分工体系(division system)及主要业务流程(main business processes)。
> 2. 掌握旅行社设立的程序及要求(procedures and requirements for the establishment of travel agencies)。

> 构建优质高效的服务业新体系，推动现代服务业同先进制造业、现代农业深度融合。
>
> ——党的二十大报告摘录

✓本章课程视频讲解　　✓实训指导书
✓线上课堂链接　　　　✓优秀学生作品精选
✓本章训练题库　　　　✓时政新闻
✓本章拓展资源

第一节　旅行社的基本业务与分工体系
Section One　The Basic Business Structure and Division System of Travel Agencies

1　Basic Business Structure of Travel Agencies

According to Travel Agency Regulations(the third revision of "Decision of the State Council on Amending and Repealing Some Administrative Regulations" on November 29, 2020), "Travel agency refers to business entities that attract, organize and receive tourists, provide tourists with relevant tourism services, engaged in domestic tourism business, inbound tourism business or outbound tourism business."

一、旅行社的基本业务

根据《旅行社条例》(2020年11月29日《国务院关于修改和废止部分行政法规的决定》第三次修订)规定:"旅行社,是指从事招徕、组织、接待旅游者等活动,为旅游者提供相关旅游服务,开展国内旅游业务、入境旅游业务或者出境旅游业务的企业法人。"旅行社开展的业务主要有以下几个方面。

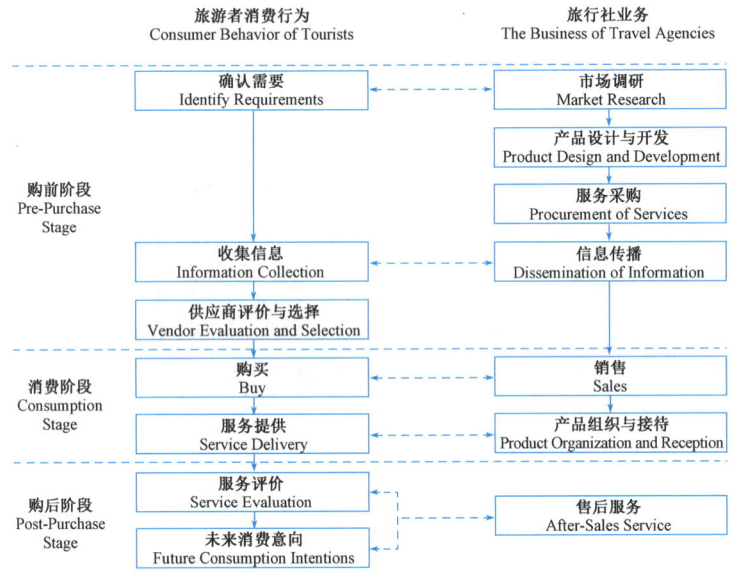

图1-1　旅行社基本业务流程图
Basic Business Flowchart of Travel Agencies

1.1　Tourism Market Survey and Forecast

(一)旅游市场调研与预测

旅游市场调研即运用科学的方法和手段,有目的地针对旅游市场需求的数量、结构特征等信息以及变化趋势(quantity, characteristics and trend of tourism market demands)所进行的调查与研究。

经济全球化(economic globalization)背景下,市场的无国界化(borderless market)导致市场范围迅速扩大,消费者的需求也越来越多样化和多变化(becoming more and more diversified and changeable),如何分析市场、发现市场和确定市场已是企业关注的关键问题。对于旅游企业而言,充分"透视"旅游市场(to fully "see through" the tourism market)并成功地开发和满足旅游市场需求,即开展旅游市场调查与预测,是旅游企业经营管理的前提条件(the prerequisite for the operation and management of tourism enterprises)。

旅游市场调研与预测有利于旅游企业获取正确的市场信息,提前作出应变安排,从而有效避免旅游企业制定错误的营销策略,最大限度地谋求利益,但是这项业务常常被旅游企业所忽视。

(二)旅行社产品设计与开发

1.2　Research and Design for Travel Agency Products

按照旅行社业务流程,第二项基本业务是产品设计与开发(research and design),包括产品设计、产品试产与试销(pilot production and sale)、产品投放市场(product launching)和产品效果检查评估(effect evaluation)四项内容。首先,旅行社根据旅游市场需求的调查分析和预测(analysis and forecast),结合本旅行社的业务特点、经营实力及各种旅游服务供应的状况,设计出各种能够对旅游者产生较强吸引力的产品(design a variety of attractive products);其次,进行小批量试产和试销,以考查产品的质量(investigate the quality of the products)和旅游者对其喜爱的程度(the degree how much tourists love them);再次,当产品试销成功后(after successful trial sale),旅行社将产品批量投放市场(put the mass products into the market),以便扩大销路(expand sales),加速产品投资的回收(accelerate the recovery of product investment)和赚取经营利润(earn profits);最后,旅行社定期对投放市场(put into the market)的各种产品进行检查和评价,并根据结果对产品进行完善和改进。

(三)旅游服务的采购业务

1.3　The Tourism Procurement

旅行社的第三项基本业务是旅游采购。旅游采购业务是指旅行社为了生产旅游产品而向有关旅游服务供应部门或企业购买各种旅游服务项目的业务活动。旅行社的采购业务主要涉及交通(transportation)、住宿(accommodation)、餐饮(ca-

Tourism procurement business refers to the business activities of travel agencies purchasing various tourism services from relevant tourism service providers or companies in order to produce tourism products.

tering)、景点游览(tourist attractions)、娱乐和保险(entertainment and insurance)等部门。另外,针对组团业务,旅行社还需要向旅游路线沿途的各地接待旅行社采购接待服务(local reception agencies along the travel routes)。

1.4 Tourism Products Distribution Business

(四)旅行社产品的分销业务

旅行社产品销售是旅行社的第五项基本业务,包括制定产品销售战略、选择产品销售渠道、制定产品销售价格和开展旅游促销四项内容。首先,旅行社应对其所处的外部环境(external environment)和企业内部条件(internal conditions)进行SWOT分析,在此基础上制定产品销售战略;其次,旅行社根据所制定的产品销售战略(formulate sales strategy)和确定的目标市场选择适当的产品销售渠道(choose appropriate channels for products);再次,旅行社根据产品成本(product costs)、市场需求(market demand)、竞争者状况(competitors' conditions)等因素制定产品的价格;最后,旅行社根据其经营实力和目标市场确定和实施旅行社的促销战略(determine and implement their promotion strategies),并选择适当的促销手段以便将旅行社产品的信息传递到客源市场(transfer the information of the products to the source market),引起旅游者的购买欲望(arouse tourists' purchasing desire),销售更多的产品。

1.5 Promotion Management for Travel Agencies

(五)旅行社促销管理

缺乏有效的信息沟通(lack effective information communication),消费者和用户对旅游企业的情况便一无所知,旅游产品最终将难以实现销售。促销的本质和核心(the essence and core of promotion)是信息沟通,而这种沟通大多是通过企业的促销活动来实现的。促销管理是以提高销售额为目的,吸引、刺激消费者消费的一系列计划、组织、领导、控制和协调管理的工作(a series of planning, organization, leadership, control and coordination management)。促销通过利用媒体广告、人员推销、公共关系等方式进行阶段性造势,并刺激销量、塑造品牌(stimulate sales and shape the brand)。促销管理是市场营销管理中最复杂、最富技巧,也最具风险的一个环节,当然也是有才华的企业家最能大显身手的领域。每家企业、每个企业家都可以在这一领域中显示其独特个性,以创造市场销售的奇迹(in order to create a miracle of market sales)。

（六）旅行社接待业务

1. 团体接待业务

团体旅游接待业务是旅行社的第四项基本业务。旅行社通过向旅游团队提供接待服务（provide reception services），最终实现包价旅游的生产与销售（achieve the production and sales of package tour）。团体旅游接待业务由生活接待服务和导游讲解服务（interpretation service）构成。

2. 散客旅游业务

旅行社的第五项基本业务是散客旅游业务。这是一项以散客旅游者为目标市场的旅游服务业务。散客旅游业务包括单项旅游服务业务、旅游咨询业务和选择性旅游服务业务。

（七）旅行社的售后服务

售后服务，从字面上来理解就是在产品销售的基础上，为消费者提供的后续服务的总和。售后服务主要有三种表现方式：一是对旅游者进行信息追踪，例如打问候电话（make greeting calls），填写意见征询单（fill in consultation forms）；二是旅游服务质量管理及处理旅游投诉（handle tourism complaints）；三是给旅游者传递旅行社信息，例如给旅游者发送节日问候，定期寄送旅行社宣传材料以及邀请顾客参加旅行社的开放活动（participate in the opening activities）等。

旅行社售后服务是指旅行社在旅游活动结束之后，继续向游客提供的一系列服务，以主动解决客人遇到的问题，以及加强同客人的联系。旅行社仅有高质量的接待服务（high-quality reception service）是不够的，良好的售后服务是优质接待工作的延续，可向游客提供新的信息并从游客那里得到意见反馈（receive feedback from tourists），不仅可以维持和扩大原有的客源，还可以不断更新产品内容，提高接待服务水平，让旅行社在激烈的市场竞争中（in the fierce market competition）立于不败之地。

二、旅行社的分工体系

旅行社的分工体系是指不同类别的旅行社在各个市场区域和旅游产品流通环节中所扮演的角色及其相互之间的关系。随着旅行社行业规模的不断扩大，行业内部也开始经历一个长期演变的生产分工过程（experience a long-term evolution of

---

1.6 Reception Services in Travel Agencies

1.6.1 Group reception business

1.6.2 Individual tourist business

Individual tourist business includes single tour service business, tourism consulting business and selective tour service business.

1.7 After-Sales Service

2 The Division System of Travel Agencies

2.1 Vertical Division System

The vertical division of labor system is composed of travel agencies performing different functions, which is successively undertaken and complementary in time and divided into travel operators, travel wholesalers and travel retailers.

the division of production process)。由于各国旅行社行业发展水平(development level)和经营环境(operating environment)的不同,旅行社行业分工的形成机制(formation mechanism)和具体分工状况存在较大差异(great differences),并由此形成了全球范围内(on a global scale)具有一般代表意义的(general representative significance)垂直分工(vertical division)体系和水平分工(horizontal division)体系。

(一)垂直分工体系

欧美发达国家的(developed countries in Europe and America)旅行社,其分工基本是在旅行社的发展进程中自然形成的(naturally),大都采用垂直分工体系(adopt the vertical division system)。垂直分工体系由执行不同职能的旅行社组成,这些职能在时间上先后承接并具有互补关系,分为旅游经营商、旅游批发商和旅游零售商。

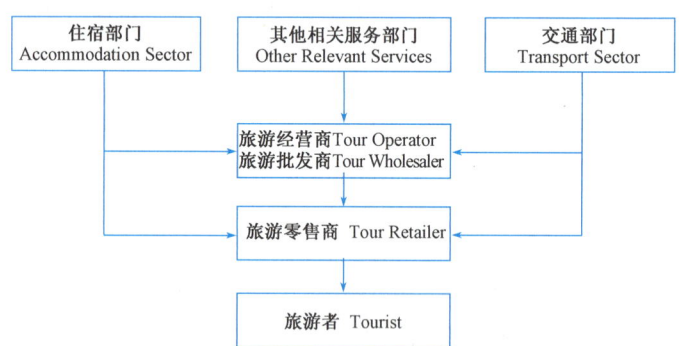

图1-2 垂直分工模式下的旅行社服务体系
Travel Agency Service System Based on Vertical Division of Labor

Tourist operator is a travel agency that designs, organizes and sells tourist products.

(1)旅游经营商是指那些设计、组织并销售旅游产品的旅行社。它们按照预先设计的旅游线路和年度销售计划(based on pre-designed tourist routes and annual sales plans),以优惠的价格向交通部门、酒店和旅游景点等部门预订产品,批量购买(purchase in bulk),然后对其进行编排和组合,形成不同的旅游产品(organize and combine them into different tourism products),通过旅游代理商销售给旅游者。拥有自己零售网点的经营商也可以自行销售产品。这类旅行社的规模较大,数量相对较少,利润来自其包价产品的成本加价(cost plus)。

(2)旅游批发商是指通过购买并组合现成的服务(purchase and combine ready-made services),形成新的包价旅游产品

(form new package tour),借助中间人(如旅游零售商)出售包价旅游产品的旅行社(sell package tour products through intermediaries such as tourism retailers),一般不从事零售业务(generally not engaged in retail business)。

(3)旅游零售商是指直接面向广大公众从事旅游零售业务的中间商,一般不预定旅游供给部门的产品,也不组合旅游产品(do not order the products of the basic tourism supply department, nor do they combine tourism products),而是通过签订契约(through the signing of contracts)销售旅游经营商或旅游批发商的旅游线路(sell tourist routes of tour operators or tour wholesalers),或代理饭店、航空公司等部门的产品,然后从经营商或批发商或者其他的供给部门那里以佣金的形式取得报酬(get remuneration in the form of commissions from operators or wholesalers or other supply departments)。

Tourism retailers directly engage in tourism retail business for the general public.

(二) 水平分工体系

旅行社的水平分工体系是与市场机制主导下(under the leadership of the market mechanism)的垂直分工体系相对应的一个概念,它由执行同一职能(perform the same function)的旅行社按照服务的市场和业务范围分化而成。一般表现形式通常是在政府行业管理力量的干预下(usually under the intervention of government management),旅行社被分为若干等级和类别(divided into several levels and categories),原本统一的旅游服务市场也被划分为入境旅游、国内旅游和出境旅游等若干子市场,这样,每一类别或等级的旅行社对应经营相应的子市场。

2.2 Horizontal Division System

Several sub-markets such as inbound tourism, domestic tourism and outbound tourism

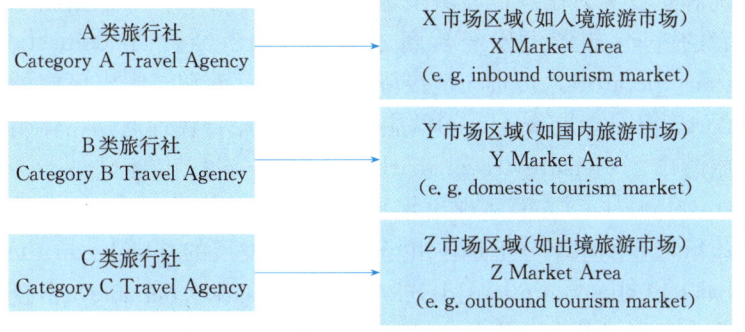

图1-3 政府主导下的旅行社水平分工体系
Government-Led Horizontal Division System in Travel Agencies

以中国为例(take China as an example),1985年,《旅行社

管理暂行条例》(Interim Regulations on the Administration of Travel Agencies)颁布,将旅行社划分为一类、二类和三类社,其中一、二类社为国际旅行社,三类社为国内旅行社。1996年10月,国务院颁布《旅行社管理条例》,将旅行社按经营业务范围划分为国际旅行社(international travel agencies)和国内旅行社(domestic travel agencies)两类,取消了一类社和二类社的界限(erase the boundaries)。尽管有以上两种分类方法,但是各类旅行社的基本业务都涉及经营活动的每个环节,既具有旅游批发商组织包价旅游产品的职能,又包括旅行代理商产品销售的职能,两者的区别仅在于服务市场领域差异。

需要指出的是,在垂直分工基础上,欧美的旅游批发商和旅行代理商(travel wholesalers and travel agents)根据市场状况和企业实力在各自领域中也进行了水平分工。如根据旅游者的流向,旅游批发经营商分为国内旅游经营商(domestic tour operators)、负责入境接待的旅游经营商和组织出境旅游(organize outbound tour)的旅游经营商;旅行代理商则在休闲旅游市场(leisure travel market)和商务旅行市场(business travel market)方面呈现出水平分工的发展态势。不过,欧美旅行社业的水平分工是在市场需求不断发展的基础上(on the basis of the continuous development of market demand),由企业自发形成的专业化分工,这与我国旅行社的水平分工体系在形成机制和表现形式上有本质区别。

This is fundamentally different from the horizontal division of labor system of travel agencies in China.

第二节 旅行社的设立
Section Two The Establishment of Travel Agencies

一、旅行社的设立要求及程序

(一) 基本要求

根据《旅行社条例》(Travel Agency Regulations)第六条规定,申请设立旅行社,经营国内旅游业务和入境旅游业务的,应当具备下列条件:

(1) 取得企业法人资格(corporate legal person status);

(2) 有不少于30万元的注册资本(no less than 300,000 RMB of registered capital)。

(二) 基本程序

根据《旅行社条例》第七条规定,申请设立旅行社,经营国内旅游业务和入境旅游业务的,应当向所在地省、自治区、直辖市旅游行政管理部门或者其委托的设区的市级旅游行政管理部门提出申请,并提交符合本条例第六条规定的相关证明文件(submit relevant certification documents)。受理申请的旅游行政管理部门应当自受理申请之日起20个工作日内做出许可或者不予许可的决定(decide whether to grant or not within 20 working days)。

予以许可的(permit is granted),向申请人颁发旅行社业务经营许可证(issue travel agency business operation license to the applicant),申请人持旅行社业务经营许可证向工商行政管理部门办理设立登记;不予许可的,书面通知申请人(be notified in writing)并说明理由。

(三) 经营出国旅游业务的条件

根据《旅行社条例》第八条规定,旅行社取得经营许可满两年(has obtained a business license for two years),且未因侵害旅游者合法权益受到行政机关罚款以上处罚的,可以申请经营出境旅游业务(apply for the operation of outbound tourism business)。

---

1 Requirements and Procedures for the Establishment

1.1 Basic Requirements

Applicants for the establishment of travel agencies to operate domestic and inbound tourism businesses shall meet the following requirements.

1.2 Basic Procedure

Those who apply for the establishment of travel agencies to operate domestic and inbound tourism businesses shall apply to the local tourism administrative departments.

1.3 Conditions for Travel Agencies to Operate Travel Services Abroad

申请经营出境旅游业务的,应当向国务院旅游行政主管部门或者其委托的省、自治区、直辖市(province, autonomous region or municipality directly under the Central Government)旅游行政管理部门提出申请(be submitted to),同第七条向申请人换发(renew)旅行社业务经营许可证,旅行社应当持换发的旅行社业务经营许可证到工商行政管理部门办理变更登记;不予许可的,书面通知申请人并说明理由(notify the applicant in writing and explain the reasons)。

1.4 The Establishment of Branches and Service Networks

(四) 分社及服务网点的设立

1. 分社的设立

1.4.1 The establishment of branches

根据《旅行社条例》第十条规定,旅行社设立分社(establish a branch)的,应当向分社所在地的工商行政管理部门办理设立登记,并自设立登记之日起3个工作日内(within three working days)向分社所在地的旅游行政管理部门备案。

旅行社分社的设立不受地域限制(is not subject to geographical restrictions)。分社的经营范围不得超出设立分社的旅行社的经营范围(operation range)。

1.4.2 The establishment of service networks

2. 服务网点的设立

根据《旅行社条例》第十一条规定,旅行社设立专门招徕旅游者、提供旅游咨询(specialize in attracting tourists and providing tourism consultation)的服务网点(service networks)(以下简称旅行社服务网点)应当依法向工商行政管理部门办理设立登记手续(go through the formalities for registration),并向所在地的旅游行政管理部门备案。

旅行社服务网点应当接受旅行社的统一管理(shall be under the incorporated management),不得从事招徕、咨询以外的活动(shall not engage in activities other than solicitation and consultation)。

1.5 Change of Registration Matters of Travel Agencies

(五) 旅行社登记事项的变更

根据《旅行社条例》第十二条规定,旅行社变更名称、经营场所、法定代表人(legal representative)等登记事项或者终止经营(terminate its business)的,应当到工商行政管理部门办理相应的变更登记或者注销登记(corresponding registration of change or cancellation),并在登记办理完毕之日起10个工作日内,向原许可的旅游行政管理部门备案,换领或者交回旅行社业务经营许可证。

(六) 质量保证金的相关规定

1. 质量保证金的缴存

根据《旅行社条例》第十三条规定,旅行社应当自取得旅行社业务经营许可证之日起 3 个工作日内,在国务院旅游行政主管部门指定的银行(bank designated by the tourism administrative department)开设专门的质量保证金账户(open a special quality deposit account),存入质量保证金,或者向作出许可的旅游行政管理部门提交依法取得的担保额度不低于相应质量保证金数额(not less than the corresponding quality deposit)的银行担保(bank guarantee)。

经营国内旅游业务和入境旅游业务的旅行社,应当存入质量保证金 20 万元(deposit 200,000 RMB quality deposit);经营出境旅游业务的旅行社,应当增存质量保证金 120 万元(increase the quality deposit of 1.2 million RMB)。质量保证金的利息属于旅行社所有(interest on the quality deposit is owned by the travel agency)。

第十四条规定,旅行社每设立一个经营国内旅游业务和入境旅游业务的分社,应当向其质量保证金账户增存 5 万元(deposit 50,000 RMB more in its quality deposit account for each branch that operates domestic and inbound tourism business);每设立一个经营出境旅游业务的分社,应当向其质量保证金账户增存 30 万元(300,000 RMB more in its quality deposit account for outbound tourism business)。

2. 质量保证金的使用

根据《旅行社条例》第十五条规定,有下列情形之一的,旅游行政管理部门可以使用旅行社的质量保证金(use the travel agency's quality deposit):旅行社违反旅游合同约定(violate the travel contract),侵害旅游者合法权益(infringe the legitimate rights and interests of tourists),经旅游行政管理部门查证属实的;旅行社因解散、破产(disbandment, bankruptcy)或者其他原因造成旅游者预交旅游费用损失的。

1.6 Relevant Provisions of Quality Deposit

1.6.1 Quality deposit

1.6.2 Use of quality deposit

1.6.3 Other provisions of quality deposit

3. 质量保证金的其他规定

根据《旅行社条例》第十六条规定，人民法院判决、裁定及其他生效法律文书(other effective legal documents)认定旅行社损害旅游者合法权益(infringe the legitimate rights and interests of tourists)，旅行社拒绝或者无力赔偿的(unable to compensate)，人民法院可以从旅行社的质量保证金账户上划拨赔偿款(allocate the compensation funds from the quality deposit account)。

根据《旅行社条例》第十七条规定，旅行社自缴纳或者补足质量保证金之日起三年内未因侵害旅游者合法权益(infringe the legitimate rights and interests of tourists)受到行政机关罚款以上处罚的，旅游行政管理部门应当将旅行社质量保证金的缴存数额降低50%(reduce 50% of the amount of the quality deposit)，并向社会公告(make a public announcement)。旅行社可凭省、自治区、直辖市旅游行政管理部门出具的凭证减少其质量保证金。

根据《旅行社条例》第十八条规定，旅行社在旅游行政管理部门使用质量保证金赔偿旅游者的损失(compensate tourists for their losses)，或者依法减少质量保证金后，因侵害旅游者合法权益(infringe the legitimate rights and interests of tourists)受到行政机关罚款以上处罚的，应当在收到旅游行政管理部门补交质量保证金的通知之日起5个工作日(within five working days)内补足质量保证金。

根据《旅行社条例》第十九条规定，旅行社不再从事旅游业务的，凭旅游行政管理部门出具的凭证(certificates issued by the administrative department)，向银行取回质量保证金。

根据《旅行社条例》第二十条规定，质量保证金存缴、使用(deposit and use of)的具体管理办法由国务院旅游行政主管部门和国务院财政部门(the tourism administrative department and the financial department under the State Council)会同有关部门(in conjunction with relevant departments)另行制定。

（七）外商投资旅行社的设立要求及程序

1.7 Requirements and Procedures for the Establishment of Foreign-Funded Travel Agencies

外商投资旅行社，包括中外合资经营旅行社(Sino-foreign joint venture travel agencies)、中外合作经营旅行社(Sino-foreign cooperative travel agencies)和外资旅行社(foreign-funded travel agencies)。外商投资旅行社适用《旅行社条例》

的相关规定。

根据(In accordance with)《旅行社条例》第二十二条规定，外商投资旅行社申请经营旅行社业务，应当向所在地省、自治区、直辖市旅游行政管理部门提出申请(apply to the tourism administration)，并提交符合本条例第六条规定条件(meet the requirements)的相关证明文件(submit relevant certification documents)。省、自治区、直辖市旅游行政管理部门应当自受理申请之日起30个工作日内审查完毕(complete the examination within 30 working days)。予以许可(agree to establish)的，颁发旅行社业务经营许可证；不同意设立(disagree with)的，书面通知申请人(notify the applicant in writing)并说明理由(explain the reasons)。

根据《旅行社条例》第二十三条规定，外商投资旅行社不得经营中国内地居民出国旅游业务以及赴香港特别行政区、澳门特别行政区和台湾地区旅游的业务，但是国务院决定或者我国签署的自由贸易协定和内地与香港、澳门关于建立更紧密经贸关系的安排另有规定的除外。

Foreign-invested travel agencies shall not operate the overseas tourism business of Chinese mainland residents and the tourism business of Hong Kong, Macao and Taiwan.

二、旅行社设立的影响因素

（一）外部因素

外部因素指旅行社自身无法控制，而又必须受其约束的因素。影响旅行社设立的外部因素主要有两个方面：行业环境因素(industry environmental factors)，是指存在于旅行社内部(exist within travel agencies)的，影响、制约着旅行社的存在与发展的因素，主要涉及旅游业的发展现状、行业内的竞争对手、潜在的竞争对手(potential competitors)、旅游服务供应部门等；其次是宏观环境因素，指存在于旅行社行业之外的，却又对旅行社的存在与发展产生直接影响(have a direct impact on the existence and development)的各种因素，包括宏观经济环境、人口环境、科技环境、政治法律环境(political and legal environment)、国际环境等。

（二）内部因素

内部因素是指旅行社自身可以控制的因素。影响旅行社设立的内部因素包括资金筹措、营业场所、协作网络、信用状况、客源渠道、员工配置等。

2 Factors Affecting the Establishment of Travel Agencies

2.1 External Factors

2.2 Internal Factors

Internal factors include fund raising, business places, collaborative networks, credit conditions, source channels, and staffing.

三、旅行社的选址及营业场所设计

(一) 旅行社营业场所选址

3 Site Selection and Design of Business Places

3.1 Site Selection of Business Places

关于旅行社选址方面的研究不多。美国空中交通协会(ATC)就旅行社选址的规定如下：第一，旅行社不能设在家中，必须设在公众出入方便的商业区(commercial areas)并保证正常的营业时间；第二，旅行社不能与其他业务部门合用办公室(can't share offices with other business departments)而且必须有独立的出口(must have independent exits)；第三，如果没有直接通向街道的通道(there is no direct access to the street)，旅行社不能设在饭店内。

美国旅游学者帕梅拉·弗里蒙特(Pamela Fremont)根据自己的实践经验(experience)，认为旅行社的选址可以参考以下几个因素：一是旅行社应该设在繁华的商业区(bustling commercial areas)，以便吸引过往行人(attract passing pedestrians)；二是旅行社营业处应该有足够的停车场地，便于公众停留(facilitate public parking)；三是尽量避免选择旅行社林立的地区，以减少竞争压力(reduce competition pressure)；四是旅行社应该选择中等收入家庭(middle-income families)相对集中(are relatively concentrated)的地区，且附近有较大规模的企业，以便吸引人们参加旅游；五是旅行社营业场所以底楼(the ground floor)为好，以方便顾客。

It is necessary to consider the customer flow conditions, traffic conditions and competitors.

旅行社营业场所是为方便宣传(propaganda)、招徕和接待国内外旅游者而专门设立的，作为旅行社重要的销售和形象窗口(important window of sales and images)，必须有一个好的地理位置，才能做到有效推广和有效销售(in order to effectively promote and sell)。从西方国家旅行社的选址经验来看，需要综合考虑客流条件、交通条件以及竞争对手情况。

(二) 旅行社营业场所设计

3.2 Design of Business Places for Travel Agencies

在1987年美国市场营销协会召开的服务营销年会上，由肖斯坦克(Shostack)提出的"服务蓝图方法"(service blueprint method)在设计和开发新型服务方面见解独到(unique insights)，引起了理论界和实业界(theoretical and industrial circles)的重大关注。

服务蓝图是详细描画服务系统与服务流程的图片或地图。

服务过程中涉及的不同人员可以理解并客观使用它,无论他们的角色或个人观点如何。服务蓝图由四个主要的行为部分和三条分界线构成。四个主要行为部分包括顾客行为(customer behavior)、前台员工行为(front office employee behavior)、后台员工行为(back-office employee behavior)和支持过程(support processes),三条分界线分别为互动分界线(interactive boundaries)、可视分界线(visual boundaries)和内部互动线(internal interaction lines)。

可以借助服务蓝图工具来进行场所设计。营业场所的前台是为旅游者提供服务的场所,营业场所的后台是旅行社的员工处理内部事务(handle internal affairs)的地方。接待区域的功能可以划分为互动区域(interactive area)和自助区域(self-service area)两个区域。

Service blueprints are a picture or map that details the service system and service flow.

It consists of four main parts of the act and three dividing lines.

The service blueprint tool helps to design the site.

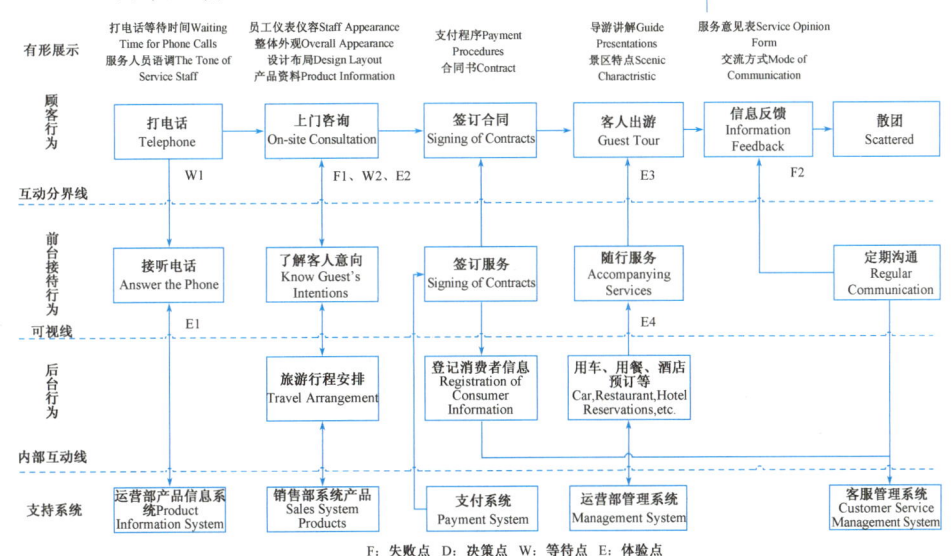

图1-4 旅行社服务蓝图及重要质量节点图
Travel Agency Service Blueprint and Important Quality Node Diagram

(三)旅行社的CIS形象战略

Corporate的名词形式是Corporation,意思是社会、公司、企业等;Identity的动词形式是Identify,意思是识别、鉴别等。所以CI可译为"企业或机构的识别"。CI在发展的过程中不断得以完善,逐渐形成了Corporate Identity System,即"企业的识别系统",即人们通常所说的CIS战略。旅行社实施CIS形象战略:一是参与国际市场竞争的需要,二是建立旅游管理品牌的需要。

3.3 CIS Image Strategy of Travel Agencies

To implement CIS image strategy, travel agencies need to participate in the international market competition, and establish the brand of Tourism Management in China.

| CIS strategy generally consists of three elements: MI, BI and VI. | CIS 战略一般由三大要素组成：理念识别（MI）、行为识别（BI）和视觉识别（VI），三个要素是相互联系的统一整体。企业理念是企业的精神和灵魂，理念就是指企业经营管理的观念，也是 CIS 战略的核心；行为识别（behavior identification）是企业动态的识别形式（dynamic identification form），企业的各种活动要充分体现出企业的理念，这样才能塑造出良好的企业形象；视觉识别（visual identification）是企业的静态识别形式（static identification form），企业的标志、标准色（logo and standard color of a company）是通过视觉系统将企业的形象传递给大众的。行为识别和视觉识别只有在具备了正确的思想内容（correct ideological content）、充分反映了企业的精神和理念时才能发挥更大的作用。 |

实训项目 01 旅行社设立申请书制作

Project 1　Submit an Application to Establish a Travel Agency

一、实训目的（Training Objectives）：

1. 培养学生社会认知能力，了解旅行社设立程序和要求。
2. 提升沟通交流能力，了解事务办理流程和规范。
3. 培养学生严谨细致的工作作风、团结合作的精神。

二、实训学时（Training Period）：2～8 学时

三、实训地点（Training Place）：旅行社情景实训室或校外走访调研

四、实训设备（Training Equipment）：联网计算机、移动硬盘或 U 盘。

五、项目描述（Project Description）：

学生拟设立一家旅行社，需要了解旅行社设立的程序、需要的资料，以及资料的内容和格式要求，并制作旅行社设立申请书文案，用 PPT 汇报制作文案成果。

六、实训任务及要求（Tasks and Requirements）：

实训任务一览表

序号	实训任务名称	实训学时	实训地点
01	一、设立旅行社申请书	2	旅行社情景实训室或者社会走访调研
02	二、可行性研究报告		
03	三、企业名称预先核准通知书		
04	四、旅行社法定代表人履历及身份证明		
05	五、设立旅行社投资人的证明		
06	六、管理人员资格审核备案表		
07	七、×××旅行社章程		
08	八、资金信用证明		
09	九、缴纳旅行社质量保证金承诺书		
10	十、营业场所和设施设备情况表		

注：教师可根据需要选用实训项目和学时。

七、实训成果（Practical Results）：

1. 每组完成旅行社设立申请书 WORD 电子文档 1 份和展示 PPT 电子档 1 份。

2. 将上述两个文件放入文件夹,命名为:"班级名称+小组编号+旅行社设立申请书实训作业"。

八、考核标准(Assessment Criterion):

项目	考核内容和要求	分值	得分
表现	按时完成任务,工作积极主动,具有合作精神	20	
内容	内容全面、真实、精确	40	
格式	格式规范、语言简洁、样式美观	20	
创新	有创意,有市场潜力	20	
小计		**100**	

第二章 旅游市场细分、选择与定位
Chapter Two Segmentation, Targeting and Positioning in Tourism Market

【学习目标】 **Learning Objectives**

1. 了解旅游市场细分（market segmentation）的目的、原则、意义（purpose, principle and significance）；

2. 掌握旅游市场细分的一般原理和方法（general principles and methods）；

3. 理解如何选择目标市场及进行市场定位（target market and market positioning）。

> 坚持以人民为中心的发展思想。维护人民根本利益，增进民生福祉，不断实现发展为了人民、发展依靠人民、发展成果由人民共享，让现代化建设成果更多更公平惠及全体人民。
>
> ——党的二十大报告摘录

✓ 本章课程视频讲解　　　✓ 实训指导书
✓ 线上课堂链接　　　　　✓ 优秀学生作品精选
✓ 本章训练题库　　　　　✓ 时政新闻
✓ 本章拓展资源

第一节 旅游市场细分
Section One Segmentation of the Tourism Market

1 Origin and Development of Market Segmentation

1.1 Generation of Market Segmentation

Market segmentation is mainly accomplished by three steps: market segmenting, market targeting and market positioning.

1.2 Development of Market Segmentation

Differentiated marketing stage began in the 1920s and ended at the end of World War Ⅱ.

一、市场细分的产生与发展

（一）市场细分的产生

市场细分是以消费需求的某些特征或变量为依据，区分具有不同需求的顾客群体的过程。市场细分工作主要由市场细分、目标市场选定和市场定位三个步骤完成。处于同一细分市场的消费群被称为目标消费群，相对于大众市场（mass market）而言，这些目标子市场的消费群就是分众（sub-market customers）。市场细分理论是由美国著名市场学家温德尔·史密斯（Wendell R. Smith）于1956年提出（put forward）的，之后便一直成为市场营销的主导理论（dominant theory）。

（二）市场细分的发展

"市场细分"概念的发展历经了三个阶段（three stages）：大众营销阶段、差异化营销阶段及目标市场营销阶段。

大众营销阶段（mass marketing stage）始于西方工业革命（Industrial Revolution），结束于20世纪20年代。在这个时期，大量生产规格品种单一的产品（produce products with single specifications），并通过众多的渠道进行分销（distribute through numerous channels），进而吸引大量消费者购买。在特定的市场形势下，这是行之有效的方法。由于成本和价格的降低，市场急速扩张（market expanded quickly），最终获得了丰厚的利润（eventually gain significant profits）。

差异化营销阶段始于20世纪20年代，终于第二次世界大战结束。这个时期，由于科学管理方法和规模化生产（large-scale production）的广泛应用（extensive application），商品普遍供大于求（in excess of demand），企业利润下降（lead to the decline of company profits）。因此，企业开始设计、生产和提供（design, produce and provide）不同于竞争对手的产品，主要表现在外观、质量、款式和规格上（the differences mainly showed in appearance, quality, style and specifications)。通过这种方法,企业希望能够提高产品的市场竞争力(market competitiveness),吸引更多的客户(attract more customers)。值得注意的是,在这个阶段,企业只关注产品差异,而不是客户需求差异(focus on product differences rather than customer demand differences)。结果大大降低了达到预期效果的可能性,不能显著(significantly)提高产品的适销性。

无节制的差异化(uncontrolled differentiation)导致企业成本急剧上升,但又不知道差异化的"终点"(end point)该在哪里,从而导致了差异化困惑(confusion of differentiation)。在这个阶段,除了生产和产品概念外,一个新的概念,即营销概念(marketing concept)应运而生。第二次世界大战结束后,主要西方国家的市场形势已转变为买方市场(change into the buyer's market)。针对目标市场的需求特点,采用适当的营销组合策略开发适销对路的产品,在消费需求差异化的基础上进行产品差异化(carry out product differentiation),即目标市场营销(target marketing)。

二、旅游市场细分标准

2 Standards for Segmentation of the Tourism Market

市场细分变量(market segmentation variables)可概括为四个大类:地理细分变量、人口细分变量、心理细分变量和行为细分变量。

表 2-1 旅游市场细分的标准
Criteria of Tourism Market Segmentation

细分标准 Segmentation Criteria	细分变量 Segmentation Variables
地理因素 Geographical Factors	地理位置、城镇大小、地形、地貌、气候、交通状况、人口密集度等 Geographical location, town size, topography, landform, climate, traffic situation, population density, etc.
人口统计因素 Demographic Factors	年龄、性别、职业、收入、民族、宗教、教育、家庭人口、家庭生命周期等 Age, gender, occupation, income, nationality, religion, education, family population, family life cycle, etc.
心理因素 Psychological Factors	生活方式、性格、购买动机、态度等 Lifestyle, personality, purchase motivation, attitude, etc.

（续表）

细分标准 Segmentation Criteria	细分变量 Segmentation Variables
行为因素 Behavioral Factors	购买时间,购买数量,购买频率,购买习惯(品牌忠诚度)、对服务、价格、渠道、广告的敏感程度等 Buying time, quantity, frequency, habit (brand loyalty), sensitivity to service, price, channel, advertisement, etc.

2.1 Geographical Factors

（一）地理细分变量

按地理变量细分(subdividing by geographical variables)，就是按消费者所在的地理位置(geographical location)、地理环境等变数来细分市场。因为处在不同地理环境下的消费者，对于同一类产品往往会有不同的需要与偏好(different needs and preferences)。

The international tourism market is divided into primary market, secondary market and opportunity market according to the tourist flow from different countries.

例如，根据不同国家来源的游客流量，国际旅游市场可分为一级市场、二级市场和机会市场。一般来说，一级市场占(accounts for)目的地国接待游客总人数的 40%～60%。二级市场是指在目的地接待国家(in destination countries)接待游客总人数中占较大比例(account for a large proportion)的旅游市场，特点是有较大的市场潜力，潜在需求(potential demand)还没有完全转变为现实需求(realistic demand)。机会市场，也叫边缘市场(marginal market)，是指一个目的地国家计划新开拓的(newly developing market)市场。特征是：该市场的旅游人数与日俱增，但前往本目的地的人数很少，有待于进一步开发的旅游市场。

2.2 Geographical Factors

（二）人口细分变量

按人口统计变量细分，就是按年龄、性别、职业、收入、家庭人口、家庭生命周期、民族、宗教、国籍等变数，将市场划分为不同的群体。由于人口变数比其他变数更容易测量，且适用范围比较广(have a wide range of applications)，因而人口变量一直是细分消费者市场(subdivide customer markets)的重要依据(important basis)。

例如根据家庭生命周期所处阶段的不同，可将市场细分为以下六个细分市场：① 年轻的单身汉(young bachelors)，有空闲时间，喜好运动、旅游，但不甚富裕；② 没有小孩的年轻夫妇

(young couples without children),有较高的购买力,有空闲时间(have plenty of time),一般进行度假旅游;③ 有小孩的年轻夫妇(young couples with children under age 6),孩子小,很少空闲时间,难以外出旅游;④ 有七八岁小孩的夫妇(couples with children aged above 7),如果家庭收入好,则常以小包价的方式旅游;⑤ 中年夫妇,小孩已长大自立(middle-age couples with independent children),家庭收入好,往往选择观光旅游、游船旅游的方式;⑥ 老年夫妇(elderly couple)往往有可观的储蓄,通常对休闲旅游感兴趣,而且更有可能出国旅游(more likely to take overseas tour)。

(三) 心理细分变量

2.3 Psychological Factors

按心理因素细分,就是将消费者按其生活方式、性格、购买动机、态度等变数细分成不同的群体。旅游者心理因素十分复杂(complex),不仅与旅游者的收入水平有关,而且与旅游者的文化素养(cultural literacy)、社会地位(social status)、价值观念、职业(occupations)等因素密切相关(closely related to)。以旅游者的心理特征(psychological characteristics)来细分,具体变量因素有气质性格、生活方式、价值取向、购买动机、偏好等。

Lifestyle, personality, purchase motivation, attitude and other factors

以性格细分变量(personality subdivision variable)为例,消费者性格(customer personality)可以分为外向与内向(extrovert and introvert)、乐观与悲观(optimism and pessimism)、自信(self-confidence)、顺从(compliance)、保守(conservatism)、急进(rush)、热情(enthusiasm)、稳重(stability)等。性格外向、容易感情冲动(emotionally impulsive)的消费者往往好表现自己,因而喜欢购买能表现自己个性的产品(express their personality);性格内向的消费者则喜欢大众化,往往购买比较平常的产品;富于创造性和冒险心理的消费者(creative and adventurous customers),则对新奇、刺激性强的(novel and exciting)旅游产品特别感兴趣。

Temperament, personality, lifestyle, value orientation, purchase motivation, preference and so on

(四) 行为细分变量

2.4 Behavioral Factors

消费者购买行为的差异细分是根据消费者购买产品的时间、数量、购买频率、消费者忠诚度(loyalty of customers)等变量,将其划分为不同的群体。

例如按消费者购买旅游产品的频率(frequency)情况,旅游者可分为较少购买的旅游者、多次购买的旅游者和经常购买的

High loyalty, medium loyalty, transfer loyalty and non-loyalty

旅游者。这一变量也可用来反映旅游者对某一旅游产品的忠诚度(reflect tourist loyalty to a certain tourism product)。企业也可按照忠诚度将消费者细分为高度忠诚者、中度忠诚者、转移忠诚者、无忠诚度者。

表 2-2 旅游者忠诚状况的特征描述
Characteristic Description of Tourist Loyalty

忠诚度 Loyalty	特征描述 Feature Description	购买模式 Purchasing Model
高度忠诚 Absolute Loyalist	始终购买一种品牌 Purchase a brand unswervingly	A→A→A→A→A→A
中度忠诚 Medium Loyalist	忠诚于两种或三种品牌 Be loyal to two or three brands	A→A→B→B→A→B
转移忠诚 Transfer Loyalist	从偏爱一种品牌转换到另一种品牌 Change from a preference for one brand to another	A→A→A→B→B→B
无忠诚度 Non-Loyal Person	对任何一种品牌都不忠诚 Not loyal to any brand	A→C→E→B→D→B

第二节　旅游目标市场选择
Section Two　Tourism Market Targeting

1　Criteria of Tourism Market Targeting

一、旅游目标市场选择的依据

目标市场是指旅游企业在市场细分的基础上,选择并集中资源以满足其特定需求(satisfy their needs)的消费者群体。选择目标市场的第一步是分析评估各细分市场(analyze and evaluate the market segments),评估依据包括各细分市场规模和增长率(growth rate)、细分市场结构吸引力(attractiveness)以及旅游企业营销目标和资源(marketing objectives and resources)。

（一）各细分市场规模和增长率

潜在细分市场（potential market segments）要具有适度规模（appropriate scale）和合适的预期增长率（expected growth rate），才具有一定的市场发展潜力，成为旅游企业进入的驱动力。

市场规模和预期增长率是一个相对的概念，对实力雄厚的大企业来说，是指规模大、增长速度快的细分市场（large-scale and fast-growing sub-markets）；而对中小企业（small and medium-sized companies）而言，由于其资源和实力有限，则指不被大企业看好的、规模较小、增长速度比较平缓的市场（small-scale and slow-growing markets）。

（二）细分市场结构吸引力

哈佛大学商学院波特教授指出（point out），影响一个市场或一个细分市场的长期盈利因素主要有行业竞争、替代产品、购买者和供应者（industry competition, alternative products, buyers and suppliers）等几个因素。细分市场结构吸引力可视为对该市场利润的期望值。期望值高，则吸引力大。而吸引力的大小则是上述几种要素在细分市场上的强度函数。

（1）竞争者状况（competitor status）。如果某一细分市场已经存在许多强有力并具有进攻性的竞争者（aggressive competitors），则不太具有吸引力。

（2）替代性产品状况（alternative products status）。如果在一个细分市场上目前或将来存在许多替代性产品的话，则吸引力有限（limited-attractive segment market）。

（3）购买者的能力状况（buyer's ability status）。购买者的砍价能力（bargaining ability）也会影响细分市场的吸引力。

（4）供应商的状况（suppliers' status）。如果在一个细分市场上存在一个强有力的供应商，能控制生产所需的原材料与服务的价格，以及它们的质量和数量，这个细分市场也是缺乏吸引力的。

（三）旅游市场营销目标与资源

除对细分市场进行深入细致的评估（carefully evaluation）外，旅游企业还须明确自身的经营目标和拥有的资源（clarify their own business objectives and resources）。对适合企业经营目标的细分市场，旅游企业还要考虑自身的生产能力

1.1 Scale and Growth Rate of Segmented Markets

Market size and expected growth rate are relative concepts.

1.2 Segmented Market Structure Attraction

The degree of attraction is a function of the strength of several factors in the market segmentation.

1.3 Tourism Marketing Target and Resources

(should consider their own production capacity)、拥有的资源和技术,不能选择企业自身无法满足的细分市场,否则就会得不偿失。

二、旅行社产品目标市场选择模式

2　Market Targeting Model of Tourism Products

旅行社在对不同细分市场进行评估后,必须对进入哪些市场和为多少个细分市场服务进行决策(make decisions)。旅行社可考虑的目标市场选择模式通常有五种。

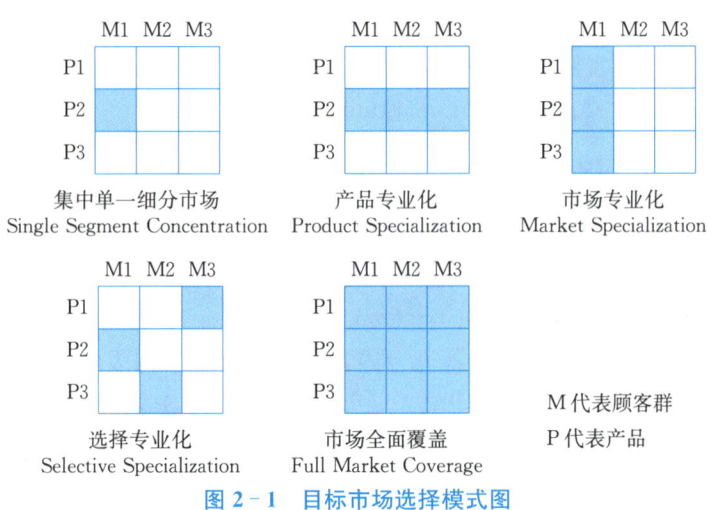

图 2 - 1　目标市场选择模式图
Market Targeting Models

（一）市场集中化

2.1　Single Segment Concentration

Only produce a certain product for a certain customer group, and specially filling a certain part of the market.

市场集中化是指一个企业只生产某一种产品,只供应给某一顾客群,专门填补某一部分市场。较小的企业通常选择这一战略(smaller companies usually choose this strategy)。

（二）产品专业化

2.2　Product Specialization

产品专业化是指企业集中生产一种产品,并向所有顾客销售这种产品(company concentrates on producing a product and sells it to all customers)。该模式优点是生产成本、调研、管理、促销费用低,缺点是目标过分集中(too centralized),全部资源和力量都投在一种产品上,企业承担的风险较大,主要适用于资金实力较弱的小企业。

（三）市场专业化

2.3　Market Specialization

市场专业化是指企业专门服务于某一特定顾客群,尽力满足他们的各种需求。市场专业化经营的产品类型众多,能有效地分散经营风险。但由于集中于某一类顾客,当这类顾客的需求下降(decline)时,企业也会遇到收益下降的风险(encounter the risk of revenue decline)。

(四) 选择专业化

企业选择若干具有良好盈利潜力(good profit potential)和结构吸引力(structural attractiveness),且符合企业目标和资源的细分市场作为目标市场,其中每个细分市场与其他细分市场之间很少或根本没有任何联系(have little or no connection with others)。这种策略能分散企业经营风险(can separate the business risk),即使其中某个细分市场失去了吸引力,企业还能在其他细分市场盈利,适合拥有较强资源和营销实力的企业使用。

(五) 市场全面覆盖

企业力图用各种产品满足各种顾客群体(all segments of the market)的需求,即以所有的细分市场作为目标市场,例如服装商场为不同年龄层次的顾客提供各种档次的服装。一般只有实力强大的大企业才能采用这种策略。

第三节 旅游市场定位
Section Three Tourism Market Positioning

一、旅游市场定位的方法

(一) 旅游市场定位的含义

"定位"由艾尔·列斯(Al Ries)和杰克·特劳特(Jack Trout)提出。他们把定位看成对现有产品的创造性实践(creative practice)。在他们看来,定位是以产品为出发点,如一种商品、一项服务、一家公司、一所机构,甚至一个人。但定位的对象不是产品,而是潜在顾客的思想。就是说把一个产品的某个形象放在潜在客户(potential customers)的大脑中(in the brain)。

艾尔·列斯理论的两个基础(two foundations):一是人们

Specialize in serving special customer group and try its best to meet their various needs.

2.4 Selective Specialization

Selective specialization is suitable for the companies with strong resources and marketing strength.

2.5 Full Market Coverage

1 Methods of Tourism Market Positioning

1.1 Definition of Tourism Market Positioning

只看他们所期望看到的事物（people only want to see what they expect to see），即知觉对感觉的影响；二是为了不被复杂生活所压倒（in order not to be overwhelmed by complex life），人们通常会在头脑中对事物进行顺序（people will usually put an arrangement in their minds）。

定位理论（positioning theory）产生的一个重要背景是产品信息及广告的爆炸性增长（explosive growth）。相似商品（similar types of goods）的涌现以及名牌商品被仿制（imitation of famous brand goods），使得突出和区分产品特性（highlight and recognize the characteristics）和优势变得更加困难。同时，消费者面对被各种商品充斥的社会，只能采取所谓单纯化策略方可进行有效的消费选择（make effective consumption choices）和生存适应（survival adaptation）。

> When customers are faced with overwhelming commodities and advertisements by simplification strategy, they adopt a certain classification method to make individual commodities typed, and naturally establish a simple and orderly product run according to the recognition of brand image.

单纯化或简化策略使消费者面临铺天盖地的商品和广告时，依照对品牌形象的认知，采取某种分类方式，使个体的商品类型化自然而然地建立起一个个简单有序的产品阶梯。在这个阶梯上，排在最上面的（rank first）产品品牌，要比其后第二位、第三位等的产品具有高得多的形象地位（much higher image status），是消费者心中的理想品牌（ideal brand in the minds of customers），从而更易为消费者选择。

定位就是要力图使被定位对象攀上这个已存在于消费者心中的形象阶梯（to climb the image ladder that already exists in the minds of customers），从而被消费者认知，进而形成某种形象。

旅游市场定位是指旅游企业根据目标市场上的竞争者和企业自身状况，从各方面为本旅游企业的旅游产品和服务创造一定条件（create certain conditions），进而塑造一定的市场形象，以求在目标顾客心目中（in the minds of the target customers）形成一种特殊的偏好。旅游市场定位有利于树立企业及其产品的市场特色，使其在消费者心目中形成一个与众不同的印象（unique impression in the minds of customers），从而影响顾客的消费行为。同时，旅游市场定位是旅游企业制定营销组合策略（formulate marketing mix strategy）的基础。市场定位主要考虑两方面因素：消费者重视的属性；与竞争者的区别（attributes that customers attach importance to and differences from competitors）。

（二）常用方法

1. 根据产品特色或特殊用途进行定位

这是最为常见的一种定位方法，即根据自己产品的某种或某些优点，或者根据目标顾客所看重的某种或某些利益去进行定位。

2. 根据"质量—价格"定位

"质量—价格"反映了消费者对企业产品实际价值的认同程度，即对产品"性价比"（cost-effectiveness）的分析判断（analysis and judgment）。此种定位有两种情况：强调质量与价格相符（focus on the consistency between quality and price）；质高价低（high quality and low price）。

3. 根据产品使用者进行定位

企业主要针对某些特定顾客群进行的促销活动（promotional activities），以期在这些顾客心目中建立起企业产品"专属性"（exclusive）特点，激发顾客的购买欲望（stimulate customers' desire）。

4. 借助竞争者进行定位

一个企业可通过将自己同市场声望较高的（high market prestige）某一同行企业进行比较，借助竞争者的知名度（rely on the visibility of competitors）来实现自己的形象定位。

二、旅游市场定位的步骤

（一）确定定位的层次

对于旅游企业及旅游目的地而言，一般应考虑三个层次的定位：组织定位、产品线定位以及单一产品定位。企业不需要同时在所有层次上定位（position at all levels），重要的是要选准定位的层次，以有效提高定位的准确度和效率。

（二）确定产品和服务的特征

当市场定位的层次确定之后，就应根据目标市场的需要选定能够使本企业产品和服务区别于（different from）竞争对手的产品特征（product characteristics），即目标顾客最看中的核心"利益点"（interest point）。

（三）绘制定位图，确定定位位置

当选定了作为产品和服务差异化的产品特征后，企业要为

1.2 Common Methods

1.2.1 According to product characteristics or special uses

1.2.2 Based on "quality—price"

1.2.3 According to the users of the product

1.2.4 According to competitors

2 Steps for Tourism Market Positioning

2.1 Determine the Level of Positioning

Organizational positioning, product line positioning and single product positioning

2.2 Identifying the Characteristics of Products and Services

2.3 Draw Positioning Maps to Determine the Position

A simple and effective way is to mark the key attributes of company and competitors on the same map to form a special "positioning map".

这些特性寻找最佳的市场位置。一个简单有效的办法就是把企业的关键属性与竞争对手的属性标注在同一张图上,形成专门的"定位图"。

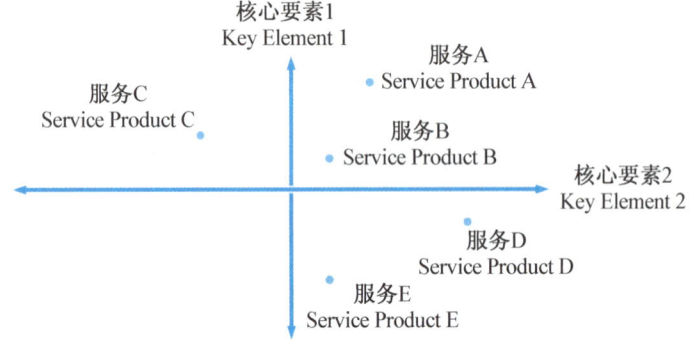

图 2-2 旅游企业市场定位图
Market Positioning Map of Tourism Company

2.4 Implementation of Positioning

The positioning should avoid the following mistakes: over low positioning, over high positioning, confusing positioning and the authenticity of positioning.

(四)实施定位

企业成功定位,一方面要强化执行并注意与整个营销策略的协调一致(pay attention to the coordination with the marketing strategy);另一方面要控制定位过程(control the positioning process),及时纠正定位过程中出现的问题(correct the problems in the positioning process)。企业在定位过程中应避免以下几种错误:定位过低、定位过高、定位混乱、定位的真实性问题。

实训项目02 旅行社产品目标市场分析报告

Project 2　Conduct a Target Market Analysis Report for Travel Agency Products

一、实训目标(Training Purpose)：

1. 认识STP营销的内容、方法和步骤及其在市场营销中的作用，了解与STP营销有关的概念，掌握市场细分的方法，并在营销实践中运用；

2. 掌握最终消费品市场与生产资料市场细分的标准；学会市场细分、目标市场选择、市场定位的方法；

3. 通过训练，锻炼学生认识问题、分析问题、解决问题的能力，培养学生实事求是、独立思考、勇于创新的精神。

二、实训学时(Training Period)：2～8学时

三、实训地点(Training Place)：旅行社情景实训室

四、实训设备(Training Equipment)：联网计算机、移动硬盘或U盘、A4绘图纸、铅笔、橡皮。

五、项目描述(Project Description)：

为了开发本地及周边旅游市场，需要根据企业实力等多种因素，有针对性地开发市场。市场细分是目标市场营销的起点和基础，是企业市场营销战略的平台。市场细分的实质是细分消费者的需求，在买方市场时代的条件下，旅行社企业要以消费者不同的消费需求对市场进行细分，然后把需求基本相同的消费者归为一类，这样就可以把某种产品的整体市场划分为若干个细分市场，然后进行市场选择与定位，提高企业的运行效率。项目完成后需要制作相应的文档并用PPT汇报实训成果。

六、实训任务及要求(Tasks and Requirements)：

实训任务一览表

序号	实训任务名称	实训内容	实训学时	实训地点
01	市场细分	在买方市场时代的条件下，旅行社企业根据消费者不同的消费需求把某种产品的整体市场划分为若干个细分市场	2	旅行社情景实训室
02	市场选择	目标市场确定的条件，目标市场确定的方法，目标市场进入的战略	2	

（续表）

序号	实训任务名称	实训内容	实训学时	实训地点
03	市场定位	调查研究影响市场定位的因素，确认目标市场的竞争优势；选择竞争优势与定位策略；准确地传播企业的定位观念	2	
注：教师可根据需要选用实训项目和学时。				

根据班级人数，每组可适当编制2~6人规模。每组组内分工，通过组内讨论，制作完成旅行社产品目标市场分析报告，并在课堂上展示。

七、实训成果（Practical Results）：

1. 每组完成旅行社产品目标市场分析报告WORD电子文档1份和展示PPT电子档1份。

2. 将上述两个文件放入文件夹，命名为："班级名称＋小组编号＋旅行社产品目标市场分析实训作业"。

八、考核标准（Assessment Criterion）：

项目	考核内容和要求	分值	得分
表现	按时完成任务，工作积极主动，具有合作精神	20	
内容	内容全面、真实、精确	40	
格式	格式规范、语言简洁、样式美观	20	
创新	有创意，有市场潜力	20	
小计		100	

第三章　旅行社产品研发与设计
Chapter Three　Research and Design for Travel Agency Products

> 【学习目标】 **Learning Objectives**
>
> 1. 了解旅行社产品概念及内涵（concept and connotation）；掌握旅行社产品的不同形态（different forms）；
> 2. 掌握旅游路线的设计流程（design process），能够运用原则分析与简单设计旅游线路（design simple tourism routes）；
> 3. 掌握相关评估工具（relevant evaluation tools）的使用，能够比较不同旅行社产品的优劣。

> 加大文物和文化遗产保护力度，加强城乡建设中历史文化保护传承，建好用好国家文化公园。坚持以文塑旅、以旅彰文，推进文化和旅游深度融合发展。
>
> ——党的二十大报告摘录

✓本章课程视频讲解　　✓实训指导书
✓线上课堂链接　　　　✓优秀学生作品精选
✓本章训练题库　　　　✓时政新闻
✓本章拓展资源

第一节　旅行社产品的含义与类型
Section One　Definition and Types of Travel Agency Products

一、旅行社产品的内涵

1 Connotation of Travel Agency Products

（一）旅行社产品的内涵

1.1 Connotation of Travel Agency Products

The concepts between travel agency products and tourism products are largely overlapping.

旅游产品是旅行社赖以生存的基础，旅游产品开发是旅行社一项基本的、重要的业务。旅行社产品主要是指服务形态产品。旅行社产品与旅游产品的概念在很大程度上重合在一起。

从旅游需求角度（from the perspective of tourism demand）来看，旅行社产品指旅游者花费一定的时间、费用和精力所获得的满足其旅游欲望（spend a certain amount of time, cost and energy to meet their desire）的一段旅游经历和感受。

从旅游供给角度（from the perspective of tourism supply）来看，是指旅游经营者凭借一定的旅游资源、旅游设施和其他相关媒介（certain tourism resources, tourism facilities and other related media），向旅游者提供其在旅游活动中各种需要（meet their various needs）的诸多产品和服务的总和。

（二）旅行社产品的主要构成

1.2 Main Composition of Travel Agency Products

In all kinds of products of travel agencies, the travel routes are the basic product of travel agencies, so they are often used to refer the products of travel agencies.

在旅行社的各类产品中，旅游线路产品是旅行社的基础产品，因而常被用来特别指代旅行社的产品。它通常由以下几部分构成：旅游交通（transportation）、旅游住宿（accommodation）、旅游餐饮（catering）、游览观光（sightseeing）、娱乐项目（entertainment）、购物项目（shopping）、导游服务（tour guide services）等。

二、旅行社产品分类

2 Classification of Travel Agency Products

旅游产品分为两类：一类是单项旅游产品（individual tourism products），一类是整体旅游产品（overall tourism products）。单项旅游产品是指住宿产品、饮食产品及交通、游览娱乐等方面的产品或服务;整体旅游产品是指满足旅游者旅游活动中全部需要的产品或服务。对于旅行社来说,旅行社线路产品是旅行社产品的重要组成部分,其类型有多种划分标准。

For travel agencies, travel routes are an important part of travel agency products. There are many kinds of classification criteria for the types of tourism products.

表 3-1 旅行社产品的形态分类
The Classification of Travel Agency Products Forms

划分依据 Classification Basis	主要表现形态 Main Forms
组织形式 Organizational Form	团体线路产品、散客线路产品 Group tourist products and individual tourist products
产品组合程度 Product Portfolio Degree	全包价旅游产品、半包价旅游产品、小包价旅游产品等 Full package tour, semi package tour, small package tour, etc.
消费档次 Consumption Level	豪华档旅游产品、标准档旅游产品、经济档旅游产品 Luxury tourism products, standard tourism products and economic tourism products
地理范围 Geographical Scope	国内旅游线路产品、国际旅游线路产品 Domestic and international tourism products
线路起止特征 Line Start-Stop Characteristics	流线型线路产品、环型线路产品、辐射型线路产品 Streamline products, loop line products, radiation products
旅游活动天数 Days of Tourist Activities	一日游、二日游、三日……多日游线路产品 One-day tour, two-day tour, three-day tour…multi-day tour
按旅游目的分 Purpose of Tourism	商务型旅游产品、观光型旅游产品、探亲型旅游产品、宗教型旅游产品、探险型旅游产品、生态型旅游产品、度假型旅游产品、文化型旅游产品、健身型旅游产品等专项旅游产品 Business tour, sightseeing tour, family visiting tour, religious tour, exploratory tour, ecological tour, vacation tour, cultural tour, fitness tour and other special tourism products

依据产品包含的内容,旅行社产品可以分为包价旅游(package tour)、非包价旅游(non-package tour)。包价旅游产品有全包价旅游线路产品、半包价旅游线路产品、小包价旅游线路产品和

Package tour products include full package products, half-package products, mini-package tour and zero-package tour products.

零包价旅游线路产品等。以下是包价旅游线路产品的分类。

表 3-2 各种包价旅游产品的比较
Comparisons of Various Package Tours

产品类型 Product Types	付费方式 Payment Method	交通 Transportation	餐饮 F&B	住宿 Lodging	导游 Tour Guide	门票 Tickets	人数 Number of People
团体包价 Group Package	一次性预付 One-time Advance Payment	✓	✓	✓	✓	✓	≥10
散客包价 Individual Package		✓	✓	✓	✓	✓	<10
半包价 Half-package	预付 Pay in Advance	✓	含早餐 Breakfast included	✓	✓	✓	×
小包价 Mini-package		✓		✓	×	×	<10
零包价 Zero-package		✓	×	×	×	×	×
单项服务 Single Entrusted Service	零星现付 Sporadic Cash Payment	×	×	×	×	×	×

2.1 Full Package Tour

Tourists pay the travel agency for all related service items included in the travel itinerary in advance, and the travel agency will fully do all related service items in the journey.

2.2 Half-package Tour

The benefit of half-package tour is that it reduces the intuitive price of products.

(一) 全包价旅游

旅游者将涉及旅游行程中一切相关服务项目的费用统包起来预付给旅行社,由旅行社全面落实旅程中的一切相关服务项目。全包价旅游产品中的一切相关服务项目包括食、住、行、游、购、娱各环节及导游服务,办理保险与签证等。

(二) 半包价旅游

半包价旅游是指在全包价旅游的基础上扣除中、晚餐费用(即不含中、晚餐项目)的一种包价形式(a kind of package price that reduces the expense of lunch and dinner)。半包价旅游的优点是降低了产品的直观价格,提高了产品的竞争力,也更好地满足了旅游者在用餐方面的不同要求。

（三）小包价旅游

小包价旅游也称可选择性旅游（optional tour），或自助游（self-help tour）。它由非选择部分和可选择部分构成（consist of the non-selective part and the selective part）。前者包含城市间交通（长途交通）和市内交通（短途交通）及住房（含早餐）；后者包括景点项目、娱乐项目、餐饮、购物及导游服务。小包价旅游具有经济实惠、手续简便（simple procedure）和机动灵活（flexible）等特点，深受旅游者的欢迎（very popular）。

（四）零包价旅游

零包价旅游是一种独特的产品形态（unique product form），多见于旅游发达国家。参加这种旅游的旅游者必须随团前往和离开旅游目的地，但在旅游目的地的活动是完全自由的，形同散客。参加零包价旅游的旅游者可以获得团体机票价格的优惠（can get the discount of the group ticket price），并可由旅行社统一代办旅游签证。

（五）单项服务

单项服务是旅行社根据旅游者具体要求而提供的各种有偿服务（a variety of paid services），旅游者需求的多样性决定了旅行社单项服务内容的广泛性。常规性的服务项目（routine service items）主要包括导游服务（tour guide service）、接送服务（pick-up service）、代办交通和文娱票据（transport and entertainment bills service）、代订客房（room booking）、联系参观游览项目、代办签证、代办旅游保险等。旅游单项服务的对象主要是零散的旅游者。单项服务又称委托代办业务（entrusted service），旅游者可采取当地委托、联程委托和国际委托等不同的方式交旅行社办理。

三、专项旅游

消费者对旅游产品的选择与其自身的消费能力、兴趣爱好和可支配时间直接相关（directly related to their consumption ability, hobbies and disposable time）。当支付能力较低时，往往选择"充实经历感"（enrich experience）的观光旅游为主。随着收入的提升和经历的丰富，旅行的选择逐渐向内在审美与愉悦的"度假"需求延伸。专项旅游产品便是这样一种适应旅游

2.3　Mini-package Tour

Non-selective part includes inter-city traffic (long-distance traffic) and city traffic (short-distance traffic) and accommodation (including breakfast).

2.4　Zero-package Tour

Tour participants in this kind of tour must go and leave the destination together with the group.

2.5　Single Entrusted Service

The diversity of tourists' needs determines the difference of the content of individual services of travel agencies.

3　Specific Tour

Tourists will tend to choose the "vacation" tour which can bring them inner aesthetics and pleasure.

者个性化、多样化需求（personalized and diversified needs of tourists）特点，具有广阔发展前景的旅游产品（wide prospects for development）。

Special tourism products include business tour, conference tour, sports tour, adventure tour, cooking tour, medical tour, tea tour, painting and calligraphy tour, religious tour and so on. In recent years, many well-known special tourism products have been developed in China, such as new century dawn trip, seabed wedding, large crossing Taklimakan Desert trip, exploration tour of Shangri-La, and so on.

专项旅游产品包括商务旅游、会议旅游、体育旅游、探险旅游、烹饪旅游、医疗旅游、品茶旅游、书画旅游、宗教旅游等。近年来我国旅行社开发的知名专项旅游产品有迎接新世纪曙光之旅、海底婚礼之旅、横穿塔克拉玛干大沙漠之旅、香格里拉探秘之旅等。

专项旅游是个性化旅行的代表形态（the representative form），是人们从泛旅行度假到精细旅行过渡（transition from pan-travel to fine travel）的开始。专项旅行相对传统意义的观光与度假而言（compared with the traditional sightseeing and vacation），更侧重于旅行产品设计的专业性（professional product design），以及旅行者与旅行目的地结合的"深度"。例如红色旅游，主要是指以中国共产党领导人在革命和战争时期建树丰功伟绩所形成的纪念地、标志物（monuments and landmarks）为载体，以其所承载的革命历史、革命事迹和革命精神（evolutionary history, deeds and the revolutionary spirit）为内涵，组织接待旅游者开展缅怀学习、参观游览的主题性旅游活动（thematic tourism activities）。

4　Service Innovation

四、服务创新

4.1　Current Situation of Service Innovation of Travel Agencies

（一）旅行社服务创新现状

目前，旅行社的服务产品管理方面存在以下问题：首先，旅行社缺乏针对顾客需求的创新（lack innovation in response to customer demands）；其次，旅行社产品单一（monotonous），相关景区（点）没有建立适合自身主题的新型服务或产品，消费者参与度低，体验感不足；再次，旅行社没有匹配高质量的售后服务（lack high-quality after-sales services），导致消费者的信任度降低（leads to a decrease in consumer trust），而旅行社企业缺乏对此现象的足够关注（lack sufficient attention to this phenomenon）；最后，旅行社在信息技术开发和应用方面，从认知态度到应用水平等方面（from cognitive attitudes to application levels），都存在明显不足。

4.2　Service Innovation Direction

（二）服务创新方向

根据实地调查（field investigations）以及相关文献，旅行社

Chapter Three Research and Design for Travel Agency Products

的服务和管理创新主要表现在(mainly manifests in)对软/硬管理技术的深入接纳(in-depth acceptance)、整合开发和运用(integrated development and application),具体涵盖信息技术、网络、交通、通讯、软件开发等等各个方面。国家文化与旅游部明确提出,各地要根据市场新变化新需求,积极引导和支持旅行社创新产品和服务。

综合来看,旅行社要优化产品供给,加快推进线上线下融合(accelerate the integration of online and offline),借助大数据、人工智能(artificial intelligence)、移动通信(mobile communication)等新技术新手段,开展云直播、云旅游、新媒体营销(carry out cloud live streaming, cloud tourism, and new media marketing),及时推出品质化、定制化、个性化产品和服务(high-quality, customized, and personalized products and services),推动行业高质量发展。

第二节　旅行社产品的开发流程
Section Two The Development Process of Travel Agency Products

一、影响旅行社产品开发的因素

1　Factors Influencing the Product Development

旅行社产品,是指为满足旅游者旅游过程中的需要,凭借一定的旅游吸引物和旅游设施(certain attractions and facilities)向旅游者提供的各种有偿服务,亦即旅游线路或旅游项目。旅行社产品是一种以无形服务(intangible service)为主体内容(main content)的特殊产品,是由吃、住、行、游、购、娱各种要素构成的"组合产品"(composite products)。

旅行社产品的形态是多种多样的,但无论哪种产品的开发,都是在资源赋予(resource endowment)、设施配置(facility allocation)、可进入性(accessibility)和旅游需求(tourism demand)等多种因素的制约下进行的。成功的旅行社产品设计主要体现在行程安排合理和价格具有竞争力(reasonable tour and reasonable price)两个方面。

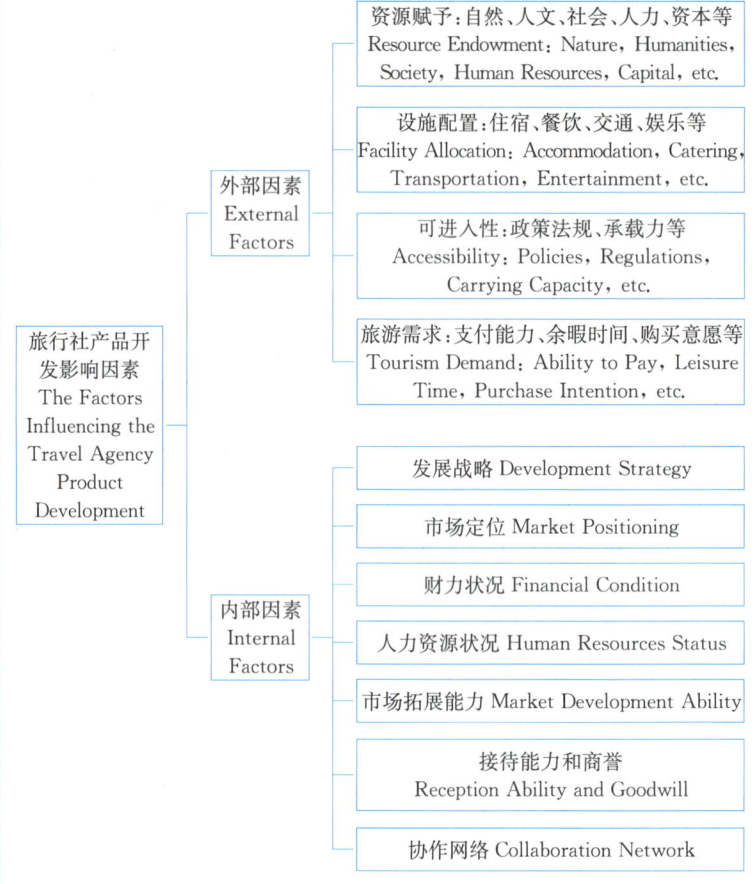

图 3-1 旅行社产品开发影响因素
Factors Influencing the Product Development

1.1 Resource Endowment

Mainly include: natural resources, human resources and social resources.

1.2 Facility Allocation

1.3 Tourism Demand

(一) 资源赋予

资源赋予是指一个国家或地区拥有旅游资源的状况,主要包括:自然资源、人文资源、社会资源。

(二) 设施配置

设施配置是指与旅游者的旅游活动密切相关的服务设施和服务网络的配置状况(allocation of service facilities),主要包括住宿、交通、餐饮和娱乐等方面,它们是旅游者实现旅游目的的中间媒介(intermediaries),而且本身也会增添旅游乐趣,构成旅游生活的重要部分。

(三) 旅游需求

旅游需求是指消费者在一定时期内以一定价格(at a

certain price in a certain period of time)愿意购买的旅游产品的数量,从根本上需要具备"有钱""有闲"和"便利"三方面条件,但也有更深层次的规律可循,通常有以下三种观点:

(1) 收入决定论(Income determinism)。人均(per capita) GNP 300 美元以上,产生近地旅游;1 000 美元以上,近国旅游;3 000 美元以上,远国旅游。

The GNP is more than US＄300, resulting in near-field tourism; more than US＄1 000, near-country tourism; more than US＄3 000, far-country tourism.

(2) 出行距离论(Travel distance theory)。以定居地为中心确定出行半径,获得在同一支付水准下的最大效益。比如国内公民出游,以中国为中心画一个圆(draw a circle centered on China),可去韩国、日本、俄罗斯、东南亚等国,在比较价格、考虑兴趣后作出决定(make a decision after comparing prices and preferences)。

(3) 需求差异(Demand difference)、偏好论(Preference theory)。不同的顾客群有不同的需求,旅行社提供的东西,必须是他们感兴趣的东西。

(四) 旅行社实力

1.4 Strength of Travel Agencies

旅行社自身的实力也是制约旅游产品开发的重要因素。我国旅行社的经营状况多数是小规模、低层次、单体作坊式的。众多中小型旅行社无法提供旅游新产品开发所需的人才、资金及相当的营销投入(the advantages of talents, funds and considerable marketing investment)。

Most of travel agencies in China are small-scale, low-level, single workshop-style business.

二、旅行社产品开发流程

2 The Development Process of Travel Agency Products

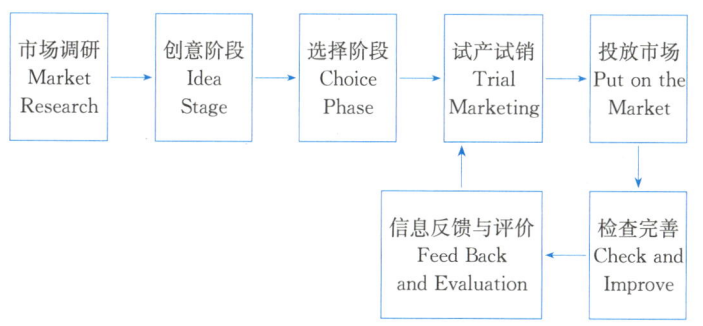

图 3-2 旅行社产品开发流程图
Flow Chart of the Development Process of Travel Agency Products

(一) 市场调查

2.1 Market Research

1. 旅游市场需求调查

2.1.1 Survey of tourism market demand

(1) 旅游客源市场的需求状况、旅游者的流向(flow direc-

tion)、外出旅行的规模(scale of outgoing travel)、旅游方式的变化、市场需求的发展趋势等情况;

(2) 旅游者的消费结构(consumption structure)及其发展变化趋势(development trend);

(3) 国家经济政策的变化对旅游市场需求结构产生的影响;

(4) 旅行社各种营销策略引起的竞争者的销售变化及其对市场需求量的影响。

2.1.2 Survey of tourists' consumption behavior

2. 旅游者消费行为调查

旅游者在进行个体旅游决策和购买、消费、评估、处理旅游产品时的种种行为表现,统称为旅游者消费行为(tourists' consumption behavior)。消费者研究要解答七个问题,可以采用"7O"调查法("7O" survey method)来进行信息收集:旅游者的类别(tourists' categories)、购买对象(purchasing objects)、购买目的(purchasing objectives)、购买组织(purchasing organizations)、购买方式(purchasing methods)、购买时机(purchasing occasions)、购买渠道(purchasing outlets)。

2.1.3 Competition survey

3. 竞争情况调查

竞争情况调查需要弄清楚同行业竞争者的数量与规模(clarify the number and scale of competitors),竞争者产品的种类、数量、成本、价格和利润水平(price and profit level),竞争者产品的市场占有率(market share)及其发展趋势,竞争者采取的竞争策略(competitive strategies)和手段,每个竞争者具有的优势和劣势。

2.2 Draft Plans

(二) 方案的拟定

2.2.1 Product creativity

1. 产品创意的产生

在服务企业,实际传递服务(deliver services)、与顾客打交道(deal with customers)的职员可能是改进和完善现有服务的最佳创意来源(best creative source)。方法包括:头脑风暴法(brainstorming)、雇员与顾客征求意见法(employee and customer consultation)、竞争者产品分析法(competitor product analysis)、观察法(observation)。

There should be a regular mechanism to ensure that ideas are preserved and developed.

无论新创意来源于组织内部还是外部,应该有一套常规机制以确保创意的保存与发展。这一机制可能包括:常规的新服务开发部门或职能负责产生新创意(generating new ideas)、为员工和顾客设立建议箱(suggestion boxes)、新服务开发小组常规性会面、在顾客和员工之间进行的调查、为确定新服务而进行的常规性竞争分析(regular competitive analysis)。

2. 构思的筛选

筛选的目的在于权衡,尽早发现和放弃(identify and discard)不良构思,找出可能成功(are likely to succeed)的构思。筛选工作应避免误弃(error abandonment)和误选(error selection)两种偏差。筛选工作可以先凭借经验进行筛选(亦称粗筛)(rough screening),在此基础上进一步进行评分筛选(亦称精筛)(fine screening)。评分模型一般包括评分因素、评分等级、因素权重和评分人员四个基本要素,对不同构思进行评分时,评分者往往需要讲述自己判分的理由,这是吸取他人经验并增长才干的机会。

2.2.2 Idea screening

The screening work should avoid two kinds of errors.

The scoring model generally includes four basic elements: scoring factors, rating, weight and scoring personnel.

表 3-3 旅行社产品构思筛选示例表
Example List of Product Conception Screening for Travel Agencies

评价因素 Evaluation Factors	因素权重 Factor Weight	评价等级 Evaluation Grades					得分 Score
		5	4	3	2	1	
销售前景 Sales Prospects	0.25		✓				1.00
营利能力 Profitability	0.25			✓			0.75
竞争能力 Competitive Power	0.20			✓			0.60
开发能力 Development Capability	0.20		✓				0.80
资源保障 Resource Guarantee	0.10		✓				0.40
总 计 Total	1.00						3.55

上表以相对指数评分模型(relative index scoring model)为例介绍构思筛选过程(screening process of ideas)。此模型以直观判断为基础(based on the natural judgment),根据经验确定一些评价因素与评分等级(evaluation factors and grades)来对构思进行筛选。

表 3－4　不同评分人员得分表
Scoring Sheet for Different Raters

构思 Conception	人员权重 Personnel Weight	评分 Evaluation Score	得分 Score
1			
2			
3			

In terms of the final score grade, 0～2 is inferior, 2.01～3.5 is medium, and 3.51～5 is good. The minimum acceptable score is 3.

从最终得分等级来看,0～2 为劣,2.01～3.5 为中,3.51～5 为良,可接受的最低评分为 3 分。

3. 构思的可行性论证

2.2.3　Feasibility study

可行性论证包括技术上的可行性(technical feasibility)、经济上的可行性(economic feasibility)、政策法规上的可行性(policy and regulation feasibility)。以上三条中任何一条得不到满足都必须舍弃(must be thrown away)该构思。

2.2.4　Draw up product plan according to product originality

4. 根据产品创意拟定产品方案

旅行社在拟定新产品方案的过程中,应注意以下几点:国家发展旅游事业的方针、政策和有关法律(guidelines, policies and relevant laws),是旅行社新产品设计中必须首先考虑的因素;各类旅行社在业务范围和专长方面都存在差异,旅行社应根据自身的特点和条件设计新产品,有针对性地搜集资料;各种信息必须全面(comprehensive)、系统(systematic),避免挂一漏万、支离破碎。

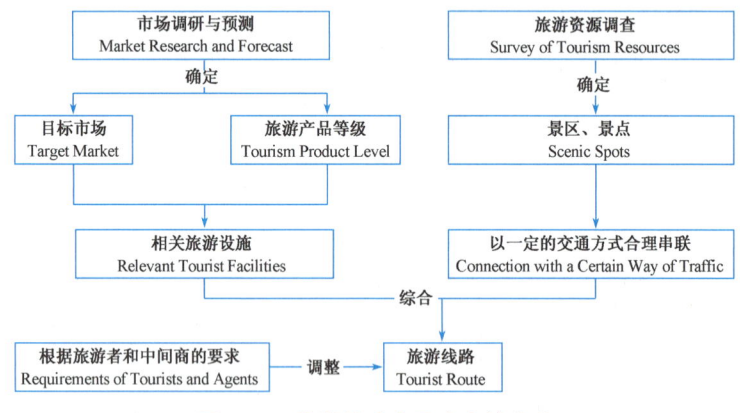

图 3－3　旅游线路产品方案的产生
Production of Tourist Route Scheme

(三) 方案的选择

1. 定性分析

从定性角度看,旅行社在选择方案时应考虑以下标准(take into account the following criteria):有利于(至少无害于)当地社会、经济的发展;有利于占有市场(occupy the market)、增加销售(increase sales);有利于提高旅行社的竞争力;有利于刺激中间商或代理人的销售热情(stimulate the sales persons' enthusiasm);有利于保证原有产品的正常发展。

2. 定量分析

定量分析的核心问题是准确计算各种方案(various schemes)所需的成本和可能达到的利润额。

例如,某旅行社拟开发某条旅游线路,该旅行社对线路的需求量大致估计为高、中、低和很低四种情况,每种情况出现的概率无法预测(unpredictable)。为了开发此条线路,旅行社设计出4种方案,计划经营3年。根据计算,各方案的损益额(profit and loss of each scheme)如表3-5所示。

2.3 Plan Selection

2.3.1 Qualitative analysis

2.3.2 Quantitative analysis

表 3-5 线路设计方案损益分析对比表
Profit and Loss Analysis and Contrast Table of Line Design Scheme

单位:千元/Unit:1 000 *yuan*

损益额 Profit and Loss	方案 1 Plan 1	方案 2 Plan 2	方案 3 Plan 3	方案 4 Plan 4
高 High	600	800	350	400
中 Middle	400	350	220	250
低 Low	0	−100	50	90
很低 Very Low	−150	−300	0	50

(1) 等概率法(Equal probability method)

所谓等概率法,就是假定每种市场需求状况发生的概率相同。由此可得各方案的损益额为:

方案(Plan)1=1/4 ×(600+400+0−150)=212.5
方案(Plan)2=1/4×(800+350−100−300)=187.5
方案(Plan)3=1/4×(350+220+50+0)=155
方案(Plan)4=1/4×(400+250+90+50)=197.5

根据计算结果可以判断,方案1为最优方案。

(2) 最大的最小值法(Maximum-minimum method)

使用最大的最小值法时,首先确定各个方案在不同市场需求状况下的最小收益值(determine the minimum profit value

The so-called equal probability method is to assume that the probability of occurrence of each market demand situation is the same.

of each scheme under different market demands),然后在其中选择收益值最大的方案(select the maximum profit value)作为最优方案(the optimal scheme)。各方案的最小收益值分别为：

方案(Plan)1＝－150

方案(Plan)2＝－300

方案(Plan)3＝0

方案(Plan)4＝50

由此可以判断，方案4为最优方案。

(3) 最大的最大值法(Max maximum value method)

使用最大的最大值法时，首先确定各个方案在不同市场需求状况下的最大收益值(determine the maximum profit value of each scheme under different market demand conditions),然后在其中选择收益值最大的方案作为最优方案(then choose the scheme with the maximum profit value as the optimal one)。各方案的最大收益值分别为：

方案(Plan)1＝600

方案(Plan)2＝800

方案(Plan)3＝350

方案(Plan)4＝400

由此可以判断，方案2为最优方案。

(4) 乐观系数法(Optimistic coefficient method)

在使用最大的最小值法和最大的最大值法时决策者根据自己对未来的判断进行决策，但决策过程缺少对未来各种状况发生可能性的程度判断(lack of judgments about the possibility of future situations)。设乐观系数(optimistic coefficient)为 $a(0 \leqslant a \leqslant 1)$，则 $1-a$ 为悲观系数(pessimistic coefficient)。乐观系数表示对最大值发生可能性的程度判断(judge the degree of possibility of maximum occurrence),悲观系数表示对最小值发生可能性的程度判断(judge the degree of possibility of minimum occurrence)。

设 $a=0.2$，则 $1-a=0.8$，那么各方案损益额分别为：

方案(Plan)1＝0.2×600＋0.8×(－150)＝0

方案(Plan)2＝0.2×800＋0.8×(－300)＝－80

方案(Plan)3＝0.2×350＋0.8×0＝70

方案(Plan)4＝0.2×400＋0.8×50＝120

由此可以判断，方案4为最优方案。

(四) 试产试销

产品试产与试销的目的主要有三个:了解产品的销路,检验市场经营组合策略的优劣,发现问题并解决问题。

(五) 投放市场

旅行社在将产品正式投放市场(put their products into the market),实现产品商业化(commercialize their products)时,应充分考虑目标市场的选择、销售渠道策略、促销策略(promotion strategy)和价格策略(price strategy)等因素。

(六) 检查完善

表 3-6 旅游线路综合评价表
Comprehensive Evaluation Table of Tourist Routes

分析项目 Analysis Items	分析结果 Analysis Results			问题 Problems	措施 Measures
	现状 Present	预测 Forecast	评分 Score		
1. 竞争能力 Competitive Power	竞争性强弱 Competitiveness					
	价 格 Price					
	成 本 Cost					
	质 量 Quality					
	服 务 Service					
	信 誉 Reputation					
2. 销售增长率 Sales Growth Rate					
3. 市场占有率 Market Share					
4. 获利能力 Profitability					
5. 经营实力 Business Capacity					
6. 综合评价 Overall Merit					

2.4 Trial Production and Sales

There are three main purposes for trial production and trial sale: to know about the sales of products, to examine the advantages and disadvantages of market operation and combination strategy, to find out problems and solve problems.

2.5 Put into the Market

2.6 Check and Improve

第三节 旅行社产品的评价与筛选
Section Three Evaluation and Screening of Travel Agency Products

Screening existing products is an important part of travel agency product innovation and also the basis of developing new products.

Generally, travel agencies adopt the four-quadrant evaluation method or matrix evaluation method to analyze and evaluate the existing products.

1 Four-Quadrant Evaluation Method

筛选现有产品是旅行社产品创新中的一项重要内容,也是开发新产品的基础。旅行社产品设计人员应根据市场调查(market survey)和预测结果(prediction results),对现有产品进行分类和比较,从中选出畅销产品(best-selling products)、经济效益好的产品和有发展前途的产品,并淘汰滞销产品(eliminate unmarketable products)、经济效益差的产品(products with poor economic benefits)和没有发展前途的产品(products without promising development)。旅行社在筛选产品过程中,一般采用四象限评价法或矩阵评价法对现有产品进行分析和评价。

一、四象限评价法

四象限评价法是在美国波士顿咨询集团(BCG)设计的"市场导向型产品检测模型"(market-oriented product testing model)基础上加以改进后提出的。

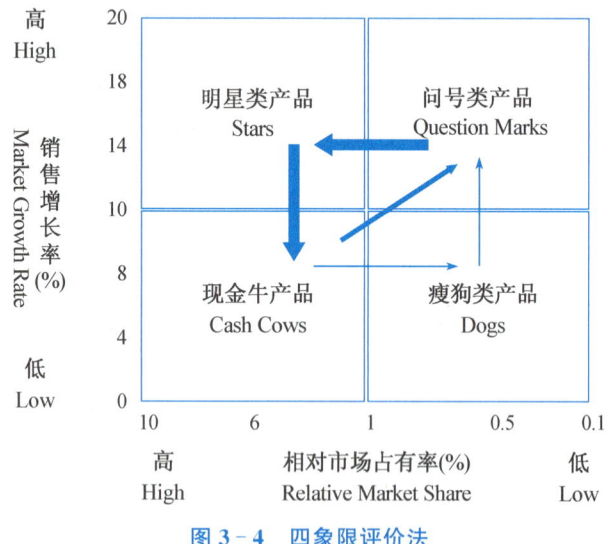

图3-4 四象限评价法
Four-Quadrant Evaluation Method

(一)"明星类"产品

此类产品市场占有率高、销售增长率也高(high sales growth rate)。这类产品处于迅速增长阶段(可形象地称之为"明星类"产品),为维持其发展需要投入大量资金(need huge invest),因此也是占用资金较多的产品。之所以要投入大量资金,是因为它们有希望成为第二类产品(have the potential to be the cash cow products)。

(二)"现金牛类"产品

此类产品市场占有率高、销售增长率低。这类产品由于市场占有率高,盈利多,现金收入多,可以带来大量现金,企业可用此类商品带来的现金支持其他需要现金的产品(products in need of cash)。因此,每个企业都十分重视这类"当家产品"(attach great importance to this kind of "master product")。

(三)"问号类"产品

此类产品市场占有率低(low market share),销售增长率高(high sales growth rate)。多数产品最初都属此类产品(Most products initially fall into this category)。为提高市场占有率,企业需要加大生产,加强推销,因而需要大量现金,要靠(rely on)"现金牛类"产品来支持。为此,企业应慎重考虑(carefully consider)这样做是否合算(这类产品被形象地称为"问号类"产品)。企业无疑要支持(no doubt need to support)这类产品中确有发展前途的产品,但不宜过多,以免资金分散(disperse funds),效益降低(reduce benefits)。

(四)"瘦狗类"产品

此类产品市场占有率低、销售增长率也低。这类产品是微利(low-profit)、保本(cost-saving),甚至亏本的(loss-making products)产品,因而被称为"瘦狗类"产品。

由于绝大多数产品存在着市场生命周期(have market life cycle),以上四类产品在矩阵图(matrix diagram)中的位置也会随着企业的经营策略而不断变化。这些可供选择的企业投资策略通常有以下四种。

1. 发展

目标是提高产品的相对市场占有率(relative market share)。为达此目标,有时甚至不惜放弃短期收入(at the

---

1.1 Star Products

1.2 Cash Cow Products
For high market sharing and profit, and bringing a large amount of cash, these kind products are figuratively called cash cow products.

1.3 Question Mark Products

1.4 Thin Dog Products

expense of short-term income)。这种策略特别适用于"问题类"产品,与有效的促销组合相结合(combine with effective promotion strategy),使它们尽快转化为"明星类"产品。

2. 维持

目标是维持产品的相对市场占有率。这种策略特别适用于"现金牛类"产品,尤其是其中的大"金牛"。因为这类产品能够提供大量现金(provide a lot of cash)。此类产品大多处于市场生命周期的成熟阶段(in the mature stage of the life cycle),采取有效的营销措施(take effective marketing measures)维持相当长一段时间是完全可能的。

3. 收割

目的在于尽可能多地追求短期利润(pursue as much short-term profit as possible),而不顾长期效益(regardless of long-term benefits)。这种策略特别适用于弱小的"现金牛类"产品,这类产品很快就要从成熟期转入衰落期(go from maturity to decline),前途暗淡,所以要趁这类产品在市场上仍有一定地位时尽可能从它们身上获取更多的现金收入(try to get as much cash from them as possible)。同样道理,这种策略也适用于下一步计划放弃的"问号类"和"瘦狗类"产品。具体方法包括减少投资、降低质量、减少促销费用、提高价格等。至于由此所带来的后果,则不予考虑(not taken into account)。

4. 放弃

目的是清理、变卖现存产品(clean up and sell existing products),不再生产,并把各种资源用于生产经营其他经济效益好的产品(use all kinds of resources to produce and operate other products with good economic benefits)。显然,这种策略适用于没有发展前途的(have no future),或者妨碍企业增加盈利(block companies from increasing profits)的某些"问题类"或"瘦狗类"产品。

二、矩阵评价法

矩阵评价法又称通用电气公司模型(general electric company model)、多因素业务矩阵法(multi-factor business matrix method)、GE矩阵法(GE matrix method)。它是用两个由多种因素综合评价得出的指标——市场吸引力和竞争力指标,来建立矩阵对企业目前业务组合进行分析的一种方法。

这种方法是对波士顿方法的一种改进(the improvement on the Boston method),将分析因素从两个因素变为多种因素(make the analysis factors become multiple factors from two factors),从而使分析更加全面,结论更为可靠(the analysis is more comprehensive and the conclusion is more reliable)。

对市场吸引力和企业不同业务的竞争能力进行综合评价,需要考虑许多因素。如对市场吸引力进行评价,会考虑市场规模(market size)、市场增长率(market growth rate)、竞争程度(degree of competition)、技术壁垒(technical barriers)和环境影响(environmental impact)等因素;对企业不同业务的竞争能力,会考虑市场占有率(market share)、产品质量(product quality)、品牌声誉(brand reputation)、生产效率(production efficiency)、促销与分销能力(promotion and distribution ability)、产品成本(product cost)和管理能力(management ability)等因素。通过评价两方面所包含的各种因素的权重和评分值(1~5),再进行加权平均,即可求得市场吸引力和企业不同业务竞争能力的综合评分(comprehensive scoring of market attractiveness and different business competitiveness)。需要注意的是,对不同企业的不同业务单位(different business units),评价市场吸引力和竞争能力要考虑的因素是不同的。根据企业不同业务单位的综合评分,结合该业务的市场规模及企业的市场占有率,就可以反映一个企业目前经营的业务组合状况(the current business portfolio)。

(一) 吸引力评价

吸引力评价共分四个步骤(four steps):首先,确定产生吸引力的重要因素(determine the important factors that generate attraction),一般包括发展潜力、市场规模、获利能力、竞争激烈程度等;其次,确定权数(determine the weight),给每个因素一个权数表示其对旅行社的相对重要性;再次,评估产品中每一项因素的吸引力(evaluate the attractiveness of each factor in the product),通常采用1~5个等级,数字越高越有吸引力;最后,确定产品的整体吸引力(determine overall attractiveness of the product),旅行社为其全部产品中的各个产品计算出一个总权数(calculate a total weight)。

two indexes, market attractiveness and competitiveness, which are obtained from the comprehensive evaluation of multiple factors.

2.1 Attractiveness Evaluation

表3-7 吸引力评价示例表
Sample Table of Attractiveness Evaluation

产品吸引力标准 Product Attraction Standard	权数 Weights	系数 Coefficient (1—5)	加权数 Weighting Coefficient
产品市场规模 Product Market Scale	0.10	3	0.30
产品发展潜力 Product Development Potential	0.30	5	1.50
产品获利能力 Profitability of Products	0.20	4	0.80
产品成本 Product Cost	0.05	5	0.25
产品销售渠道 Product Sales Channels	0.10	5	0.50
竞争激烈程度 Degree of Competition	0.20	3	0.60
产品所处周期阶段 Product Cycle Stage	0.05	2	0.10
合计 Total	1.00		4.05

2.2 Competitiveness Evaluation

2.2.1 Determine the sum of product weights

Product competitiveness evaluation includes two aspects, namely, determining the sum of product weights and product comparisons.

(二)竞争力评价

1. 确定产品加权数总和

产品竞争力评价包括两个方面,即确定产品加权数总和与产品比较。首先,确定产品加权数总和,分四个步骤:一是找出产品在市场竞争中成功的关键因素(find out the key factors to make the product successful in the market competition);二是根据所起作用的重要程度(according to the importance),给每个因素规定权数(determine the weight of each factor);三是计算各项因素的加权数(calculate the weighted number of each factor),评价时采用1~5级评分标准,数字越高越有竞争力;四是计算出加权数总和并用其表示产品的竞争能力指数(calculate the sum of weighted numbers and use them to represent the competitiveness index of products)。

表3-8 产品竞争力评价示例表
Examples of Product Competitiveness Evaluation

关键性成功因素 Key Success Factors	权数 Weights	系数 Coefficient (1—5)	加权数 Weighting Coefficient
市场份额 Market Share	0.15	5	0.75
专业知识含量 Professional Knowledge	0.15	2	0.30
产品知名度 Product Awareness	0.15	4	0.60
接待服务水平 Reception Service Level	0.20	5	1.00
价格的竞争性 Competitiveness of Prices	0.25	5	1.25
经营成本 Operating Cost	0.10	3	0.30
合计 Total	1.00		4.20

2. 产品比较

完成上述各项分析后,将旅行社全部产品绘成各种圆圈,标在产品位置图内。纵向表示产品吸引力(vertical direction means product attractiveness),横向表示产品竞争力(horizontal direction means competitiveness)。每个圆圈的中心点位置由该产品的产品吸引力和产品竞争力两个得分决定(the center position of each circle is determined by the two scores of attractiveness and competitiveness),圆圈大小与该产品销售总额成正比(size of the circle is proportional to the total sales),阴影部分表示产品在市场上所占的份额(the shadow part represents the market share)。

处于左上方(upper left)三个区的业务单位,如图中的A、B两个业务单位,市场吸引力和竞争能力均较高(high market attractiveness and competitiveness),企业应加强投资(strengthen investment to promote),以促进其发展;对于处于左下角到右上角(lower left corner to the upper right corner)对角线上(business units of main diagonal)三个区的业务单位,如图中的C、D业务单位,其市场吸引力和竞争能力总体上居中(market attractiveness and competitiveness are generally in the middle),企业应有选择地投资(invest selectively),以促进其发展,使其一部分能转向竞争能力较强的区域,或者继续为企业多赚利润;右下方(zones on the lower right)三个区的

2.2.2 Product comparison

After completing the above analysis, draw all tourism products into various circles and mark them in the product location map.

业务单位,如图中的 E、F 业务单位,其市场吸力和竞争能力均较低(have low market attractiveness and competitiveness),在正常情况下应逐步缩减其投资,或采取放弃策略(gradually reduce their investment or adopt the abandonment strategy)。

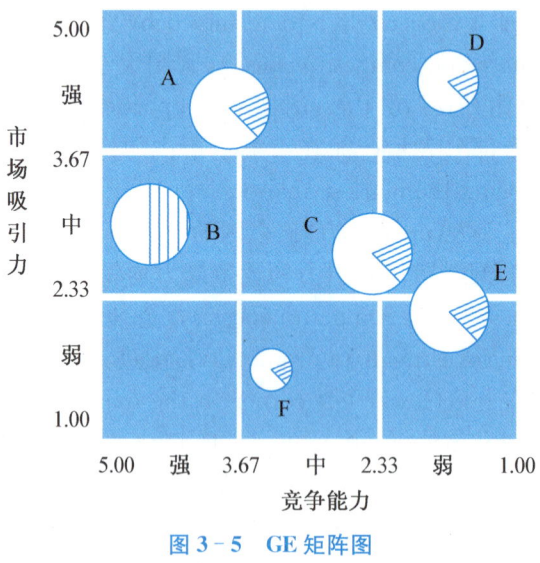

图 3-5　GE 矩阵图
GE Matrix Diagram

实训项目03 旅行社产品设计与开发

Project 3　Prepare a Presentation on the Design and Development of Travel Agency Products

一、实训目标(Training Objectives)：

1. 通过实训加深对旅行社产品设计相关理论知识的理解。

2. 提高旅游资源采录整理能力；学会使用信息技术手段制作旅游地图或者手绘旅游线路地图，学会设计常规旅行社产品与主题旅行社产品，提高旅行社产品成本核算和定价能力。

3. 培养以人为本的服务意识、严谨求实的工作作风、创新求异的思维方式。

二、实训学时(Training Period)：2～8学时

三、实训地点(Training Place)：旅行社情景实训室

四、实训设备(Training Equipment)：联网计算机、移动硬盘或U盘、A4绘图纸、铅笔、橡皮。

五、项目描述(Project Description)：

为了开发以本地及周边旅游目的地的旅行社产品，设计产品主题，采录并整理旅游资源(包括自然、人文景点、景观等)，进行旅游地图制作，形成旅行社产品，并用PPT汇报采集成果。

六、实训任务及要求(Tasks and Requirements)：

实训任务一览表

序号	实训任务名称	实训内容	实训学时	实训地点
01	设计线路主题或创意	通过讨论，对旅游线路的性质、大致内容和设计思路等各方面因素作出高度概括	2	旅行社情景实训室
02	采录旅游资源	针对一定地域范围，收集旅游资源(包括自然、人文景点、景观等)，用PPT展示	2	
03	手绘旅游地图或电脑制作	形成旅游线路，手绘旅游线路地图，标识出游览点之间的距离与行车时间	2	
04	设计旅行社产品	通过讨论，设计1～2个旅行社产品，并开展PPT展示活动	2	

注：教师可根据需要选用实训项目和学时。

七、实训成果(Practical Results)：

1. 每组完成旅游线路产品策划书WORD电子文档1份

和旅游产品展示PPT电子档1份。

2. 将上述两个文件放入文件夹,命名为:"班级名称+小组编号+旅行社产品设计与开发实训作业"。

八、考核标准(Assessment Criterion):

项目	考核内容和要求	分值	得分
表现	按时完成任务,工作积极主动,具有合作精神	20	
内容	内容全面、真实、精确	40	
格式	格式规范、语言简洁、样式美观	20	
创新	有创意,有市场潜力	20	
小计		100	

第四章　旅行社计调与采购管理
Chapter Four　The Operations and Procurement of Travel Agencies

【学习目标】　**Learning Objectives**

1. 了解旅行社计调业务流程（operation business process）；
2. 了解旅游服务采购（procurement of tourism service）的概念、流程及内容；
3. 掌握旅行社产品的定价方法（pricing methods）。

必须完整、准确、全面贯彻新发展理念，坚持社会主义市场经济改革方向，坚持高水平对外开放，加快构建以国内大循环为主体、国内国际双循环相互促进的新发展格局。

——党的二十大报告摘录

✓本章课程视频讲解　　✓实训指导书
✓线上课堂链接　　　　✓优秀学生作品精选
✓本章训练题库　　　　✓时政新闻
✓本章拓展资源

第一节 旅行社计调业务概述
Section One An Overview of the Operations of Travel Agencies

Product design and marketing, reception and accounting are three major businesses of travel agencies.

计调在旅行社三大业务(产品的设计与宣传销售、接待业务、财会业务)中属于不太稳定的一类,其业务范围(business scope)常随着旅行社功能的加强而延伸(extending with the enhancement of travel agency functions),因此,不同的业务类别对计调的要求也不尽相同。最初,旅行社除了为旅游者安排旅行游览外,主要是为社会团体和零星客人代订机、车票,安排食宿,即承接与旅游有关的各种单项委托业务。

Undertake a variety of individual entrustment business related to tourism.

随着业务范围的扩大(enlargement),旅行社开始设立(set up)专职岗位或部门(full-time position or department)。计调开始对外代表旅行社同旅游供应商(上下游行业)建立广泛的协作网络,签订有关协议,取得代办人身份(get agent identity),以保证提供旅游者所需的各项委托事宜,并协同处理有关计划变更和突发事件(plan changes and emergencies);对内做好联络和统计工作,为旅行社业务决策和计划管理提供信息服务(information service)。至此,计调业务作为旅行社的主要业务地位得以确立。

Operators began to, on behalf of travel agencies, make collaboration network (upstream and downstream industry) with travel suppliers.

一、旅行社计调业务的含义

1 Definition of the Operations of Travel Agencies

计调是计划、调度的简称(abbreviation of planning and scheduling),是旅行社业务的命脉,是为完成接待计划和相关信息统计,承担旅游服务采购和有关业务调度工作,是旅行社经营活动的重要环节。旅行社通过外联招徕客源(attract customers through external connection),而接待前的准备工作则由计调人员承担(preparation before reception is undertaken by operators)。担任计调的人员在岗位识别上通常被称为计调员、线控、团控、担当等(operators are usually called line controller, group controller and responsible person)。旅行社计调有广义和狭义之分(There are broad sense and narrow sense of travel agency operators)。

广义来看(in broad sense),旅行社计调业务既包括计调部门为业务决策而进行的信息提供(information provision)、调查研究(investigation and research)、统计分析(statistical analysis)、计划编制(plan formulation)等参谋性的工作,又包括为实现计划目标而进行的统筹安排(overall arrangement)、协调联络(coordination and liaison)、组织落实(organization and implementation)、业务签约(business contract signing)、监督检查(supervision and inspection)等业务性工作。

狭义(in narrow sense)来看,计调业务主要指旅行社在接待业务中,为旅游团安排各种旅游活动所提供的间接性服务(indirect services),包括安排食、住、行、游、购、娱等事宜,选择旅游合作伙伴(partners)和导游,编制和下发(compiling and issuing)旅游接待计划、旅游预算表(tourism budget tables),以及为确保这些服务而与其他旅游企业或有关行业、部门建立合作关系(establish cooperative relations)等。

二、旅行社计调业务的职能

旅行社作为旅行行业的中介组织(intermediary organization),一般通过向其他旅游服务企业(tourism service enterprises)采购旅游服务要素(tourism services elements),然后加上自己的导游服务(tour guide services)再销售出去。因此,除导游服务以外,旅行社产品的构成要素几乎全部采购自其他旅游供应商(tourism suppliers)。

综合来看(generally speaking),旅行社计调具有以下几种基本职能(basic functions):① 选择职能(selecting functions),在众多的采购对象中选择最理想的合作伙伴,从而优化组合成一个最佳服务系统(optimize an optimal service system),以保证最优服务质量(service quality);② 签约职能,采取签订经济合同的形式来保持合作关系的稳定性;③ 联络职能(liaison function),以便及时、准确、无误地处理各类突发问题(deal with all kinds of emergencies);④ 统计职能(statistical function),旅游业务逐月、逐季、逐年(monthly, quarterly and year by year)的定量统计和分析,可以检查旅行社经营业务的实际情况,从而发现并及时解决问题,同时了解客源的流向、流量(flow direction and flow scale of customers),作为旅行社进行经营决策的依据(as the basis to make decisions);⑤ 创收职能(income-generating function),虽然计调部门不是旅行社的直接创收部门(indirect income-generating department),但能够

2 Functions of the Operations of Travel Agencies

Sign contracts to maintain the stability of cooperative relations in the form of economic contracts.

间接创收(indirectly generate income),增加经济效益,这也是计调部门的一项重要职能。

3 Work Flow of the Operations of Travel Agencies

三、旅行社计调的工作流程

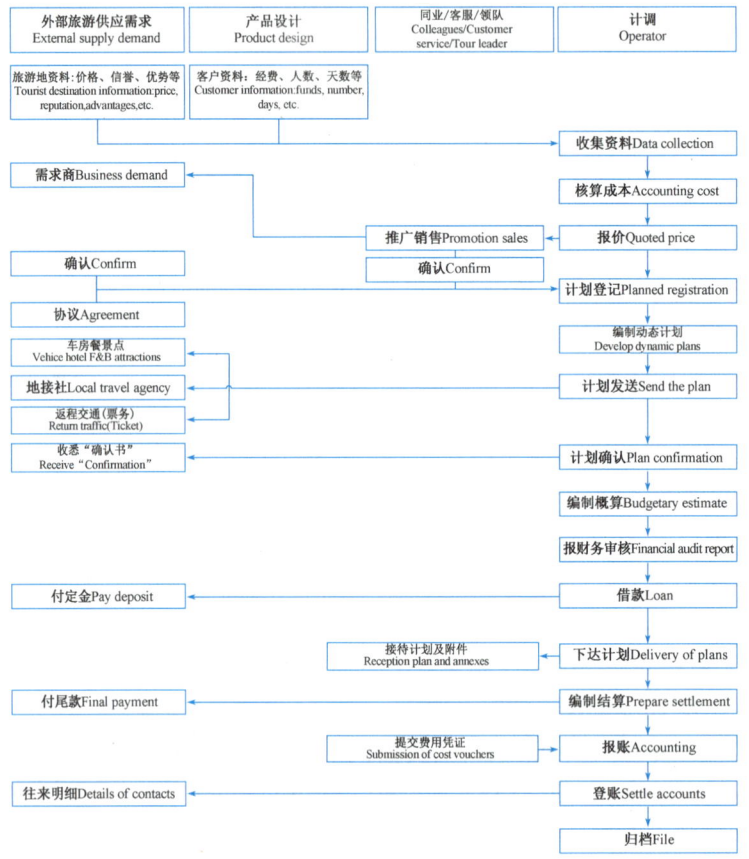

图 4-1 旅行社计调业务流程
Work Flow of the Operations of Travel Agencies

3.1 Collect Customers' Demand Information

（一）搜集客户需求资料

客户的资料(customer information)主要包括旅游者经费预算、人数、天数,以及其他要求等(tourist budget, tourist number, days, and other requirements)。

3.2 Design and Quotation of Travel Routes

（二）线路设计及报价

在客户需求(customers' demand)的基础上,根据对方询价编排线路(arrange tour routes according to tourists' inquiry)。

如车价、导服费、餐费、保险费(insurance)等,然后一起加起来,再利用成本加成法(cost addition method)等定价方法确定线路价格(route price)。以"报价单"(Quotation Sheet)提供相应价格信息(报价)。

(三) 计划登录

将团号(group number)、人数(number of people)、国籍(nationality)、抵/离机(车)时间等相关信息录入(log)当月团队动态表(group dynamic table)中。

(四) 编制团队动态表

编制接待计划,将人数、陪同数、抵/离航班(车)时间、住宿酒店、餐厅、参观景点、地接旅行社、接团时间及地点、其他特殊要求等逐一登记在"团队动态表"中。

(五) 计划发送

向各有关单位发送计划书,逐一落实。

(1) 用房(Housing):根据团队人数、要求,向协议酒店(cooperative hotel)或指定酒店发送"订房计划书"并要求对方书面确认(written confirmation)。如遇人数变更,及时发出"更改件"(Amendment),也需要对方书面确认;如遇酒店无法接待,应及时通知(inform)组团社(organizing agency),经同意后调整至同级别酒店(adjust to the same level hotel after approved)。

(2) 用车(Car):根据人数、要求安排用车,向协议车队(cooperative automobile company)发送"订车计划书"(Booking Plan)并要求对方书面确认。如遇变更,及时发出"更改件",也要求对方书面确认。

(3) 用餐(Dining):根据团队人数、要求,向协议餐厅(cooperative restaurant)发送"订餐计划书"。如遇变更,及时发出"更改件",并要求对方书面确认。

(4) 地接社(Local reception agency):向协议地接社发送"团队接待通知书"并要求对方书面确认。如遇变更,及时发出"更改件",并要求对方书面确认。

(5) 返程交通(Return traffic):仔细落实并核对计划,向票务人员下达"订票通知单",注明团号、人数、航班(车次)、用票时间、票别、票量,并由经手人签字。如遇变更,及时通知票务人员。

3.3 Log in the Plans

3.4 Compile Group Dynamic Tables

Prepare the reception plan, and register the requirements in the group dynamic table one by one.

3.5 Send Plans

Send the proposal to the relevant units for the implementation one by one.

Send the team reception notice to the cooperative reception agency.

Carefully implement and check the plan, and issue the "booking notice" to the ticket staff.

3.6　Plan Confirmation

（六）计划确认

逐一落实完毕后（或同时），编制接待"确认书"（compile the reception confirmation letter），加盖确认章（affix the confirmation stamp），发送至组团社（tour wholesaler）并确认组团社收到。

3.7　Budgetary Estimate

Prepare team budget estimates. Indicate cash charges and purposes.

（七）编制概算

编制团队"概算单"。注明现付费用、用途。送财务部经理审核，填写"借款单"（Loan Form），与"概算单"（Budget Estimate Form）一并交部门经理审核签字，报总经理签字后，凭"概算单""接待计划""借款单"向财务部（borrow money from finance department）领取借款。

3.8　Release Plan

（八）下达计划

编制"接待计划"及附件（prepare reception plan and annex），由计调人员签字并加盖团队计划专用章（Signature and seal），通知导游人员领取计划及附件。附件包括（attachments include）：名单表、向协议单位提供的加盖作业章的公司结算单（Company Settlement Form）、导游人员填写的"陪同报告书"（Accompanying Report）、游客（全陪）填写的"质量反馈单"（Quality Feedback Form）、需要现付的现金等，票款当面点清（count face to face）并由导游人员签收。

3.9　Settlement Establishment

Fill out the company's Team Settlement Form and affix the company's special financial stamp after examination.

（九）编制结算

填制公司"团队结算单"，经审核后加盖公司财务专用章，于团队抵达前将结算单传真至组团社进行催收（fax to the tour wholesaler for collection）。

3.10　Reimbursement

The operator shall examine the details "Accompanying Report", fill out the "Tour Expense Summary Sheet" and "Final Account Sheet".

（十）报账

团队行程结束，导游员凭"接待计划"（Reception Plan）、"陪同报告书"（Accompanying Report）、"质量反馈单"（Quality Feedback Form）、原始票据（original bills）等及时向部门计调人员报账。计调人员详细审核导游填写的"陪同报告书"，以此为据填制"团费用小结单"及"决算单"，交给部门经理审核签字后，交财务部并由财务部经理审核签字，总经理签字，向财务部报账。

(十一) 登账

部门将涉及该团的协议单位的相关款项(relevant payment)及时登录到"团队费用往来明细表"(Group Expense Exchange List)中,以便核对(for verification)。

(十二) 归档

整理该团的原始资料(sort out the group's original information),每月底将该月团队资料登记存档,以备查询。

第二节 旅行社产品要素采购及供应链管理
Section Two The Procurement of Travel Agency Products and Supply Chain Management

旅行社产品要素采购是旅行社部门最基本的业务之一(one of the most basic businesses),其采购成效直接关系到旅行社产品的价格和企业经营活动的成败。

一、旅行社产品要素采购的概念

采购是指在需要的时间和地点,以最低成本(at the lowest cost)、最高效率(with the highest efficiency)获得最适当数量和品质的物资或服务(obtain the most appropriate quantity and quality of goods or services),并及时交付(deliver)部门使用的过程。旅游服务采购是指旅行社为了组合旅游产品(combine tourism products),而以一定的价格向其他旅游企业或与旅游业相关的其他行业和部门购买相关旅游服务项目(purchase relevant tourism service items from other tourism enterprises)的行为。

旅行社是一种旅游中介组织(tourism intermediary organization),并不直接经营旅游活动中的交通、食宿、游览、娱乐等服务项目,采购旅游服务也就成为旅行社经营活动的一个重要方面。旅行社产品要素采购的并不是具体的商品或实物(specific commodities or physical objects),而是某种设施或服务在特定时间内的使用权。

3.11 Entry Account

Timely log the information into the relative sheet.

3.12 File

Record the team's information at the end of each month for reference.

Its effect is directly related to the price of travel agency products and the success of business activities.

1 Definition of Procurement of Travel Agency Products

What the travel agency purchases is the right to use certain facilities or services in a specific period of time.

旅行社产品要素采购是旅行社通过合同或协议形式(through the form of contract or agreement),以一定价格(at a certain price)向其他旅游服务企业及相关部门定购食、宿、行、游、购、娱等服务要素的行为,以保证旅行社向旅游者提供所需的旅游产品。目前旅行社采购的项目主要有交通服务(transportation service)、住宿服务(accommodation service)、餐饮服务(catering service)、景点游览服务(scenic spot tour service)、娱乐服务(entertainment service)、保险(insurance)、出入境手续(entry and exit procedures)等内容。

二、旅游服务采购的策略

旅行社与其他旅游服务供应部门或企业之间的关系是一种商品交换的关系(a kind of commodity exchange relationship),都应遵循市场经济规律(follow the law of market economy)。旅行社采购时,必须遵循:保证供应原则(principle of ensuring supply),应从数量充足、质量保障和时间即时性三个方面加以努力;成本领先原则(principle of cost leadership),在激烈的市场竞争中占据成本优势;互惠互利原则(principle of reciprocity and mutual benefit),以实现合作最优化和降低总成本的目标(achieve the goal of optimizing cooperation and reducing total cost)。旅行社在实际采购活动中,采购人员可根据具体情况灵活运用采购策略。

(一)集中采购

集中采购(centralized procurement)是旅行社以最大的采购量去争取最大的优惠价格(strive for the maximum preferential price with the maximum procurement volume)的一种采购方法。集中采购的主要目的是通过扩大采购批量,减少采购批次(reduce procurement batches),从而降低采购价格和采购成本(reduce procurement prices and procurement costs)。集中采购策略主要适用于旅游温、冷点地区(warm and cold spots)和旅游淡季(off-season)。

(二)分散采购

分散采购(decentralized procurement)主要适用于两种情况:市场处于供不应求(market is in short supply)的旺季,目的是为了保证供应;市场处于供过于求(supply exceeds demand)的淡季,目的是为了降低成本。分散采购也是旅行社采购活动中经常使用的一种采购策略。一种是所谓近期分散采购(recent decentralized procurement),就是一团一购的采购方式。第二种分散采购就是旅行社设法从许多同类型旅游服务供应部门或企业获得所需旅游服务的一种采购方法(obtain required tourism services from many service suppliers)。

(三)建立采购协作网络

建立采购协作网络,通常可以使旅行社获得稳定的供给(obtain stable supply);在供不应求的情况下,旅行社获得的各种紧缺服务项目的机会比别人多(have more opportunities to obtain a variety of services than others);在供过于求的情况下,旅行社可以获得更加优惠的交易条件(more favorable trading terms)。旅行社在建立采购协作网络的过程中,必须坚持三个原则(must adhere to three principles):第一,协作网络必须比较广泛,覆盖面比较广(wide coverage);第二,运用经济规律,在互利互惠的基础上长期合作(long-term cooperation);第三,加强公关活动(strengthen public relations activities),建立良好的人际关系(establish good interpersonal relations)。

2.3 Establish a Network for the Procurement Collaboration

三、旅行社采购方式

随着旅游电子商务(tourism e-commerce)和会展旅游(MICE tourism)的发展,旅行社采购的方式也越来越多,越来越便捷。目前,旅行社常用的采购方式主要有以下四种。

3 Purchasing Method in Travel Agencies

(一)蹲点考察

蹲点考察是指旅行社的采购人员深入旅游服务项目的供应企业(supply enterprises)或部门,实地了解情况(know the situation on the spot),建立采购协作关系的采购方式,是旅行社采购的传统方式。这种采购方式最大的优点是能确保旅游服务项目的质量(ensure the quality of tourism service projects),但缺点是要花费较大的人力、财力资源(financial resources)和时间。

3.1 Spot Investigation

It is the traditional way to establish the purchasing cooperation relationships.

(二)电话咨询

电话咨询是指旅行社的采购人员通过电话去了解旅游企

3.2 The Procurement Based on Telephone Consultation

This kind of procurement should be based on the good business reputation.

业的服务供应情况,建立采购协作关系的采购方式。这种采购方式非常便捷高效(convenient and efficient),但是由于缺乏实地考察(lack of field investigation),所以很难把握服务项目的质量(grasp the quality of service)。因此这种方式采购应该建立在对方拥有良好商业信誉的基础之上。

3.3 The Procurement Based on Network

It is the main procurement mode of most small travel agencies.

(三) 网络采购

网络采购是指旅行社的采购人员通过网络搜索(network search)方式,了解旅游企业的服务供应情况,从而建立采购协作关系的采购方式。这种采购方式是近年来伴随旅游电子商务的快速发展而兴起,并且成多数小型旅行社的主要采购方式。网络采购不仅方便快捷,而且成本低(low cost)、选择多(more options)。但是这种采购方式也存在服务质量风险(service quality risks)。

3.4 The Procurement in Tourism Fairs

It is a favorite procurement method for large- and medium-sized travel agencies.

(四) 旅游交易会采购

近年来,旅游交易会(tourism fairs)、旅游博览会(tourism expositions)层出不穷,它不仅是旅游企业的营销机会(marketing opportunities),同时也是旅游企业寻求合作伙伴(seek partners),建立业务协作关系(establish business cooperation relations)的良机。这种采购方式虽然成本较高,但方便集中采购和面对面的业务洽谈(convenient for centralized procurement and face-to-face business negotiation),成为大中型旅行社青睐的一种采购方式。

4 Travel Agency Supply Chain Management

四、旅行社供应链管理

供应链管理(supply chain management,简称SCM)是一种先进的集成管理思想(integrated management theory),兴起于制造业。在注重时效(pay attention to timeliness)的市场环境中,单靠企业自身力量与优势无法立足,必须充分利用外部资源(make full use of external resources),注重与合作伙伴的合作(focus on cooperation with partners),发挥各企业的核心专长(give play to the core expertise of each enterprise),把自身弱势领域外包给合作伙伴(outsourcing to partners),从而提高整体效率实现共赢(win-win)的目标。近年来,旅游业也投入到这股供应链管理的浪潮中,旅行社作为旅游业的代表企业也顺应了这一趋势(conforming to this trend)。

（一）供应链管理的定义

供应链管理是通过对信息流(information flow)、物流(logistics)、资金流(capital flow)控制将供应商(suppliers)、制造商(manufacturers)、分销商(distributors)、零售商(retailers)直到最终用户(end user)连成一个整体的管理模式，它是一种新的管理模式，是企业的集合并注重企业间的合作。我国《国家标准物流术语》指出供应链管理是指对供应链涉及的全部活动即商流、物流、信息流和资金流进行计划、组织、协调与控制的活动。

（二）旅行社供应链管理的必要性

供应链结构一般由一个主导企业充当核心(a leading enterprise acts as the core)，把其他企业吸引到核心企业周围形成一个网链(form a network chain)。核心企业在供应链中发挥着信息交换中心与物流、资金流调度中心的角色(it plays the role of information exchange center, logistics and capital flow scheduling center)。供应链运作的好坏直接关系到整个供应链竞争力的大小，很大程度上取决于供应链上核心企业的影响力(influence of core enterprises)。

旅行社作为连接旅游需求与供给的纽带(as a link between tourism demand and supply)，在旅游产品生产和消费之间起着举足轻重的作用(plays a decisive role)。旅行社由于在整个旅游服务供应链上的特殊职能(special functions)，既直接和消费者接触，又同时充当旅游服务供应商企业的中介(acting as an intermediary for tourism service providers)，决定着旅行社在旅游信息汇集、客流调度等方面拥有独特的优势(unique advantages)，使其成为旅游服务供应链上的核心。

旅行社作为旅游企业群体的主导企业(dominant firm)，从功能上具备成为核心企业的条件。现实中，需要旅行社经营者、旅游供应商、政府等部门齐心合力，着力扩大旅行社规模(strive to expand the scale of travel agencies)，加强旅行社产品开发能力(strengthen the product development capability)，提高旅行社市场开拓能力(improve the market development ability)，不断提升旅行社商业信誉(enhance the commercial reputation)，逐步树立起旅行社在旅游供应链中的核心地位，发挥核心作用，成为供应链核心企业，从而对其他节点具有吸引力，有效提升整体旅游企业的市场核心竞争力。

4.1 Definition of Supply Chain Management

4.2 Necessity of Supply Chain Management of Travel Agencies

4.3 Network Structure of Tourism Supply Chain

(三) 旅游供应链的网络结构

旅游供应链(tourism supply chain)是一个由不同旅游活动的参与者组成的旅游组织网络(tourism organization network),该网络既包括私营企业(private enterprise),也包括公共部门(public sector)。关于旅游供应链的描述大体有两种:旅游供应链和旅游服务供应链。其实二者并无明显区别,可以通用。目前,国内外学者达成的一个普遍的共识是,旅游供应链是一个涉及多个行业的网络结构(network structure)而非链条结构(chain structure)。

旅游供应链网络结构是指由供应链成员按照旅游产品和服务的供应方向排列起来并表明各级供应商和顾客之间关系的网络构成。传统旅游供应链的网络结构是由旅游供应商(travel supplier)、旅游运营商(travel operator)、旅游代理商(travel agent)和旅游者等多个主体构成,其中虚线框(dashed box)里的制造商是旅游间接供应商(tourism indirect supplier),食宿行游购娱供应商是直接供应商(direct supplier),如图所示。

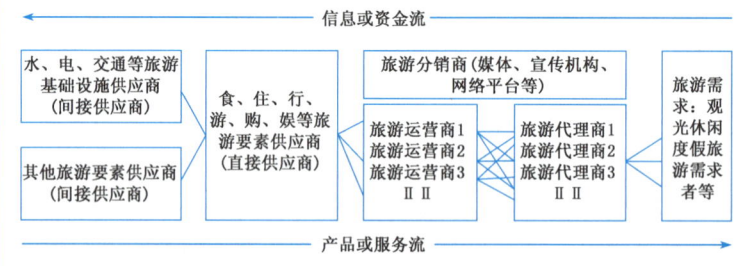

图 4-2 旅游供应链典型网络
Typical Network of Tourism Supply Chain

随着计算机、PC互联网、移动互联网的普遍使用,以及电子商务技术的应用,旅游供应链节点企业间的关系发生了很大变化,网络平台成为连接旅游供应商和旅游者之间的一种新型渠道,例如旅游供应链出现的新型中间商,即电脑预定系统(computer reservation system,简称CRS),它同时具有旅游运营商和代理商的职能,新型旅游供应链的网络结构更加突出了网络系统的重要性。

第三节 旅游服务采购的内容
Section Three The Components of Tourism Service Procurement

旅行社采购的项目主要有交通服务、住宿服务、餐饮服务、景点游览服务、购物服务、娱乐服务、地接服务、保险服务等内容。

Items purchased by travel agencies mainly include transportation service, accommodation service, catering service, scenic spot tour service, shopping service, entertainment service, local reception service, insurance service etc.

图 4-3 旅游服务采购的内容
Contents of Tourism Service Procurement

一、交通服务

1 Transportation Service

旅行社旅游交通采购业务主要包括航空(aviation)、铁路(railway)、公路(highway)和水运交通服务(water transportation services)采购。旅行社应取得有关交通部门的代理资格(obtain the agency qualification),以便顺利采购到所需的交通服务。

二、旅游住宿服务

2 Travel Accommodation Service

旅游住宿服务的费用在旅行社产品总费用中位居第二(rank second in the total cost),住宿服务是旅行社采购中又一重要内容。住宿服务的采购业务主要包括选择住宿服务设施(selection of accommodation facilities)、选择预订渠道(selection of booking channels)、确定客房租住价格(determination of room rental prices)和办理住宿服务预订手续(accomodation services)四项内容。

3　Food and Beverage

三、餐饮服务

国内旅行社在采购餐饮服务时，一般采用定点的办法（sentinel procurement method）。所谓定点是指旅行社经过对采购的餐馆、酒店进行综合考察（comprehensive inspection）筛选后，和被选择的餐馆、酒店进行谈判，就旅行社的送客人数（number of guests）、各类旅游者、旅游团队的就餐标准（dining standards）、付款方式（payment method）等达成协议。

4　Tour and Visit

四、游览与参观

旅游和参观是旅游者在目的地进行的最基本和最重要的旅游活动（most basic and important tourism activities）。旅行社采购人员应对本地区的重要游览景点和参观单位进行考察和比较（compare the important scenic spots and visiting units），并根据其不同特点分别同这些景点、单位进行联系，保证旅游者正常游览参观（ensure the normal visit of tourists）。在进行景点采购时，应与对方洽谈（negotiate with the partners）的具体内容通常包括以下几个方面：门票价格与优惠政策（ticket price and preferential policies）、结算方式与时间（payment method and time）、部分限流量景区预订与取消预订的方式与时间要求（requirements about booking and cancellation）、违约责任等（liability for breach of contract）。

5　Shopping and Entertainment Services

五、购物和娱乐服务

在购物和娱乐的采购中，采购人员一定要树立正确的观念（establish correct concepts），全面认识（fully understand）购物、娱乐和旅游产品之间的关系。进行购物服务采购时，应与对方商谈（discuss with partners）以下内容：游客自由选择权的保障（protection of tourists' free choice）、利润提成的方式（methods of profit commission）及结算方式（payment）、停车费用（parking fees）、违约责任（liability for breach of contract）等。

在采购娱乐服务时，应商谈以下内容：服务内容与时间（service content and time）、门票价格与优惠政策（ticket prices and preferential policies）、结算方式与时间（payment method and time）、预订与取消预订的方式与时间要求（booking and cancellation requirements)、违约责任(liability for breach of contract)等。

六、地接服务

地接服务采购是指组团旅行社(tour wholesaler)向目的地旅行社(destination travel agency)采购接待服务的一种业务,在行业内通常称为选择地接社。组团社应根据游客的需求及发展趋势(demands and development trends),有针对性地在各旅游目的地旅行社中选择比较,接待社应具备以下条件(should meet the following conditions)才能够作为合作伙伴。首先是有诚信(good faith),必须具备良好的信誉(must have good prestige);其次是有较强的接待能力(strong reception ability),能够采购到组团社委托其采购的各项旅游服务并提供优质的导游服务;再次是收费合理(reasonable charges),接待社的收费不能过高甚至超过旅游者和组团社的承受能力(affordability)。在进行一段时间的考察和合作(investigation and cooperation)后,应设法同那些表现上乘的接待社签订合作协议,建立长期合作关系(establish long-term cooperative relations)。

七、旅游保险

根据《旅行社条例》(Travel Agency Regulations)及相关法律(relevant laws),旅行社应该为旅游者提供规定的保险服务。由计调部门(Operations Department)负责采购保险服务。旅游保险的主要险种有以下几种。

(一) 旅行社责任保险

旅行社责任保险是指旅行社根据保险合同的约定,向保险公司(insurance companies)支付保险费(pay insurance premiums),保险公司对旅行社在从事旅游业务经营活动中,致使旅游者人身、财产遭受损害(damage to tourists' personal and property)应由旅行社承担的责任,承担赔偿保险金(indemnity insurance)责任的行为。

(二) 旅游意外保险

旅游意外保险,是指旅游者个人向保险公司支付保险费,

6 Local Reception Service

Select and compare among travel agencies in various tourist destinations.

7 Travel Insurance

7.1 Travel Agency Liability Insurance

Caused by travel agencies when they engage in tourism business operations.

7.2 Travel Accident Insurance

It refers to the insurance premium paid to the tourists by the insurance company.	一旦旅游者在旅游期间(during the travel period)发生意外事故,由承保的保险公司按合同约定,向旅游者支付保险金的保险行为。
	(三)航空旅客意外伤害保险
7.3 Air Passenger Personal Accident Insurance	航空旅客意外伤害保险,简称"航意险",属自愿投保的个人意外伤害保险(voluntary personal accident injury insurance)。
	(四)中国境外旅行救援意外伤害保险
7.4 Overseas Travel Rescue Accident Insurance	中国境外旅行救援意外伤害保险,属附加性保险(additional insurance),即附加在主保险合同上的保险险种(attached to the primary insurance)。

第四节　旅游产品定价
Section Four　Pricing Strategies for Tourism Products

There is no brand loyalty in the world that cannot be offset by two cents of discount.	定价是一门科学。菲利普·科特勒(Philip Kotler)认为,世上没有减价两分钱不能抵消的品牌忠诚。旅游产品价格是否科学、准确、合理(scientific, accurate and reasonable),影响着旅游景区在区域旅游市场(the regional tourism market)所占的份额(share),决定着旅游景区的经济效益(economic benefits)。

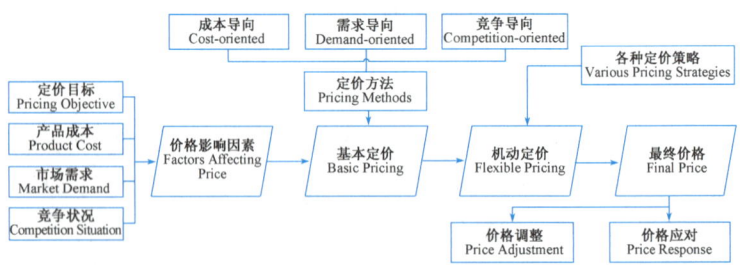

图 4-4　旅游产品定价流程图
Flow Chart of Tourism Products Pricing

The following five steps should be generally followed.	科学确定(scientifically determine)旅游产品的价格,一般要遵循以下五个步骤:首先研究目标市场旅游消费者的购买行为(purchase behavior);其次评估(evaluate)旅游企业旅游产

品的成本;再次分析旅游企业所处的市场环境(market environment),然后在此基础上确定旅游产品的定价目标(pricing target);最后选择旅游产品定价的方法及策略(method and strategy of pricing)。

一、影响旅游产品价格的因素

(一)旅游产品定价目标

旅游产品的定价目标(pricing target)是旅游企业营销目标(marketing target)的基础,是旅游企业选择定价方法(choose pricing methods)和制定价格策略(formulate pricing strategies)的依据,具体来说,定价有以下几种目标。

1. 利润导向目标

利润导向目标是旅游产品定价的目标之一,具体可以分为以下几种形式:① 投资收益定价目标(investment income pricing target),即旅游企业在一定时间内使旅游产品的价格有利于企业获取预期的投资报酬率(obtain the expected rate of return);② 短期最大利润定价目标(short-term maximum profit pricing target),即旅游企业通过制定较高价格,在较短时期内使企业利润最大化(maximize their profits in a relatively short period);③ 长期利润定价目标(long-term profit pricing goal),即旅游企业着眼于长期总利润水平(long-term total profit level)的逐步提高来确定旅游产品的销售价格(determine the sales price)。

2. 销售导向目标

销售导向目标是指制定旅游产品价格的主要目的是为巩固和提高市场占有率(consolidate and improve market share)、维持和扩大旅游产品的市场销售量(maintain and expand the market sales)。采用这种定价目标的旅游企业一般规模较大、实力较强,它们为扩大生产规模(expand the scale of production)、降低单位产品成本(reduce the cost),以及巩固其市场地位(consolidate their market position),往往在单位旅游产品上给予旅游者更多的优惠(give more preferential treatment to tourists),以争取与吸引旅游者。销售导向目标下所制定的价格,低于利润极大化的目标下的价格,但操作得当,可以使旅游企业的旅游产品达到某一特定的预期市场占有率(reach a certain expected market share),从而为旅游企业提供长期较大利

1 Factors Influencing the Price of Tourism Products

1.1 Target of Tourism Product Pricing

1.1.1 Profit-oriented Objectives

1.1.2 Sales-oriented objectives

润的可能性(possibility of long-term and large profits)。

3. 竞争导向目标

竞争导向目标是指旅游企业在分析自身旅游产品竞争能力(competitiveness)和竞争地位的基础上,以对付竞争对手(deal with competitors)和保护自身作为制定价格的目标。对于实力较弱的中小旅游企业(small and medium-sized tourism enterprises),容易招致实力雄厚的竞争对手的强力反抗(lead to strong resistance from powerful competitors),但实力雄厚的旅游企业,采用此种定价目标则容易以低价阻止竞争对手进入市场(prevent competitors from entering the market)或迫使较小企业减少市场份额甚至退出市场(withdraw from the market)。

1.1.3 Competition-oriented objectives

1.1.4 Social responsibility oriented goals

Put profit target in a relatively secondary position, emphasizing the goal of maximizing social efficiency.

4. 社会责任导向目标

社会责任导向目标指以社会责任为着眼点制定旅游产品价格,而将利润目标列于相对次要位置,强调社会效率最大化的目标。目前,世界各国倡导(advocate)对与环境保护(environmental protection)关系密切的某些旅游产品采用此种导向目标的定价方法。例如,关于生态旅游产品(ecotourism products)的定价,国际惯例是根据旅游环境的承载能力(carrying capacity)来限制游客规模和确定旅游产品的价格,主要目的不是营利(profitable),而是关注旅游生态环境的持续健康发展(sustainable and healthy development)。

1.2 Cost of Tourism Products

It is formed by the material consumption and labor remuneration spent in the process of production and logistics.

Obviously, the cost of tourism products is the critical point of accounting profit and loss.

(二) 旅游产品成本

旅游产品成本是构成旅游产品价值和价格(the value and price of tourism products)的主要组成部分(main component),是由旅游产品的生产过程和流通过程所花费的物质消费和支付的劳动报酬形成的。旅游企业在确定旅游产品的价格时,要使总成本得到补偿(compensate the total cost),价格不能低于平均成本费用。当旅游产品的售价大于产品成本时,旅游企业就可能形成盈利;反之(on the contrary),旅游企业的销售收入(sales revenue)不能弥补其劳动消耗(cannot make up for their labor consumption),旅游企业的生产将出现亏损(suffer losses)。显然,旅游产品的成本是旅游企业核算盈亏的临界点,是影响旅游产品价格最直接、最基本的因素。

1.3 Demand Elasticity of Tourism Products

(三) 旅游产品的需求弹性

旅游产品的需求弹性(demand elasticity)不仅受到产品供

求关系(restricted by the supply-demand relationship)的制约，而且受到产品需求弹性的影响。所谓旅游产品的需求弹性是指旅游产品的价格弹性(price elasticity)，即旅游产品价格的变化对市场需求量变化的影响程度。用公式表示为：需求的价格弹性＝需求量变化的百分比/价格变化的百分比。当大于1(greater than one)时，表示需求弹性较大；当小于1时(less than one)，表示旅游产品的需求弹性较小。一般说来，旅游景点产品、旅游购物、旅游娱乐的需求弹性相对较高，而旅游餐饮、旅游住宿、旅游交通的需求弹性相对较低。但是从总体说来(generally speaking)，旅游产品的需求弹性整体上是比较高的。

Price elasticity of demand= percentage of change in demand/percentage of change in price

（四）旅游产品市场竞争状况

旅游产品市场竞争(market competition)状况是指旅游产品竞争的激烈程度。旅游产品市场的竞争越激烈，对旅游产品的价格影响就越大。在完全竞争(complete competition market)中，旅游企业是被动地接受市场竞争中形成的价格，而没有定价的主动权，只能依靠提高管理水平与服务质量去扩大市场占有率。在垄断市场(monopoly market)上，某种旅游产品只是独家经营(manage exclusively)，那么其价格往往也具有垄断性(monopolistic)。某些旅游企业对旅游资源的独占性(monopoly of tourism resources)，例如对一些著名的名胜风景区的垄断性经营(monopoly management)，其制定的价格基本上是垄断性价格(monopoly price)；在寡头垄断市场(oligopoly market)中，少数几家大型旅游企业控制与操纵旅游产品的生产与经营，它们之间相互制约与限制，因而旅游产品的价格是由寡头企业控制和协议制定的。

1.4 Market Competition of Tourism Products

The more intense the competition in the market, the greater impact on the price of tourism products

二、旅游产品定价的方法

旅游企业在进行旅游产品定价时，一般遵循的原则(principles)如下：成本是价格的最下线(lowest line)，竞争对手与替代产品(alternative products)是定价的出发点(starting point)，顾客对旅游产品特有的评价是价格的上线。因此就形成了成本导向(cost orientation)、需求导向(demand orientation)、竞争导向(competition orientation)三种最基本的定价方法。

2 The Pricing Method of Tourism Products

Three basic pricing methods: cost orientation, demand orientation, competition orientation.

（一）成本导向定价法

成本导向定价法是一种传统的"将本求利"的定价方法。

2.1 Cost-oriented Pricing Method

Cost-oriented pricing method is a traditional "cost-seeking" pricing method.

This method is also conservative, passive and limited.

这种定价方法的实质是以价值为导向的,有利于旅游企业维持简单再生产(maintain simple reproduction)与进行经济核算(conduct economic accounting)。但此定价方法忽视了(ignore)市场需求、竞争、旅游消费者的心理(consumers' psychology)等因素,因而这种方法也具有保守性、被动性和局限性等特点。成本导向定价法主要包括成本加成定价法(cost-plus pricing)、投资回收定价法(investment recovery pricing)、目标收益法(target-return pricing)三种。

（二）需求导向定价法

2.2 Demand-oriented Pricing Method

需求导向定价法指的是以消费者对产品的需求程度和对产品价值的理解而形成的心理价格为定价(psychological price)依据,是一种伴随营销观念更新所产生的新型定价方法,主要包括需求差别定价法(demand differential pricing method)和理解价值定价法(understanding value pricing method)。

2.2.1 Demand differential pricing method

1. 需求差别定价法

需求差别定价法又称为价格区别对待法。这种方法主要根据产品的需求强度(demand strength)和需求弹性(demand elasticity)的差别来制定产品的价格。主要有以下几种类型：①根据旅游者的收入而进行的差别定价(differential pricing according to the different income status of tourists),如旅游景点的门票定价时针对学生、老年人实行特殊优惠价格；②根据旅游产品的产品形式进行差别定价(make differential pricing according to different forms of tourism products),常见于旅游商品定价；③根据地理位置而进行的差别定价(differential pricing according to different geographical locations)；④根据时间而进行的差别定价(differential pricing according to different time),如旅游淡旺季、双休日、黄金周制定不同价格。

2.2.2 Understanding value pricing

2. 理解价值定价法

理解价值定价法是指以消费者对产品价值的理解(consumers' understanding of product value)和认识程度作为依据来制定产品价格的方法。旅游企业采用这种方法定价的关键在于利用各种手段,在心理上增加旅游者所购旅游产品的附加值(added value),至少是使旅游产品的价格符合旅游者的理解价值(conform to the understanding value)。这就要求旅游企业定价时首先要确定好产品的市场定位(determine the market position),拉开本企业产品与竞争对手的差异,突出产品的特征(highlight the characteristics),并综合运用各种营销手段(various marketing strategies),树立深刻的市场形象(set up the profound market image),使消费者感到购买这些产品能获得更多的相对利益(gain more relative interests),从而提高他们接受价格的限度。

(三) 竞争导向定价法

2.3 Competition-Oriented Pricing Method

竞争导向定价法是指以同类产品或服务的市场供应竞争状况为依据,以竞争对手价格为基础的定价方法。采用这种方法定价,要求旅游企业在竞争的同时结合自身的(based on the market supply competition and the price of competitors)实力状况、发展战略(development strategy)等因素。在实际运用中,它主要表现为率先定价法(pioneer pricing method)、随行就市定价法(going-rate pricing)、追随核心企业定价法(follow the core enterprise pricing)。

三、旅行社产品的定价策略

3 Pricing Strategies for Travel Agency's Products

旅游产品的定价需要以科学的理论和方法(scientific theories and methods)为指导。但在激烈的竞争中,旅游企业还需要掌握一些高明的定价策略和技巧(sophisticated pricing strategies and skills)。旅行社产品定价策略指根据旅游市场的具体情况,从定价目标出发,灵活运用定价方法,使所制定的价格适应市场的状况(adapt to the market conditions),从而最终实现(achieve)既定的营销目标(marketing objectives)和企业的经营目标(business objectives)。

(一) 新产品定价策略

3.1 Pricing Strategies for New Products

一般情况下,旅行社对新产品可能会采用以下定价策略:撇脂定价法(skimming pricing),又称高价法(high-price pricing),即将产品的价格定得较高,尽可能在产品生命初期,在竞争者研制出相似产品之前,尽快回收投资并取得相当利润(recover investment and make considerable profits as soon as possible);渗透定价法(penetration pricing method),又称薄利多销策略(low profit and high turnover strategy),指产品在上市初期利用消费者求廉的消费心理,有意将价格定得很低,使新产品以物美价廉的形象(cheap and fine image)吸引顾客,占领市场,以谋取远期稳定的利润;满意定价策略(satisfactory pricing strategy),介于以上二者之间的一种定价策略,以正常

It is also known as "moderate price" or "gentleman price".

3.2　Psychological Pricing Strategy

3.3　Discount Pricing Strategy

A pricing strategy for enterprises to make certain concessions of the basic price in trading

4　Price Adjustment of Travel Agency Products

Once the price strategy and the price of products are formed, they should have certain stability.

的价格进入市场，既能得到消费者的接受，又不至于引起竞争者的注意(avoid attracting the attention of competitors)，所以这种定价策略又称为"温和价格"或"君子价格"。

(二) 心理定价策略

该策略考虑的不仅仅是经济因素，更多的是考虑消费者的心理因素。消费者对产品的认可并不单纯从产品的质量和品质来进行判断(judge by the quality)，很多旅游产品只有在消费者体验后(after experiencing)才能感受其质量。因此，购买之前，产品的价格就成为唯一直观的价值(intuitive value)反映，产品价格的心理效应(psychological effect)就起很大的作用。如尾数定价/零头定价策略(mantissa pricing/zero pricing strategy)、整数定价/声望定价策略(integer pricing/prestige pricing strategy)、招徕定价/特价定价策略(solicitation pricing/special pricing strategy)、系列定价/分级定价策略(series pricing/graded pricing strategy)等。

(三) 折扣定价策略

折扣定价策略实际上是企业在交易过程中，对基本价格做出一定的让步，直接或间接降低价格，以争取顾客、扩大销量的一种定价策略。如数量折扣(quantity discount)、现金折扣/提前支付折扣(cash discount/advance payment discount)、功能折扣/交易折扣(function discount/transaction discount)、季节折扣/季节差价(seasonal discount)等。

四、旅行社产品的价格调整

价格策略和旅行社产品的价格一旦形成，应具有一定的稳定性。但随着市场相关因素的变化，旅行社会对产品的价格策略和价格进行适当调整以实现企业营销目标(achieve marketing objectives)。引起旅行社对价格进行调整的具体情况(specific conditions)通常包括以下几个方面：市场供求变化(changes in market supply and demand)、产品的需求价格弹性大(high price elasticity of product demand)、成本变化(changes in cost)、企业或产品形象发生变化(changes in enterprises or product images)、外部经济社会环境和政策环境变化(changes in external economic and social environment and policy environment)、竞争对手价格变化(changes in competitors' prices)等。

实训项目 04　旅行社计调工作方案设计

Project 4　Design a Work Programme for the Operators in Travel Agencies

一、实训目标(Training Objectives)：

1. 通过实训加深理解计调在旅行社运转中的作用及主要业务流程。

2. 理解旅游采购服务是计调最基本的业务，了解旅游服务采购的内容、流程及注意事项。

3. 培养以人为本的沟通交流能力、创新求异的思维方式。

二、实训学时(Training Period)：2~8学时

三、实训地点(Training Place)：旅行社情景实训室

四、实训设备(Training Equipment)：商务洽谈室、移动硬盘或U盘、A4绘图纸、铅笔、橡皮。

五、项目描述(Project Description)：

计调部在旅行社中处于中枢位置，计调业务连接内外，牵一发动全身。一般而言，计调是指为落实接待计划所进行的服务采购，以及为业务决策提供信息服务的总和。本实训项目在于训练学生对于计调工作内容、流程等方面的熟悉程度。实训项目结束后，团队合作完成计调工作方案，并用PPT汇报团队成果。

六、实训任务及要求(Tasks and Requirements)：

实训任务一览表

序号	实训任务名称	实训内容	实训学时	实训地点
01	了解计调工作任务及业务流程	通过查阅资料、企业岗位调研等方式，了解旅行社计调工作的岗位职责、工作流程等内容	2	旅行社情景实训室
02	填写相关服务采购的表格	针对已有旅行社产品，进行服务采购，调研查阅相关企业或网站，填写相关表格	2	旅行社情景实训室
03	旅行社计调方案的设计与制作	计调方案设计，并用PPT汇报	2	旅行社情景实训室

注：教师可根据需要选用实训项目和学时。

(一)根据班级人数，每组可适当编制2~6人规模。通过

组内讨论，进行相关旅游要素搭配，设计 1~2 个旅行社产品。

（二）每组选择 1 个旅游产品，组内分工，制作并完成旅行社计调工作设计方案，并在课堂上展示。

七、实训成果（Practical Results）：

1. 每组完成旅行社计调工作设计方案 WORD 电子文档 1 份和旅游计调工作设计方案展示 PPT 电子档 1 份。

2. 将上述两个文件放入文件夹，命名为："班级名称＋小组编号＋旅行社计调工作设计方案实训作业"。

八、考核标准（Assessment Criterion）：

项目	考核内容和要求	分值	得分
表现	按时完成任务，工作积极主动，具有合作精神	20	
内容	内容全面、真实、精确	40	
格式	格式规范、语言简洁、样式美观	20	
创新	有创意，有市场潜力	20	
小计		100	

第五章　旅行社分销渠道管理
Chapter Five　Distribution Channel Management in Travel Agencies

【学习目标】 Learning Objectives

1. 了解旅游中间商(tourism intermediaries)的概念与类型；
2. 理解旅行社分销渠道(distribution channels)的类型及选择标准(selection criteria)；
3. 掌握旅行社分销渠道发展的趋势(development trend)。

> 坚持和完善社会主义基本经济制度，毫不动摇巩固和发展公有制经济，毫不动摇鼓励、支持、引导非公有制经济发展，充分发挥市场在资源配置中的决定性作用，更好发挥政府作用。
> ——党的二十大报告摘录

✓本章课程视频讲解　　✓实训指导书
✓线上课堂链接　　　　✓优秀学生作品精选
✓本章训练题库　　　　✓时政新闻
✓本章拓展资源

第一节 旅游中间商的类型
Section One Types of Tourism Intermediaries

一、旅游中间商的类型

1 Types of Tourism Intermediaries

It refers to intermediaries and individuals between producers and consumers.

旅游中间商是指介于旅游生产者与消费者之间,专门从事旅游产品或服务市场营销的中介组织和个人。由于旅游中间商在旅游市场营销中的作用,旅游生产企业与这些中介组织和个人的责权关系不同,因而旅游中间商的类型也就呈多样化形态。它主要包括旅游批发商(tourism wholesalers)、旅游经销商(tourism distributors)、旅游零售商(tourism retailers)、旅游代理商(tourism agents)以及随着互联网的产生与发展而出现的在线网络服务商(online network service providers)。

There are two ways to divide tourism intermediaries.

旅游中间商有两种划分方法:一种是根据产品在销售渠道中流动时有无所有权的转移(according to the transfer of ownership of products)划分为旅游经销商(tourism distributors)和旅游代理商(tourism agents);另一种是根据销售对象(sales objects)划分为旅游批发商(tourism wholesalers)和旅游零售商(tourism retailers)。

（一）旅游经销商

1.1 Tourism Distributors

Profit comes from the gap between the purchase price and the sale price.

The product is traded once by the distributor, and the ownership of the product is transferred too.

旅游经销商是指将旅游产品买进以后再卖出的中间商,它的利润来源于旅游产品购进价与销出价之间的差额。旅游经销商与旅游产品的生产企业共同承担市场风险(market risks),其经营业绩(operating performance)的好坏直接影响到旅游生产企业经济效益(affect the economic efficiency)的高低。产品经过经销商交易一次,产品的所有权进行一次转移。由于旅游产品的特殊性,购买者得到的只是产品的使用权,而非产品的所有权。旅游经销商多种多样,最主要的有旅游批发商和旅游零售商(wholesalers and retailers)两类。

（二）旅游批发商

1.2 Tourism Wholesalers

旅游批发商往往是一些从事批发业务(engaged in wholesale business)的旅行社或旅游公司,是连接生产者与零售商或最终消费者的桥梁(bridges between producers and retailers)。按照国外旅游学界的普遍看法(general view),旅游批发商的业务是将航空公司或其他交通运输企业的产品与旅游目的地旅游企业的地面服务组合成整体性的旅游产品,然后通过某一销售途径推向广大公众。因而,旅游批发商通过大量订购旅游交通运输企业、饭店、旅游景点(tourism attractions)等企业的单项产品(individual product),将这些产品编排成多种时间、多种价格的包价旅游线路(package tour routes),然后再批发给旅游零售商,最终出售给旅游消费者。

一般来说,旅游批发商的经营范围可宽可窄,有的旅游批发商可在全国甚至在海外(home and abroad)通过设置办事处(set up offices)或建立合资企业(establish joint ventures)、独资企业(sole proprietorship enterprises)等形式进行大众化产品的促销工作,或者广泛经营旅游热点地区的包价旅游产品(package tourism products);有的旅游批发商也可在特定的目标市场中只经营一些特定的旅游产品,如专项体育活动(special sports activities)、专项节日(special festivals)活动等产品;而有的旅游批发商则可以通过某一种交通运输工具组织包价旅游(organize package tourism products),如我国的长江三峡(Three Gorges of China's Yangtze River)豪华游艇包价旅游(luxury yacht package tour)、汽车穿越塔克拉玛干沙漠包价旅游(car tour through the Taklimakan Desert)等。

在少数情况下(in a few cases),旅游批发商(tourism wholesalers)也对旅游消费者进行直接销售活动。此时旅游批发商要对旅游消费者的整体旅游活动负责(be responsible for the overall tourism activities)。旅游者旅行所必需的费用须全部计入所报价格中(be fully included in the quoted price),包括旅游消费者的食、宿、行、游、娱等活动,乃至行李搬运费(luggage handling fees)、小费(tips)等。

(三) 旅游零售商

旅游零售商是指直接面向广大旅游消费者,从事旅游产品零售业务的旅游中间商,它与旅游消费者联系最为紧密(closely related to)。为适应旅游消费者的多种需求(various demands),旅游零售商要熟悉(be familiar with)多种旅游产品的优劣、价格和日程安排(price and schedule),要了解和掌握旅游消费者的经济支付水平(the level of payment)、生活消费需要和方式等情况,以帮助旅游消费者挑选适宜于其要求的旅游

The business of the tourism wholesalers is to combine the products of airlines or other transportation enterprises with the ground services of tourism destination enterprises as a whole and to promote them to the general public through a certain sales channel.

The business scope of the tourism wholesalers could be wide or narrow.

1.3 Tourism Retailers

Tourism retailers directly face the vast number of tourism consumers and engage in the retail business of tourism products.

产品。同时，旅游零售商在市场营销活动中应具有较强的沟通能力(have strong communication ability)和应变能力(adaptability)，要与旅游目的地的饭店、餐馆、风景点以及车船公司(bus and boat companies)、航空公司等接待旅游企业保持良好的联系，能根据旅游市场及旅游消费者的需求变化而相应地调整服务(adjust the services according to tourists' demands)。

一般来说(generally speaking)，旅游零售商的主要职责(main responsibilities)为：向旅游者提供广泛的和正确无误的旅行咨询服务(travel advisory service)；做出包含海、陆、空在内的各种交通运输安排；做出旅游消费者在旅游活动过程中的食宿、观光(sightseeing)以及音乐会(concerts)、剧场入场券(theatre tickets)等特殊节目甚至行李的运送等方面的安排；制定单独旅游、个人陪同旅游(personal escort tour)、团体旅游等旅游产品；对有特殊兴趣的旅游，如宗教朝拜(religious worship)、会议旅游(convention trip)、奖励旅游(incentive tour)、业务旅游(business tour)、学生旅游和体育旅游(sports tour)等做出安排、预定；旅游活动中所涉及的一切琐碎事宜，如有关健康、保险、旅行支票(travel cheque)、语言学习资料(language learning materials)等事宜的处理和咨询。

For the same tourism enterprise, it may play different roles in different marketing channels.

旅游零售商一般为旅行社，旅游发达国家的超级市场(supermarkets)、航空公司(airlines)等往往也是旅游零售商。与一般的生产企业不同，旅游企业不一定只是批发商或零售商。对于同一个旅游企业来说，在不同的营销渠道中，它可能担任不同的角色。如A旅行社为一个来自美国的旅行团组织了一次包价旅游活动，此时，它是以旅游批发商的身份进行销售活动的；同时，它又为B旅行社的一个团队提供了当地导游的服务(local tour guide service)，那么可以说它又是旅游零售商。

1.4 Tourism Agents

It sells tourism products to tourists by acting as a tourism wholesaler.

(四) 旅游代理商

旅游代理商，是指那些只接受旅游产品生产者或供应者的委托(accept the entrustment of the producers or suppliers)，在一定区域内代理销售其产品的旅游中间商(act as agents to sell their products in a certain area)，它通过与买卖双方的洽商，促使产品的买卖活动得以实现，但从中并不取得产品的所有权(ownership of products)。旅游代理商的收入来自被代理企业支付的佣金(commission)。旅游代理商的主要职能是在其所在地区代理旅游批发商或提供行、宿、游等旅游服务的旅游企业向旅游消费者销售其产品。

旅游产品生产企业在自己推销能力不能达到的地区(where their marketing ability cannot reach),或是无法找到合适的销售对象(cannot find suitable sales targets)的情况下,利用旅游代理商的营销资源而寻求营销机会(seek marketing opportunities),因而,对代理商的利用是对经销商利用的一种补充。通过代理商转移风险的程度(degree of risk transfer)比通过经销商要低得多。一般而言,在旅游产品比较好销的情况下,利用旅游批发商等中介组织(intermediary organizations)的机会比较多,而在新产品上市初期或产品销路不太好的情况下,利用代理商的机会则比较多。在实际工作中,旅游代理商由于直接面对广大的旅游消费者,或以为旅游消费者服务为主,同时经营少量的旅游产品的批发业务(while operating a small number of wholesale business),因而旅游代理商往往又是旅游零售商,但其收入主要以收取佣金为主。

Their income is mainly based on commissions.

二、旅游中间商的管理

2 Management of Tourism Intermediaries

旅游中间商介于生产者和消费者之间,专门从事产品流通经营活动(specialize in the circulation and operation of products)、促成买卖行为发生和实现的组织和个人。对于旅游中间商的管理主要集中于两个方面:一是旅游中间商的选择问题(choice of tourism intermediaries),另一个是旅游中间商的激励问题(encouragement of tourism intermediaries)。在与中间商进行合作时,有必要建立中间商档案(set up intermediaries' archives),及时沟通信息,有针对性地实行优惠与奖励(implement preferential policies and incentives),并适时调整中间商。

(一)旅游中间商的选择

2.1 The Choice of Tourism Intermediaries

一般来说,在选择旅游中间商时,着重考虑以下几个方面问题:中间商所处的地理位置(geographical location)是否是客源相对集中(be relatively concentrated)的地方;中间商合作意向;中间商对于本旅行社的产品是否有较强的依赖程度(strong dependence on the products);中间商是否有很好的信誉和良好的声誉(good reputation)。当然,中间商的服务对象、经营方向、从业人员情况、经营管理水平及服务能力、设施设备(facilities and equipment)等因素也是需要考虑的(should be considered)。

2.2 Motivation for Tourism Intermediaries

（二）对旅游中间商的激励

旅行社在进行中间商管理时,应注意维护中间商的尊严(maintain the dignity of intermediaries),尊重中间商的利益(respect the interests of intermediaries),这是赢得中间商合作的首要前提;其次要帮助中间商增加收入;再次,给予中间商的优惠形式要多样(should be diversified),方法要灵活(flexible)。对中间商的主要激励(incentives)措施包括开展促销活动(promotion activities);进行资金资助(financial support);帮助中间商搞好经营管理,提高市场营销效果(marketing effect);提供商业信息;与中间商结成长期的伙伴关系(partnerships)等。

第二节 分销渠道的概念及类型
Section Two Definition and Types of Distribution Channels

1 Definition of Tourism Distribution Channels

1.1 Distribution Channels

一、旅游产品分销渠道的概念与内涵

（一）分销渠道

分销渠道是将产品或服务提供给消费者和商业客户过程中的各种独立组织的集合(collection of independent organizations)。图5-1显示了利用中间商实现经济效益的一个途径。接待业的分销网络(distribution network)包括合同协议和独立企业间组成的松散联盟(loose alliance)。在市场营销中,分销渠道通常被用来将商品(有形产品)从生产者转移到消费者[transfer goods (tangible products) from producers to consumers]。而在接待业与旅游业中,它经常是将消费者向产品移动(move consumers to products):饭店、餐馆、游船或飞机。

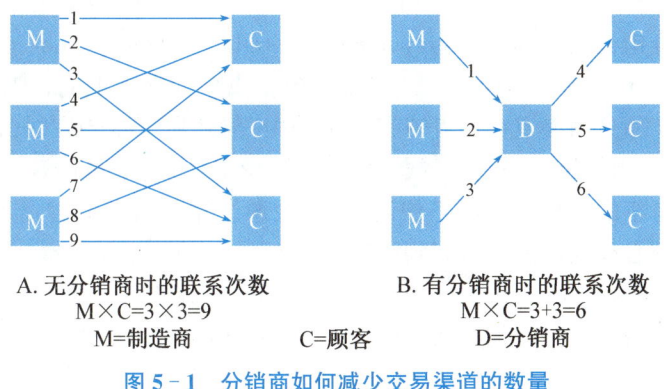

图 5-1 分销商如何减少交易渠道的数量
How Distributors Reduce the Number of Trading Channels

（二）旅游产品分销渠道

旅游企业作为一个特殊的行业（special industry），它在产品的生产和消费之间存在着时间、地点、品种、信息、价格等方面的矛盾，虽然旅游产品的销售在很大程度上（to a large extent）还是以传统的直销（traditional direct marketing）为主，即产品从生产领域直接到达消费者手中，不需要经过过多的中间环节（without too many intermediate links）。但为了解决上述矛盾（solve the above contradictions），实现企业销售目标（sales goals），中间商在其中发挥着巨大的作用。比如很多旅游景点，散客（individual tourists）只占（account for）很少一部分，而绝大多数（the vast majority of）游客是以旅行社或企事业单位与景区签订协议输送的客人。

旅游产品分销渠道又称为旅游产品的销售渠道，是指旅游产品从生产企业向旅游消费者转移的过程中所经过的路线和环节，这个路线和环节（route and link）是由一系列取得使用权或协助使用权转移的市场中介机构或个人所组成的（composed of a series of market intermediaries or individuals who acquire or assist in the transfer of the right to use）。所以，又可以说，一切与旅游商品转移相关的中介机构或个人（intermediaries or individuals）共同组成了旅游产品的分销渠道（constitute the distribution channels of tourism products）。

理解旅游产品的分销渠道应把握以下要点（grasp the following points）：① 分销渠道的起点（starting point）是生产者，终点（end point）是消费者和用户；② 分销渠道的环节是指那些参与旅游产品流通（in the circulation of tourism products）

1.2 Distribution Channels of Tourism Products

Tourism enterprises also have contradictions in terms of time, place, variety, information and price between the production and consumption of products.

的各种中间商,包括各种批发商、代理商、零售商、经纪人和实体分销机构(wholesalers, agents, retailers, brokers and entity distribution agencies)等;③ 不包括供应商和辅助商;④ 旅游产品分销渠道在销售转移的过程中,与其他实体产品(other entity products)转移不同,消费者只有有限的使用权而不发生所有权的转移。无论是旅游景点、旅游线路和旅游饭店,旅游者都必须在规定的时间到指定的地方去消费(tourists must go to a designated place at a specified time),旅游者与旅游企业的关系是一种契约关系(contractual relationship)。

二、旅游产品分销渠道的类型

2 Types of Tourism Distribution Channels

There are many kinds of distribution channels for tourism products.

在现代旅游营销实践中,旅游产品分销渠道的种类很多,不同的旅游企业和产品,选择的分销渠道是不一样的,即使相同的旅游产品其分销渠道也有差异。分销渠道可以由渠道级数来描述(be described by channel series)。每个在将产品及其所有权向最终买主(final buyer)转移的过程中承担一定工作的中间机构,就是一个渠道级。

由于生产者和最终消费者都承担了一些工作,所以他们都是渠道的组成部分。我们使用中间机构的级数(how many intermediate links there are)来表示渠道的长度(represent the length of the channel)。按照渠道中是否有中间环节或中间环节的多少的不同,分销渠道的结构大致可以划分为以下四种,如图5-2所示。

The structure of distribution channels can be roughly divided into four types.

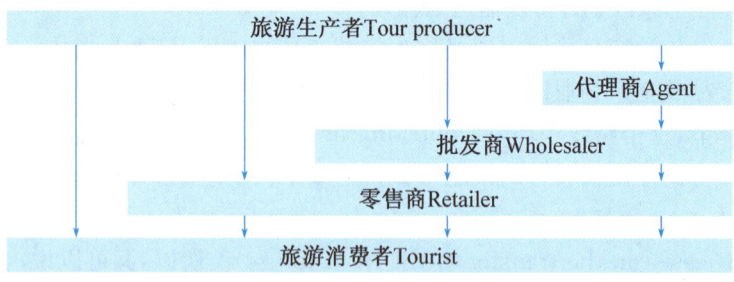

图5-2　四种结构的分销渠道
Four Structures of Distribution Channels

从上图可以看出,旅游产品分销渠道一般可以分为两类:一类是直接分销渠道(结构1)(direct distribution channel);一类是由多个中间环节构成(composed of multiple intermediate links)的间接分销渠道(结构2、3、4)(indirect distribution channels)。其中,结构3和结构4的区别就在于旅游产品的生产者委托旅游代理商来销售其产品,再由代理商出售给批发商、零售商,最后由零售商销售给消费者。

(一) 直接分销渠道和间接分销渠道

2.1 Direct and Indirect Distribution Channels

1. 直接分销渠道

图5-2中的第一条渠道称为直接分销渠道,又叫零级渠道(zero-level channel),是指旅游生产者在其营销活动中,不经过任何中介机构而直接把旅游产品销售给旅游者的分销渠道。比如,许多乘客在临上飞机前(before boarding the plane)直接在购票大厅(ticket lobby)购买机票,航空公司直接向旅客供应其产品——搭乘飞机。这是一种最简便、最快捷的分销渠道。我国许多旅游企业都采用这种分销渠道。从旅游企业的营销实践(marketing practice)中可以看到,直接分销渠道主要包括三种形式(direct distribution channel mainly include three forms):第一,在生产者现场(on the spot)直接向消费者销售其旅游产品;第二,消费者通过网络、电话、直接邮寄(by means of network, telephone and direct mail)等方式预订和购买旅游企业产品的直销方式;第三,旅游企业还通过自设的营业网点(through their own business outlets)直接向旅游者销售其产品的分销方式。

2.1.1 Direct distribution channel

This is the simplest and fastest distribution channel.

2. 间接分销渠道

间接分销渠道至少含有一个中介机构(at least have one intermediary),是旅游产品的生产者或供应者借助中间商的力量将产品转移到消费者手中的途径。图5-2中的第2、3、4条渠道都是间接分销渠道。它是旅游市场上占主导地位的渠道类型(dominant channel form),有以下三种结构。

2.1.2 Indirect distribution channel

(1) 一级渠道(结构2)(One-level channel):指旅游产品生产者与消费者之间只有一层旅游零售商中间环节的渠道,旅游生产者把旅游产品交给零售商代售,需向旅游零售商支付佣金或手续费(pay commissions or fees to the retailers)。

(2) 二级渠道(结构3)(Two-level channel):指在旅游生产者和消费者之间有两个中介机构的渠道。比如,现在国外很多旅游批发商通过大批量购买航空公司、饭店、旅游景点等业务,然后将它们巧妙组合,设计出许多迎合旅游市场消费者需求的包价旅游产品(ingeniously combine them to design many package tour products to meet the needs of consumers),但他们并不自行销售这些产品,而是通过旅游零售商或自设旅游网

With two intermediaries between tourism producers and consumers

点(self-established tourist outlets)进行销售。

（3）三级渠道(结构 4)(Three-level channel)：指在旅游产品生产者与消费者之间有三个中介机构的渠道。通常适用于一些地域偏远(remote)、规模不大(small-scale)，又需要广泛推销(need to be widely promoted)的旅游产品。在此渠道中的代理商通常是一些区域代理商或经纪人(regional agents or brokers)，他们经营规模较大，一般不直接向零售商销售，需要通过批发商转手。

此外(In addition)，还有级数更多的旅游渠道，但较少见(rare to see)。旅游分销渠道的级数表示了旅游渠道的长度，级数越高，中介机构越多，旅游渠道越长，企业就越难控制。

> The higher the series, the more intermediaries, the longer the tourism channels, and the more difficult it is for enterprises to control.

(二) 长渠道和短渠道

根据旅游产品在销售过程中所经过的中间环节的多少，我们将旅游分销渠道划分为长渠道和短渠道。显然，没有中间环节的直接旅游渠道最短；中间环节越多，渠道越长(the more intermediate links, the longer channel is)。一般把三级和三级以上的旅游渠道称为长渠道，三级以下的渠道称为短渠道。当然，这也不是绝对的(absolute)。实际上，在旅游企业的营销实践中，同一种类的旅游产品，由于市场的地理位置(geographical location)不同，采用的渠道也是不相同的；同样，同一种类的旅游产品，即使市场地理位置都相似，但还由于中间商规模大小不同等原因影响渠道的长短。

2.2 Long Channel and Short Channel

The different size of intermediaries and other reasons would still affect the length of channels.

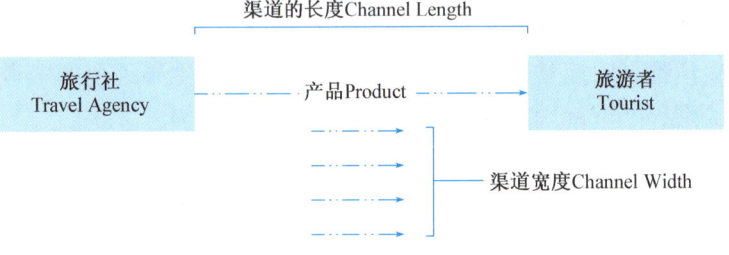

图 5-3 旅游分销渠道的长度与宽度
Length and Width of Tourism Distribution Channels

2.3 Wide Channel and Narrow Channel

(三) 宽渠道和窄渠道

旅游分销渠道的宽与窄(width and narrowness)取决于(depend on)旅游产品销售过程中每一环节选用的中间商数目的多少。旅游产品分销渠道的宽度一方面是指分销渠道中经销或代理本企业产品的中间商(intermediaries who distribute or represent their products in the distribution channels)的数目;另一方面是指本企业和中间商面向市场所设立的销售网点的数目以及分布的格局。因此,对于旅游企业来说,要想方便消费者购买(facilitate consumers to buy),扩大本企业旅游产品在目标市场上的供应范围(expand the scope of their tourism products in the target market),就要不断地(constantly)增加销售网点,加宽旅游产品的分销渠道。

旅游产品分销的窄渠道(narrow channel)是指旅游企业使用的同类中间商数目很少,分布格局比较狭窄,甚至有时在一个城市仅选择一家中间商为其分销商品,这种独家分销(exclusive distribution)的情况属于窄渠道(belongs to the narrow channel)。

对旅游产品的生产者来说,渠道级数越多,横向环节(horizontal links)越多,市场的覆盖面(market coverage)就越广,与消费者的接触面就越广,但也会增加一些费用。因此,要尽量减少不必要的环节,选择合理的分销渠道。

(四)单渠道和多渠道

根据旅游企业选择渠道种类的多少,旅游分销渠道又可分为单渠道和多渠道。一般情况下,旅游企业生产规模小或经营能力较强(small scale of production or strong management ability),可采用单渠道销售产品;反之,则可采用多渠道,以便扩大产品覆盖面(expand product coverage),大量(in large quantities)销售企业的旅游产品。

第三节 销售渠道的选择
Section Three　Selection of Sales Channels

从理论上讲(Theoretically),每个旅游企业可以选择所有种类的(all kinds of)分销渠道,然而,基于企业自身产品的特点、企业利润目标(profit objectives)、市场的不同等因素,大多数旅游企业只能选择其中一种或几种渠道,以使旅游企业的分销渠道效果达到最佳(achieve the best distribution channel effect)。

Increase sales outlets and broaden the distribution channels.

It refers to the fact that the number of similar intermediaries used by tourism enterprises is very few and the distribution pattern is relatively narrow.

As for tourism producers, it's better to minimize unnecessary links and select reasonable distribution channels.

2.4 Single Channel and Multi-Channel

一、旅游产品分销渠道选择的影响因素

1 Influencing Factors

(一) 旅游产品因素

1.1 Tourism Product Factors

The nature, type, grade, price, etc. directly affect the choice of distribution channels.

旅游产品因素包括旅游产品的性质、种类、档次、价格、等级、季节性以及旅游产品所处的生命周期的阶段等,都直接影响分销渠道的选择。对易腐的旅游纪念品(perishable tourist crafts)、高档旅游产品(high-grade tourist products)和新产品等,适宜选择较短的分销渠道(shorter distribution channel)或直销(direct marketing),以免造成损失(avoid losses)。对技术比较复杂、服务要求高的旅游产品(products with complex technology and high service requirements),如滑雪旅游(skiing tourism)、极地探险游(polar exploration tourism)、考古旅游(archaeological tourism)等,一般都需配备特殊的设施和特别的服务,也适宜采用直销或短渠道促销。反之(on the contrary),则选用较长的分销渠道(a longer distribution channel can be chosen)。对某些旅游危险品(some dangerous tourism goods)最好选择专用渠道(special channels)。

(二) 市场因素

1.2 Market Factors

Strong demand and relatively concentrated population are appropriate to choose direct channels.

市场因素包括目标市场范围(target market size)、消费者特点(consumer characteristics)、消费水平高低(level of consumption)、消费习惯(consumption habits)、地理分布(geographical distribution)、需求的季节性(seasonality of demand)及市场竞争(market competition)状况等,都不同程度地(in varying degrees)影响着旅游企业分销渠道的选择。一般来说,目标市场范围很大,需求旺盛,人口相对集中的情况下,适宜选择直接销售渠道。相反,若目标市场很大,但季节性消费明显(seasonal consumption is obvious),且购买力又小的市场,常需要中间商提供服务,适宜选择较长的分销渠道。同时,当现实旅游者(realistic tourists)较少时,为了节省流通费用(save circulation costs),可以采用较短的渠道或直销。

(三) 企业因素

1.3 Enterprise Factors

Tourism enterprises should fully consider their own factors.

企业因素指旅游企业在选择产品分销渠道时,应充分考虑企业自身的因素,包括企业的规模(enterprise size)、发展目标(development goals)、财力(financial resources)、市场声誉

（market reputation）、服务能力（service ability）及管理水平（management level）等。一般来说，企业规模大、财力雄厚、有较好的经营管理能力和丰富经验的市场营销人员，信誉好、产品质量高，在选择销售渠道方面就有较大的自由度（have greater freedom in choosing sales channels），往往选择较固定的中间商（fixed intermediaries），甚至建立自己的销售机构（sales organizations），采用短渠道销售。而那些管理水平较低的企业就要考虑通过中间商来打开产品的销路。当直接销售的预期利润（expected profit）大大超过间接销售的预期利润时，则应采用短渠道。

（四）环境因素

1.4 Environmental Factors

这是影响旅游企业选择分销渠道的外部因素（external factor）。环境因素包括宏观经济形势（macroeconomic situation），各国政府对旅游的相关政策、法律法规（laws and regulations），旅游市场竞争情况等，都对企业分销渠道的选择有很大的制约作用（have great restrictions on the choice of distribution channels）。比如，在经济不景气的情况下（in the economic downturn），旅游产品生产者要求以最快、最经济的途径把产品推向市场，就要运用短渠道策略，减少中间环节（reduce the intermediate links），提高竞争力（improve their competitiveness）。各国法律、法规的相关政策，也会影响分销渠道的选择。

以上四个因素是影响旅游产品分销渠道选择的基本要素，除此以外，旅游企业在选择分销渠道时，还要考虑中间商的实力（strength of intermediaries）以及环境的不可抗力等因素（the force majeure of the environment）。

The above four factors are the basic factors affecting the choice of distribution channels.

二、旅游产品分销渠道的选择策略

2 Strategies for Choosing Distribution Channels

旅游产品分销渠道的选择是旅游企业产品销售工作中最重要的决策之一。因为旅游企业生产的产品，只有通过适当的分销渠道（through appropriate distribution channels），才能及时、有效地把商品送到消费者手中（be delivered to consumers），实现企业经营目标（achieve business objectives）。所以，分销渠道的选择是否合理，中间环节到底多少最恰当（the most appropriate number of intermediate links），会直接影响到产品的成本、价格乃至竞争力。因此，旅游企业都十分

The choice of distribution channels of tourism products is one of the most important decisions in the product sales.
Tourism enterprises attach great importance to choose the reasonable distribution channels.

重视和研究选择合理的分销渠道策略。对旅游产品分销渠道的选择可根据行业情况、市场需求、企业实力等进行综合考虑。

2.1 Strategies of Direct or Indirect Distribution Channels

Both strategies have their advantages and disadvantages.

（一）直接分销渠道或间接分销渠道的策略

在制定分销渠道策略时,旅游企业应首先决定是采用直接分销渠道还是间接分销渠道;如果选用间接分销渠道,选用几个中间环节的间接渠道。两种策略各有利弊。

（1）直接分销渠道策略既短又快捷,成本低,有利于生产者(beneficial for producers)以相对低廉的价格出售产品,满足消费者求廉的心理(satisfy consumers' psychology of seeking cheapness);直接分销渠道策略有利于企业对市场的控制,可直接了解市场动态(market dynamics),及时调整营销策略(adjust marketing strategies);直接分销渠道中间环节较少,便于(is convenient for)企业与消费者的信息沟通,提高企业和产品的声誉。但是直接分销渠道在对消费者进行面对面宣传时,会增加销售人员(sales staff)和销售费用(sales expenses),因此,直接分销渠道要求企业有一定的人力、财力、物力资源。

（2）间接分销渠道策略有利于企业节省(save)流通领域(field of circulation)的人力、财力、物力资源,扩大企业产品的辐射面(expand the radiation of enterprise products),加速旅游企业产品和资金的流转过程(accelerate the transfer process of tourism products and funds)。但间接分销渠道策略,中间环节较多,要花费企业一部分利润,在一定程度上会影响企业的经济效益;同时,企业在选择中间商时一定要慎重,选择不好,会给企业带来极大的麻烦(bring troubles)和市场风险(market risk)。

Be careful when choosing intermediaries.

2.2 Long Channel or Short Channel Strategies

Long channel or short channel depends on the number of intermediate links in the process of transferring tourism products from producers to consumers.

（二）长渠道或短渠道策略

旅游产品分销渠道的长短,主要是以旅游产品从生产者转移到消费者过程中所经历的中间环节的多少为依据的。通常来讲,直接分销渠道和经过一个中间商的间接分销渠道被称为短渠道;经过两个以上中间商的间接分销渠道(indirect distribution channels through one level of intermediaries)被称为长渠道。如果旅游产品生产企业已经决定通过中间商来销售本企业的产品,还需对中间商的数量进行选择。当然选择时,要从旅游产品生产者的实际出发,充分研究市场、产品特点(product characteristics)、管理能力(management ability)、自身实力以及中间商能力(intermediary ability)、市场信誉等因素,量力而行,慎重选择。

(三) 宽渠道或窄渠道策略

旅游产品分销渠道的宽窄策略(wide and narrow distribution channel strategies)是指在同一个中间环节上(in the same intermediate link)有多少旅游中间商在同时为本企业销售产品的策略。一般有以下三种选择。

1. 广泛分销渠道策略

此策略又称密集分销渠道策略,是指旅游生产企业设立尽可能多的分销点(set up as many distribution points as possible),选择尽可能多的中间商(select as many intermediaries as possible),加宽分销渠道(widen distribution channels),以便扩大产品的销售量(expand the sales of products),方便旅游消费者购买(convenient for tourists to buy)。该策略的优点是方便旅游消费者购买,产品销售范围广,数量大;缺点是旅游产品生产者或供给者对渠道的控制力不足(have insufficient control over the channels),进而与中间商的关系比较松散(have loose relations with intermediaries)。

2. 独家分销渠道策略

独家分销渠道策略是指旅游产品的生产者或供给者在一定区域内只选择一家中间商经销或代销,实行独家经营。这是一种最窄的分销渠道策略。该策略的优点是旅游企业经过精细挑选,便于和中间商沟通、协作(communicate and cooperate with the intermediary),易于控制中间商和产品的价格。中间商与企业风险共担、利益共享(share risks and benefits),很能调动中间商的积极性,提高对顾客的服务质量,有利于树立良好的产品形象(establish a good image),可防止竞争者加入(prevent competitors from joining in)。但这种策略风险太大(too risky),一旦选择不当或中间商发生某种变故,企业将会陷入困境(be in a dilemma),另外这种策略灵活性太低,不利于消费者选择购买。

3. 选择性分销渠道策略

选择性分销渠道策略是指旅游产品的生产者根据自身的实力,在一定市场区域内,选择几家信誉好、销售水平高的中间商经销或代销自己的旅游产品。该策略与独家分销渠道策略相比(compared with),销售面稍宽,有利于旅游产品扩大销路,开拓市场(open up the market),展开竞争(launch competition)。与广泛分销渠道策略比,这种策略不仅能密切产销之

2.3 Wide Channel or Narrow Channel Strategies

There are generally three choices.

2.3.1 Intensive distribution channel strategy

2.3.2 Exclusive distribution channel strategy

It only chooses one intermediary to operate in a certain area.

2.3.3 Selective distribution channel strategy

Choose several intermediaries with good reputation and high sales level to distribute or sell their own tourism products in a certain market area.

间的关系(close the relationship between production and marketing),而且旅游企业可节省分销费用(save the distribution costs),易于企业对分销渠道进行控制,从而保证产品的形象和企业的信誉(ensure the image of products and the credibility of enterprises)。因而它具有广泛的适用性(wide applicability)。

三、渠道方案的评估标准

3　Evaluation Criteria for Channels

分销渠道评估的实质(essence of distribution channel evaluation)是从那些看起来似乎合理但又相互排斥的方案(seemingly reasonable but mutually exclusive schemes)中选择最能满足企业长期目标的方案。因此,企业必须对各种可能的渠道选择方案进行评估。评估标准(evaluation criteria)有三个,即经济性(economy)、控制性(control)和适应性(adaptability)。

(一) 经济性标准

3.1　Economic Criteria

经济性标准是最重要的标准,这是企业营销的基本出发点(basic starting point)。在分销渠道评估中,首先应该将分销渠道决策可能引起的销售收入增加同实施这一渠道方案所需要花费的成本作一比较,以评价分销渠道决策的合理性(evaluate the rationality of distribution channel decision-making)。

(二) 控制性标准

3.2　Controllability Criteria

企业对分销渠道的设计和选择(design and selection)不仅应考虑经济效益,还应该考虑企业能否对其分销渠道实行有效的控制(effectively control)。因为分销渠道是否稳定对于企业能否维持其市场份额(maintain their market share),实现其长远目标是至关重要的(crucial for long-term goals)。

(三) 适应性标准

3.3　Adaptability Criteria

在评估各渠道方案时,还需考虑分销渠道是否具有地区、时间、中间商等适应性。地区适应性(regional adaptability)指在某一地区建立产品的分销渠道,应充分考虑该地区的消费水平(consumption level)、购买习惯(purchase habits)和市场环境(market environment),并据此建立与此相适应的分销渠道。

时间适应性(time adaptability)指根据产品在市场上不同时期的适销状况,企业可采取不同的分销渠道与之相适应。如季节性商品(seasonal commodities)在非当令季节(in off-season)就比较适合于利用中间商的吸收和辐射能力(absorption and radiation capacity)进行销售;而在当令季节就比较适合于扩大自销比重。中间商适应性(adaptability of intermediaries)指企业应根据各个市场上中间商的不同状态采取不同的分销渠道。如在某一市场若有一、两个销售能力特别强的中间商(intermediaries with strong sales ability),渠道可以窄一点;若不存在突出的中间商(prominent intermediary),则可采取较宽的渠道。

第四节　分销渠道的发展趋势
Section Four　Development Trends of Distribution Channels

一、旅游产品分销渠道的联合趋势

1　Joint Trend of Distribution Channels

20世纪80年代以来,随着商品经济的不断发展,旅游产品分销渠道的类型也发生了很大的变化,分销渠道突破了(break through)由生产者、批发商、零售商和消费者组成(composed of producers, wholesalers, retailers and consumers)的传统模式和类型(traditional patterns and types),有了新的发展。许多国家出现了分销渠道的联合,包括纵向联合、横向联合以及集团联合等形式,中国近年来在大城市、大企业也出现不少这样的分销渠道联合。旅游企业产品分销渠道策略也将随着渠道类型的变化适时加以调整和改善。

There have been joint distribution channels, including vertical joint, horizontal joint and group joint.

（一）分销渠道的横向联合

1.1　Horizontal Joint of Distribution Channels

分销渠道的横向联合又称为水平分销渠道系统(horizontal distribution channel system),是指由两个以上的旅游产品的生产者联合起来,共同开发分销渠道的策略。这种横向的联合方式又可以分为暂时的松散式联合(temporary loose combination)和永久的固定式联合(permanent fixed combination)。旅游产品渠道的横向联合,可以很好地集中各联合企业的力量

(concentrate the strength of joint ventures),发挥群体作用,实行优势互补,共担风险,更好地开展产品的销售活动(better carry out sales activities),获取最佳效益(obtain the best benefits)。

1.2 Vertical Joint of Distribution Channels

(二) 分销渠道的纵向联合

The vertical joint of distribution channels can be divided into the following two types.

分销渠道的纵向联合又称为垂直分销渠道联合,是指由生产企业、批发商、零售商组成的统一系统。纵向联合的特点是联合各方采用一定的方法和手段实行专业化管理(carry out professional management),集中计划(centralize planning),统一行动(unite action),协调发展(coordinate development),以提高这个联合体的共同的利益为目标。分销渠道的纵向联合又分为以下两种。

一是契约型的产销联合(contract-based production-marketing alliance):指旅游产品的生产者与其分销渠道上各环节的中间商以契约的方式进行的联合(in a contractual way)。它的好处是联合双方责任、权利清晰(clear responsibilities and rights),目标一致(consistent objectives),互利双赢(win-win benefit),协调行动(coordinated action)。比如现在国内许多旅游景点开发公司与各地旅行社以一种契约的方式联合起来,共同开展旅游产品的销售工作(jointly engaged in the sales of tourism products in a contractual way)。

二是紧密型的产销一体化(close integration of production and marketing alliance):指旅游产品的生产者将旅游业务向前或向后延伸(extend the tourism business forward or backward),以兼并、入股、新建等方式(by means of mergers, shares and new construction)建立起来统一的产、供、销联合体(establish a unified production, supply and marketing consortium),使旅游产品生产者同时具备生产、批发、零售的全部功能(have all the functions of production, wholesale and retail at the same time),以实现对营销活动的全面控制和管理。

1.3 Group Joint Channel

(三) 集团联合渠道

集团联合渠道是指旅游产品的生产者以组建企业集团的形式,联合多个企业分销产品的渠道策略。由多个企业组成的企业集团具有计划、生产、销售、服务、信息和科研等多种分销功能(have many distribution functions, such as planning, production, sales, service, information and scientific research),核心层与非核心层(core and non-core layers)的内外协调能力很强(great internal and external coordination ability),分工明确(clear division of labor),协调运作,大大提高了产品分销的整体实力和企业效益。但这种渠道联合策略规模太大,容易产生信息流动慢、沟通不畅的现象(slow information flow and poor communication),导致"大企业病"(lead to "big enterprise disease")。

二、旅游产品分销渠道的发展趋势

2 Development Trend of Distribution Channels

(一)分销渠道逐步"扁平化"

2.1 Gradually "Flattened" Distribution Channels

旅游产品的分销渠道随着中国旅游营销发展的整体趋势(overall trend),逐步减少旅游产品到最终消费者的中间环节(gradually reduce the intermediate link),也就是所谓的扁平化发展。通过对流通环节的压缩,使得代理层次减少,直销的销售方式增多。渠道的扁平化对于旅游产品的生产者或供应者来说,可以减少中间环节,提高效率,节约成本。

(二)分销渠道逐步"宽化"

2.2 Gradually "Broadened" Distribution Channels

扁平化的渠道减少了中间的冗余环节(reduce the redundant links),使得渠道宽度增加(increase the channel width),最终消费者可以方便地通过若干途径获得旅游产品的信息,实现对产品的消费,而不必依赖于单一的信息来源和渠道成员(relying on a single source of information and channel members)。旅游消费者在进行消费前,多渠道获得需要的信息的同时还可对不同渠道进行比较。

(三)由总经销向终端市场建设为中心转变

2.3 Changing to Terminal Market Construction

渠道的扁平化使零售终端(retail terminals)的位置日益突出。旅游产品的生产商通过大力建设终端市场,可以更直接地接触市场,获得市场信息,降低产品价格,方便消费者购买,加强与消费者的沟通并达到吸引最终用户的目的。

By vigorously building the terminal market, producers of tourism products can contact the market more directly.

(四)网络营销日渐风靡

2.4 More and More Popular Network Marketing

进入21世纪,蓬勃发展的互联网对传统的旅游产品的分销渠道产生了巨大的冲击,网络营销日益风行(network marketing has become increasingly popular),比如网上旅游信息咨询(online tourism information consultation)、旅游景区在线

	预订(online booking)、网上预订景区门票、预订酒店等。
The vigorous development of the Internet has had a huge impact on the traditional distribution channels of tourism products.	网络营销可以使旅游企业准确掌握市场信息(accurately grasp market information);使得旅游产品的生产商与消费者之间沟通更加方便;旅游企业降低了交易成本和流通成本(reduce transaction costs and circulation costs),提高产品竞争力;可以最大限度地降低产品的积压和浪费(minimize product backlog and waste);有助于企业提供个性化的产品(help enterprises to provide personalized products)。
3 The Rise and Development of Online Travel Agencies	**三、在线旅行社的兴起与发展** **(一) 在线旅行社的定义**
3.1 Definition of Online Travel Agency	在线旅行社(Online Travel Agency),英文简称为OTA,是旅游电子商务(tourism e-commerce)领域的专业词汇。旅游消费者通过网络向旅游服务提供商(tourism service provider)预定旅游产品或服务,并通过网上支付(online payment)或者线下付费,即各旅游主体可以通过网络进行产品营销或产品销售。OTA的出现将原来传统旅行社(traditional travel agency)的销售模式放到网络平台(network platform)上,可以更加广泛地传递旅游产品信息,而且互动式的交流(interactive communication)更加方便了客人的咨询和订购,因此,得到了广泛应用(been widely used)。
3.2 Difference between Online and Offline Travel Agencies	**(二) 线上、线下旅行社的区别** 其实,OTA线上旅行社与传统旅行社的本质差别并不大(the essential difference is not big),工作性质都是为客户提供旅游服务(provide tourism services)。不过它们各自的优劣势还是很不一样的,传统旅行社有实体店面(physical store),可以通过良好的硬件配套和软服务(software and hardware support)来留住客源,让客户感到安全;但是营业受时间、空间限制,客源来源单一(single source of customers),具有不稳定性。 相较于传统旅行社,OTA则不受时间与空间的限制,客源来源广,尤其在互联网时代,网民众多,只要开通一个流量入口(open a flow inlet),就多了千万机会。OTA打破了供需双方信息严重不对称现象(serious information asymmetry),可以将更多有效信息提供给客户,从而有助于筛选出适合客户的最

优选项(filter out the best options for customers),可以节约大量交易成本(transaction costs saving),很符合现代消费者的需求。但是 OTA 的劣势也比较明显,例如缺乏实体店面支撑导致客人安全感不足(lack of security),网络用户(network users)的线上点评对销售影响较大,大数据杀熟(big data-enabled price discrimination against existing customers)、信息泄露(information leakage)、虚假宣传(false propaganda)等问题层出不穷(emerge in an endless stream)。

以目前状况来看,传统旅行社还稍微处于弱势,但是各种现象已经表明传统旅行社和 OTA 之间逐渐趋于融合(tend to merge)。线上旅行社在流量和消费的入口方面确实更胜一筹,传统旅行社需要正视在线旅游的发展,实现行业转型和升级(realize industry transformation and upgrading);传统旅行社具备了 OTA 所没有的导游、领队等资源,并且在短时间内 OTA 建立不了实体服务(physical services)、质量和品牌。双方只有实现合作共赢(achieve win-win cooperation),才能共谋旅游业的长远发展。

(三) 移动互联网在 OTA 中的应用

3.3 Application of Mobile Internet in OTA

随着 PC 互联网向移动互联网(mobile Internet)发展,移动互联网在 OTA 模式中的应用场景(application scenario)极大改善了用户的消费体验(consumption experience),主要表现为以下几个方面:

第一,移动定位服务。在旅游中基于位置的移动定位服务 LBS(location-based service)包括导航服务(navigation service)、位置跟踪服务(location tracking service)、安全救援服务(safety rescue service)、移动广告服务(mobile advertising service)、相关位置的查询服务等。例如可以通过在线旅游服务商的应用程序,实现查询附近酒店、旅游景点、娱乐设施等信息,从而实现预订、导航等服务。

第二,移动支付。移动支付(mobile payment)是指移动客户端(mobile client)利用手机等电子产品来进行电子货币支付。移动支付将互联网、终端设备、金融机构(financial institution)有效地联合起来,形成了一个新型的支付体系,不仅仅能够进行货币支付,还可以缴纳话费、水电等生活费用。移动支付开创了新的支付方式,使电子货币(electronic money)开始普及。

第三,移动信息服务。移动信息服务是指基于通信网络平

台（communication network platform），通过各种移动设备，以无线接入网络的方式（mode of wireless access network）实现信息的双向传播（two way communication）。很多人会有进入到某地自动收到当地的欢迎信息或者是交互链接的经历，这种行为可以引导实际消费行为的产生（lead to actual consumption behavior）。

实训项目 05　旅行社分销渠道设计

Project 5　Design Distribution Channels for Travel Agencies

一、实训目标(Training Objectives)：

1. 通过实训加深对旅行社分销渠道相关理论知识的理解，理解并掌握旅游分销渠道的概念和功能，熟识旅游分销渠道的类型及其优劣势；

2. 认识旅游中间商的作用，掌握选择旅游中间商的原则，以及激励和评估的策略；

3. 理解影响旅游分销渠道选择的因素，掌握并运用旅游分销渠道的选择策略，设计旅行社分销渠道方案。

二、实训学时(Training Period)：2～8 学时

三、实训地点(Training Place)：旅行社情景实训室

四、实训设备(Training Equipment)：联网计算机、移动硬盘或 U 盘、A4 绘图纸、铅笔、橡皮。

五、项目描述(Project Description)：

旅行社将其产品销售给最终消费者的途径，即为旅游销售渠道。它是由一系列参与销售并促使旅游产品向最终消费者转移且被最终消费者购买和消费的组织和个人所组成。其中，食、住、行、游、娱、购等单项旅游产品的提供者位于旅行社销售渠道的起始点；各种旅游中介组织位于旅行社销售渠道的中间环节；而最终消费者则位于旅行社销售渠道的终点。本实训目的在于让学生能够自主设计完整的旅行社分销渠道系统，并用 PPT 汇报成果。

六、实训任务及要求(Tasks and Requirements)：

实训任务一览表

序号	实训任务名称	实训内容	实训学时	实训地点
1	影响旅游产品分销渠道的因素	确定旅游分销渠道的类型及影响因素，旅游营销渠道有长、有短、有宽、有窄，旅游产品生产者在选择营销渠道时要作出正确决策，必须考虑多种因素的综合影响。	2	旅行社情景实训室
2	旅行社渠道结构设计	包括渠道的结构、层次、每个渠道层次的业务目标、代理商区域划分等。根据渠道目标结合产品因素、顾客因素、竞争因	2	

(续表)

序号	实训任务名称	实训内容	实训学时	实训地点
		素、企业因素、中间商因素的分析进行渠道长度、宽度、广度设计以及制定中间商的选择条件。	2	
3	制定渠道激励方案	认识渠道激励的内容及形式,选择渠道激励重点措施。	2	
注:教师可根据需要选用实训项目和学时。				

根据班级人数,每组可适当编制2～6人规模。通过查阅资料、社会调研和组内讨论,制作并完成旅行社分销渠道设计方案,并在课堂上展示。

七、实训成果(Practical Results):

1. 每组完成旅行社分销渠道设计WORD电子文档1份和展示PPT电子档1份。

2. 将上述两个文件放入文件夹,命名为:"班级名称＋小组编号＋旅行社分销渠道设计实训作业"。

八、考核标准(Assessment Criterion):

项目	考核内容和要求	分值	得分
表现	按时完成任务,工作积极主动,具有合作精神	20	
内容	内容全面、真实、精确	40	
格式	格式规范、语言简洁、样式美观	20	
创新	有创意,有市场潜力	20	
小计		**100**	

第六章　旅行社促销管理
Chapter Six　Promotion Management for Travel Agencies

【学习目标】 Learning Objectives

1. 了解旅行社促销(promotion)的作用及类型(role and types);
2. 理解旅行社促销的运作流程(operation process);
3. 掌握旅行社促销组合(promotion mix)策略及评估方法(evaluation method)。

> 依托我国超大规模市场优势,以国内大循环吸引全球资源要素,增强国内国际两个市场两种资源联动效应,提升贸易投资合作质量和水平。
>
> ——党的二十大报告摘录

✓本章课程视频讲解　　✓实训指导书
✓线上课堂链接　　　　✓优秀学生作品精选
✓本章训练题库　　　　✓时政新闻
✓本章拓展资源

根据现代营销的观点(according to the view of modern marketing),旅游企业不仅需要向目标市场(target market)提供具有竞争优势的(competitive)旅游产品,还需与消费者和潜在消费者(current consumers and potential consumers)保持沟通(maintain communication)。而这种沟通大多是通过企业的促销活动(promotion activities)来实现的,从而把大量的个人需求激发出来(stimulate personal needs)。

第一节　旅行社促销概述
Section One　An Overview of Travel Agency Promotion

1　Definition of Travel Agency Promotion

一、旅行社促销的概念

促销是市场营销组合的四大策略之一(one of the four major strategies of marketing mix),是指企业利用各种有效的手段和方法,使目标消费者(target consumers)认识和了解企业的产品,从而激发消费者的购买欲望(stimulate consumers' desire to buy),并最终(ultimately)促使其实现购买(lead to their purchasing behavior)。由此可见,促销的实质是传播与沟通信息(disseminate and communicate information)。那么,旅游产品促销则是指旅游企业通过一定的方式(in a certain way),将企业的旅游产品信息及购买途径传递给(pass the information to)目标顾客,从而对旅游中间商和旅游者(intermediaries and tourists)的购买行为产生影响(influence the purchasing behavior),促使他们(impel them to)了解、信赖并购买(understand, trust and purchase)旅行社产品,激发用户的购买兴趣(stimulate users' purchasing interest),强化(strengthen purchasing desire)购买欲望,甚至创造需求(create demand),从而促进产品销售(increase sales)的一系列活动(a series of activities)。旅行社促销的根本目的在于激发潜在旅游者的购买欲望(stimulate the purchase desire),最终导致购买行为的发生。旅行社促销的实质是买卖双方的信息沟通(information communication)。旅行社在向旅游消费者传递信息(information transmission)的过程中,有多种因素参与其中,

并且发挥作用。

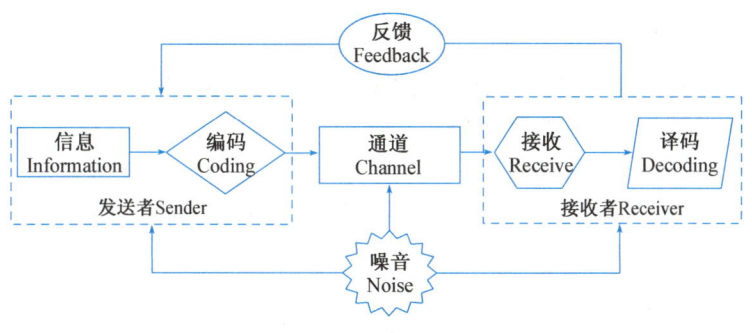

图 6-1 信息沟通过程模型
Model of Information Communication Process

二、旅行社促销的作用

旅游产品促销的重要性及其作用（importance and functions）可以从两个方面（from two aspects）来认识：第一，不论某一产品如何完美，如果不被消费者所知晓（not known by consumers），那么该产品则无异于不存在（non-existence）；第二，在同类可替代产品（similar alternative products）大量存在的今天，特别是在市场竞争激烈的情况下，某一产品及其所提供的利益被消费者所了解，无疑（undoubtedly）是该产品能获得关注（to be noticed）的必要前提（necessary prerequisite）。企业希望通过消费者自然的口碑（the natural word-of-mouth）传播来实现广阔的销路是远远不够的，必须主动对市场进行刺激。旅游产品促销（product promotion）的作用主要表现（is mainly manifested in the following aspects）在以下几个方面。

（一）提供旅游信息，沟通供需联系

旅游产品促销的直接作用是进行信息传递（to transmit information），实现旅游企业与消费者之间的沟通。通过各种促销手段，将旅游产品相关信息传递给消费者，同时也将消费者的意见反馈给企业。这不仅能使消费者了解产品销售的情况，为企业建立良好的声誉（establish a good reputation for enterprises），从而为企业产品成功销售创造条件（create conditions for the success of enterprise）；而且旅游企业也可以根据市场需求状况调整供求关系（adjust the supply and demand relationship），不断改进产品，找到更合适的市场定位（more

2 The Role of Travel Agency Promotion

It is not enough for enterprises to achieve a broad market through communication among consumers; they must actively stimulate the market.

2.1 Provide Tourism Information and Communicate Supply and Demand

appropriate market positioning)。

(二) 突出产品特点,强化竞争优势

2.2 Highlight Product Characteristics and Strengthen Competitive Advantages

随着社会经济(social economy)的发展,旅游市场竞争越来越激烈,产品同质化也较严重(homogenization of products is more serious),消费者往往不易察觉这些产品的细微差别。此时,要增加旅游产品对旅游消费者的吸引力,旅游企业就应通过促销活动,突出本企业产品的特色(highlight the characteristics)、优势以及能给消费者带来的独特利益(unique benefits),提高企业的市场竞争能力。

(三) 树立良好的企业形象,巩固市场地位

2.3 Establish a Good Corporate Image and Consolidate Market Position

恰当的(appropriate)促销活动可以树立良好的企业形象,使消费者对企业及其产品产生好感,从而培养和提高用户的忠诚度(cultivate and improve the loyalty of users),形成稳定的用户群(form a stable user group),不断扩大市场份额,巩固企业的市场地位(consolidate the market position)。旅游企业要想充分发挥促销的作用,就必须重点关注(focus on)各种促销策略的专长,灵活运用多种方法进行组合,找到一种能适合企业自身的组合策略(find a suitable strategy mix),从而产生优势互补(complementary advantages),达到事半功倍(twice the results with half the effort)的效果。

(四) 缩小淡旺季差异,稳定销售

2.4 Reduce the Difference Between Off-Season and Peak Season and Stabilize Sales

Tourism products are affected by many factors.

旅游产品受到多种因素的影响,如自然条件、政治经济因素、人文环境因素(human environment factors)等,因此也就决定了旅游产品在淡季和旺季(off-season and peak season)的需求差别较大。如旅游企业能在不同的时节对相应的旅游产品进行大规模促销和宣传,从而缩小淡季和旺季的差异(narrow the differences between off-season and peak season),稳定销售。

(五) 刺激旅游需求,引导旅游消费

2.5 Stimulate Tourism Demand and Guide Tourism Consumption

Stimulate or induce consumers' potential demand for tourism consumption.

旅游产品属于弹性需求(elastic demand)的商品。企业应针对消费者的心理动机(psychological motivation),灵活运用(flexibly use)各种有效的促销方法,激发或诱导消费者潜在的旅游消费需求,从而扩大旅游企业的销售。此外,通过企业的促销活动还可以创造需求(create demand),发现新的销售市场,使市场需求向有利于企业营销的方向发展(develop in a direction conducive to enterprise marketing)。

三、旅游促销的类型

（一）旅游目的地促销

旅游目的地促销侧重于向目标市场或有关公众（the public）传递特定旅游目的地的宣传信息，所以又称为目的地形象宣传（destination image publicity）。

（二）旅游产品促销

侧重点在于向目标市场或有关公众传递某种旅游产品的宣传信息。

（三）目的地旅行社促销

目的地旅行社促销属于旅行社的企业名号促销，这类促销是旅行社侧重于目标市场、客户或有关公众传递本企业形象的宣传信息（convey the information of the enterprise）。

第二节　旅行社产品促销运作流程
Section Two　The Procedure of Product Promotion in Travel Agencies

一、旅行社产品促销运作流程

旅行社开展促销活动可以影响旅游者或旅游中间商的购买行为，甚至直接促进旅游者或旅游中间商购买行为的发生。

3　Types of Tourism Promotion

3.1　Promotion of Tourism Destination

3.2　Promotion of Tourism Products

3.3　Promotion of Travel Agency in the Destination

1　The Procedure of Product Promotion in Travel Agencies

Promotion activities carried out by travel agencies can influence and even directly impel the purchasing behavior of tourists or tourism intermediaries.

图 6-2　有效的促销运作流程
Effective Promotion Process

有效促销的工作流程(work-flow)通常包括以下几个流程(includes the following processes)。

（一）确定目标受众

1.1 Identify Target Consumers

目标受众(target consumers)是指被挑选出来接受信息的人群。在进行促销决策时,首先要明确目标受众的范围(make clear the scope of the target consumers),即要明确要对哪些人群进行促销。对不同的目标受众(different target consumers),促销的信息、渠道、方式和媒体组合(media mix)等都有所不同。

1.2 Decide Promotion Objectives of Travel Agencies

（二）旅行社促销目标的确定

旅行社的促销目标(promotion objectives)就是旅行社在一定时期内,通过对各种促销要素的有机组合(combination of various promotion elements)而要达到的总体目的(general objective)。旅行社在一定时期内的总体促销目标是旅行社促销策略的基础和核心(basis and core of the promotion strategy),包括直接目标和间接目标。直接目标如销售额、市场份额、利润等,间接目标包括企业或产品形象、产品知名度、传播知识等。

1.3 Design Promotion Information

（三）设计促销信息

The effective promotional information is beneficial to arouse tourists' attention, stimulate tourists' consumption demand, and then promote the purchase behavior.

Information form refers to the way in which the content and structure of information are expressed.

有效的促销信息(effective promotional information)应该能够唤起旅游者对旅行社产品的注意,引起旅游者的消费兴趣,激发旅游者的消费需求,进而促使购买行为发生。在设计产品信息时,旅行社要在信息的内容、结构、形式和信息来源等方面进行合理决策(make reasonable decisions)。

信息内容包括旅行社产品的档次、价格、特点和线路安排(route arrangement)等具体内容(specific information),针对不同细分市场的旅游者,信息内容的选取要有不同的侧重。信息结构是指信息内容的次序安排。信息形式(information form)指信息的内容和结构采取何种表现方式。信息来源强调专业性、可信性和可亲性(emphasize its professionalism, credibility and accessibility)。

1.4 Choose Channels for Information Communication

（四）选择信息沟通渠道

信息沟通渠道一般包括人际沟通(interpersonal communication)渠道和非人际沟通(non-interpersonal communication

渠道两种。人际沟通渠道包括两个或更多的人相互之间直接进行信息沟通。他们可能直接面对面,也有可能是通过电话、计算机网络进行沟通。当产品价格昂贵、购买风险(purchase risk)比较高或者购买不频繁(not frequent)时,人际沟通渠道作用明显。旅行社可以采用的人际沟通手段包括人员推销(personnel marketing)和口碑效应(word-of-mouth effect)两种。

非人际沟通渠道包括媒体、氛围和事件(events)等。其中,媒体的使用频率最高(most frequently used),大多数的促销活动通过媒体来完成。然而,旅行社的门市部也是旅游者与旅行社打交道的场所,门市部的氛围会起到重要的沟通信息的作用。

(五)旅行社的促销预算

1.5 The Promotions Budget of Travel Agency

确定促销预算时应考虑的因素包括促销目标、竞争因素、可利用的资金等。制定促销预算的方法(methods of making promotion budget)可以包括以下几种:① 销售额百分比法(sales percentage method),根据一定时期内销售额的一定比例确定促销预算的方法;② 利润额百分比法(profit percentage method),原理、特点与销售额百分比法完全相同,只是用利润额代替销售额(uses profit instead of sales);③ 目标达成法(target achievement method),是以促销目标决定促销预算的方法,因此预算结果具有科学性;④ 竞争对抗法(competitive confrontation method),又叫竞争对等法(competitive-parity method),即旅行社根据竞争对手的促销预算确定本旅行社的促销预算;⑤ 支出可能法(expenditure possibility method),又称全力投入法(full devotion method),按照旅行社财力可能支付的金额,来确定促销预算。

(六)决定促销方式组合

1.6 Decide on Promotion Mix

旅行社可以采用广告(advertising)、销售促进(sales promotion)、人员推销(personnel marketing)和公共关系(public relations)等多种促销方式。联合运用(joint use of)各种促销方式有助于旅行社整体促销目标(overall promotional objectives)的实现。

(七)促销效果评估

1.7 Evaluation of Promotion Effectiveness

促销效果评估是指评价促销活动是否实现了促销目标(achieve the objective of promotion),评价促销费用的支出

	(promotion expenses)是否收到了预期的效果(receive the expected effect)。促销效果评估有针对旅行社整体促销活动经济效益的评估(evaluation of the economic benefits),也包括对具体促销方式促销效果的评估(evaluation of the promotion effect)。
2 Promotion Mix and Strategies for Travel Agencies	**二、旅行社促销组合与策略**
2.1 AIDA Rule	**(一) AIDA 法则**
AIDA refers to four processes of buying behavior, namely, arousing attention, arousing interest, cultivating desire and promoting action.	旅行社有了好的产品、优惠的价格(preferential prices)、畅通的营销渠道(smooth marketing channels),还需要以适当的促销手段吸引中间商或旅游者购买(attract intermediaries or tourists to buy)。国际推销专家海英兹·姆·戈得曼(Heinz M. Goldmann)总结(sum up)了一个非常有用的推销模式(marketing model),即 AIDA 法则,也称"爱达"公式,它是西方推销学中一个重要的公式(formula)。它的具体涵义是指一个成功的推销员必须把顾客的注意力吸引或转变到产品上(attract or transform the attention of customers to products),使顾客对推销人员所推销的产品产生兴趣,这样顾客欲望(customer desire)也就随之产生,尔后再促使其采取购买行为(promote the purchase behavior),达成交易。 AIDA 法则来自(come from)西方的营销理论(western marketing theory),它是指购买行为的四个过程,即"引起注意、激发兴趣、培养欲望、促成行动"。A 是指"注意"Attention,I 是指"兴趣"Interest,D 是指"欲望"Desire,最后一个 A 是指"行动"Action。
2.2 Four Basic Methods of Tourism Promotion	**(二) 四种最基本的旅游促销方式**
Non-personnel promotion mainly includes advertising, sales promotion, business promotion, public relations, etc.	现代旅游企业大多有着复杂的营销沟通系统(complex marketing and communication systems),其进行产品促销的策略和方法也是多种多样的,主要包括人员推销(personnel promotion)和非人员促销(non-personnel promotion)两大类。人员推销是指企业的销售人员直接接触潜在消费者,面对面地介绍(face-to-face introduction)产品,并促进其实现产品销售,是指运用人员推销,把产品推向市场。非人员促销主要包括广告、销售促进、营业推广、公共关系等。

Chapter Six Promotion Management for Travel Agencies

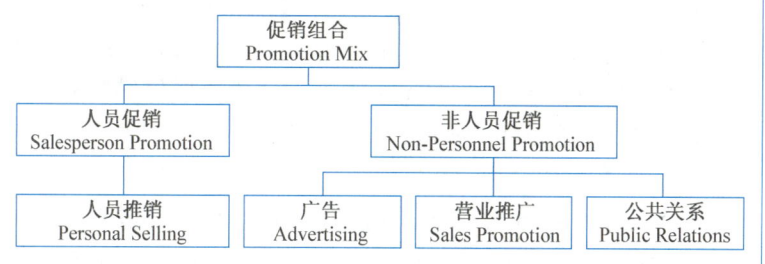

图 6-3 旅行社产品促销方式
Ways to Promote Travel Agency Products

1. 广告促销

广告促销就是通过一定的媒体,将旅行社产品介绍给潜在消费者(potential consumers),激发其购买欲望(stimulate their desire to buy),促进旅游产品销售,提高旅行社经营效益的宣传推介活动。广告促销具有传播速度快(fast dissemination)、覆盖范围广(wide coverage)、利用手段多(various means)、宣传效果好(good publicity effect)等许多优点。因此,它是旅行社产品促销中使用最频繁(most frequently used)、最广泛的(widely used)一种促销方法。旅游产品促销广告根据使用媒体的性质不同,又可以将其分为自办媒体广告(self-run media advertisements)和大众媒体广告(mass media advertisements)两种基本类型(basic type)。

根据凭借的媒介,可以将自办媒体分为户外广告牌(outdoor billboards)、广告宣传单(advertising leaflets)和印有旅行社信息的旅游纪念品(tourist souvenirs printed with the information of the travel agency)三种形式。这种形式的促销具有自主选择宣传对象(the characteristics of self-selecting targets),广告命中率高(high advertising hit rate)等特点。大众媒体主要包括电视广告(TV advertisements)、旅游杂志(travel magazines)、报纸广告(newspaper advertisements)、广播广告(radio advertisements)、互联网广告(Internet advertisements)等。

2. 直接促销

直接促销就是指旅行社通过直接与旅游中间商或潜在消费者进行接触来推动旅游产品销售的过程。直接促销是旅行社产品促销的重要方法,具有联系紧密(close connection)、机动灵活(flexibility)、反馈及时(timely feedback)、选择性强(strong selectivity)等主要特点,有利于确立同消费者之间的良好关系。直接促销主要有人员推销(personnel promotion)、

2.2.1 Advertising promotion

2.2.2 Direct promotion

电话促销(telephone promotion)、直接邮寄促销(direct mail promotion)、文化广场促销(cultural square promotion)、旅游大篷车促销(tourist caravan promotion)和会展促销(exhibition promotion)等几种形式。

3. 公共关系

公共关系促销是指通过信息沟通(through information communication),发展旅行社与社会、公众、游客之间的良好关系,建立、维护或改变(establish, maintain or change)旅行社和产品的形象,营造有利于旅行社的经营环境和经营态势(business environment and business situation)的一系列措施和行为。旅行社公共关系主要有新闻媒体公关和社会公众公关(news media public relations and social public relations)两大类型,常见的公共关系促销方法包括新闻发布、演讲、出版物、展览会、赞助公益事业以及提供旅游咨询等服务(news, speeches, publications, exhibitions, sponsorship of public welfare undertakings, provision of various services including tourism consulting services, etc.)。

4. 营业推广

在市场营销学中,营业推广又称销售促进,它是指对中间商、潜在消费者以及本企业销售人员提供短期激励(short-term incentives),以达到促成购买或努力销售的各种行为活动。销售促进是短期的促销方法(short-term promotion method),通过制定降价(price reduction)、考察旅行(incentive travel)等各种鼓励购买的优惠条件,刺激游客或中间商的促销活动。针对旅游者的方法如折价券(discount coupons)、价格折扣(price discounts)、抽奖(raffles)、不满意退款(unsatisfactory refunds)、附赠品(gifts);针对中间商的方法如价格折扣、联合促销(joint promotions)、赠品、旅游展销会(tourism fairs)、推销竞赛(marketing competitions)、免费提供宣传品、考察旅行等。销售促进的优点在于促销刺激性强、激发需求快,但由于其有效期短(short period of validity),易引起竞争,长期运用不利于产品形象(long-term use is not conducive to product image)。

(三) 促销组合和促销策略

1. 选择促销组合

对一种旅游产品而言,在促销时只使用其中一种方式往往是不够的,需要把几种不同的方式有机组合起来(combine

2.2.3 Public relations

2.2.4 Sales promotion

sales promotion also known as business promotion

The advantages of sales promotion lie in its strong and fast stimulation of customer demands.

2.3 Promotion Mix and Promotion Strategies

2.3.1 Choose promotion mix

It is often not enough to use only one way in promotion.

several different ways),综合运用,形成整体的促销攻势(form an overall promotion offensive)。这种把多种促销方式(various promotion methods)有机结合并综合运用的方式就是促销组合(combination of promotions)。

促销组合是指企业根据产品的特点和营销目标,综合各种影响因素,对各种促销方式的选择、编配和运用(choose, arrange and apply),从而获得良好的整体促销效果(overall promotion effect)的过程。影响促销组合的因素有促销目标(promotion objectives)、产品因素(product factors)、市场条件(market conditions)、促销预算(promotion budget)等。旅行社促销的四种方式各有利弊,其促销重点也各有不同,有效的旅游促销策略是几种方式的有效组合(effective combination)。

2. 制定促销组合策略

2.3.2 Make promotion mix strategies

在对上述因素综合分析(comprehensive analysis)的基础上,可以初步制定促销组合策略(preliminary formulate the promotion mix strategy)。如前述,不同的方式组合就可以形成不同的策略。但是,大体来说,这些策略可以分为两大类:推式策略(push strategy)和拉式策略(pull strategy)。

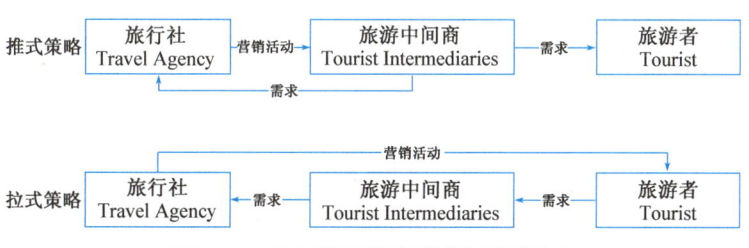

图 6-4 旅行社促销的"推"和"拉"策略
The "Push" and "Pull" Strategies of Travel Agency Promotion

(1) 推式策略

推式策略是着眼于积极地把本企业旅游产品推向目标市场,也就是指推着旅游产品经分销渠道最终达到消费者手中(reach target consumers)。推式策略的意图是旅游产品生产者或提供者劝说或诱使(persuade or induce)旅游中间商及旅游消费者来购买自己的产品,使旅游产品逐次地通过各个销售渠道(pass through various sales channels one by one),并最终抵达旅游消费者;表现为在销售渠道中,每个环节都对下一个环节主动出击,强化顾客的购买动机(strengthen the purchase motivation),说服顾客迅速购买。这种策略主要是以人员推销为主,销售促进、公共关系等与之相配合。

In the sales channels, each link will take the initiative to attack the next link.

（2）拉式策略

拉式策略是基于直接激发最终消费者对本企业旅游产品的兴趣和热情（interest and enthusiasm），形成急切的市场需求（urgent market demand），促使其主动去寻找购买途径（take the initiative to find ways to buy），然后拉引中间商纷纷经销这种产品（distribute the products）。在市场营销过程中，由于中间商与生产企业对某些新产品的市场前景有不同的看法，当新产品上市时，中间商因担心市场风险过高而不愿经销。在这种情况下，生产企业就可以先从消费者方面推销，形成巨大的市场需求，促使经销商经销（impel the distributors to sale）。拉式策略常用的方式有广告、销售促进、展览促销等。

> Once the new products launch on the market, intermediaries are reluctant to distribute because they are afraid of high market risk.

第三节　促销效果的评估
Section Three　Evaluation of the Promotion Effect

旅行社企业进行促销活动的同时，要不断对已经进行的促销活动进行效果评估，考察是否收到了预期的效果，对好的经验进行总结并加以推广（summarize and popularize the good experience）。如果发现问题，也可以及时改进，以保证促销目标的实现（ensure the realization of the promotion objectives）。

> Constantly evaluate the effect of the promotion activities.

一、促销效果评估的分类

促销效果评估（evaluate promotion effectiveness）是企业促销工作的一项重要内容，分事前评估、事中评估和事后评估（advance evaluation, in-process evaluation and post evaluation）三类，它们的特点各异，作用各异（have different characteristics and functions）。

> 1　Classification of Promotion Effectiveness Metrics

（一）事前评估

所谓（so-called）事前评估就是指促销计划正式实施之前所进行的调查测定活动（survey and measurement activities）。其目的在于评估该计划的可行性和有效性（assess the feasibility and effectiveness），或以此在多个计划中确定出最佳的方

> 1.1　Advance Evaluation
>
> There are two main methods of advance evaluation: consulting method and experimental method.

案。事前评估主要有征求意见法和试验法两种方法。

(二) 事中评估

1.2 In-Process Evaluation

事中评估亦称消费者调查(consumer surveys),是在促销活动进行过程中对其效果进行的评估法。调查内容分三个方面:首先是促销活动进行期间消费者对促销活动的反应(response to the promotion activities),可以通过现场记录(on-site records)来分析消费者参与的数量(the number of consumers involved)、购买量(purchase volume)、重复购买率(repeat purchase rate)、购买量的增幅(the increase of purchase volume)等;其次是参与活动的消费者结构,包括新、老消费者比例(the proportion of),新、老消费者的重复购买率(repeat purchase rate),新消费者数量的增幅等;再次是消费者意见,包括消费者参与动机(consumer participation motivation)、态度、要求、评价等。综合上述几方面的分析(synthesize the above analysis),就可大致掌握消费者对促销活动的反应,客观评价促销活动的效果。

(三) 事后评估

1.3 Post Evaluation

事后评估就是在促销活动告一段落或全部结束后(after the end of the promotion)对其产生的效果进行评估。常用的方法(commonly used methods)有比较法(comparative method)和调查法(investigation method)。

二、促销效果评估方法

2 Method of Evaluating Promotion Effectiveness

(一) 前后比较法

2.1 Before-and-After Comparison Method

前后评估法是对即将开展促销活动之前、之中和之后三段时间(before, during and after the promotion activities)的销售额(量)(sales volume of the three periods)进行比较来测评效果。这是最常用的消费者促销评估方法。促销前、促销期间和促销后产品的销售量变化会呈现出几种不同的情况,这说明促销产生了不同的效果。通常,可能出现的情况有以下四种。

Generally, there are four possible scenarios.

(1) 初期奏效(it works initially),但在促销中期销售就逐渐下降,到结束时,已恢复到原来销售水平(return to the original level)。这种促销冲击力强(have a strong impact),但缺乏实质内容(lack substance),没能对消费者产生真正的影响。主要原因可能是促销活动缺乏长期性(lack of long-term promotional activities)，策划创意缺乏特色(lack of characteristics in planning and creativity)，促销管理工作不力(poor management in promotion)。

(2) 促销期间稍有影响(slight impact)，但促销后期销售低于原来水平(lower than the original level)。这时促销出现后遗症(follow-up effect)，这说明(indicate)由于产品本身的问题或外来因素(external factors)，使该品牌的原有消费者构成发生动摇，而新的顾客又不愿加入(be reluctant to join)，从而在促销期满后(after the expiration of the promotion period)，销量没有上升。其中主要原因可能是促销方式选择有误(incorrect choice of promotion methods)，主管部门干预(intervention of competent authorities)，媒体协调(media coordination)出现问题、消费者不能接受，竞争者的反攻(counterattack)生效，争夺了大量消费者。

(3) 促销期间的销售情况同促销前基本一致，但促销结束后又无多大变化。这说明促销无任何影响，促销费用浪费。这种情况说明该品牌基本处于销售衰退期(sales recession)。主要原因可能是企业对市场情况不熟悉(not familiar with the market)，促销方式缺乏力度，信息传播方式方法出现问题(problems occurred in information dissemination)，产品根本没有市场等。

(4) 促销期间销售有明显增加(increase significantly)，且促销结束后销势不减或略有减少(decrease or slightly decrease)。这说明促销明显，且对今后有积极影响(have a positive impact)。促销产品的市场销量上升，增加的原因是促销对消费者产生吸引力。在促销活动结束后的一段时期内，称为有货消耗期，消费者因消耗在促销期间积累的存货而没有实施新的购买，从而商品销量在刚结束的时候略有下降，但这段时间过后，商品销量比促销前上升，说明促销取得了良好的效果，使产品的销售增加。

2.2 Market Research Method

(二) 市场调查法

这是一种企业组织有关人员进行市场调查分析确定促销效果的方法。这种方法比较适合于评估促销活动的长期效果，包括确定调查项目(determine investigation items)和调查法的实施方式(implement investigation methods)两方面内容。

(1) 确定调查项目。调查的项目包括促销活动的知名度

(popularity),消费者对促销活动的认同度(consumers' recognition),销势增长(变化)情况,企业的形象在前后变化情况(corporate image before and after promotion)等。

(2)市场调查法的实施方式。一般来说(generally speaking),采用的方法是寻找一组消费者样本(find a group of consumers as samples)和他们面谈,了解(find out)有多少消费者还记得促销活动,他们对促销的印象如何,有多少人从中获得利益(benefit from),对他们今后的品牌选择(brand choice)有何影响等。通过分析这些问题的答案,就可以了解到促销活动的效果。

(三)观察法

2.3 Observation Method

这种方法是通过观察消费者对促销活动的反应,从而得出对促销效果的综合评价(comprehensive evaluation)。主要是对消费者参加竞赛与抽奖(take part in the competition and lottery)的人员、优惠券(coupons)的回报率、赠品的偿付情况(payment of gifts)等加以观察,从中得出结论(draw a conclusion)。这种方法相对而言较为简单,而且费用较低,但结论易受主观影响,不是很精确。

三、促销效果评估的注意事项

3 Attentions in Evaluating Promotion Effectiveness

(一)评估周期

3.1 Evaluation Cycle

效果评估应采取单次评估(single evaluation)与中期评估(mid-term evaluation)相结合的方式。随着客户消费时的选择日益理性(customers' more rational choices)、信息传播的滞后(the lag of information dissemination)等原因,当月组织实施的促销即使在活动结束之后几个月仍然能够发挥一定的销售促进作用。同时,促销活动的负责人能够在一定程度上控制促销结果,例如压货(overstock)等,非常容易造成销售上升的假象。因此,在实施效果评估时,建议采取短期、中期相结合的方法(adopt a combination of short-term and medium-term methods),这样才能使效果评估更加合理、公平(reasonable and fair)。

(二)促销费用的计算

3.2 Calculation of Promotion Costs

(1)很多企业在计算促销费用往往没有计算(calculate)上

Although most enterprises will indicate that no return is allowed when implementing the promotion.

级下拨的赠品,如礼品、宣传物品等。这将使促销费用失真,不能反映促销费用的真实效果(reflect the real effect)。

（2）有部分客户在促销期内购进较大量的产品,由于滞销或其他私人原因,容易出现退货现象(尽管大部分企业在实施促销时都会注明不允许退货)。因此,建议除加强控制外,应根据历史经验(according to the historical experience)预提(in advance)退货损失,并将其列入促销费用。

（3）促销活动的关键在于事前计划(advance planning)、费用预算(cost budget)、事中控制(in-process control)。效果评估只是用于对活动结束后的总结(summarize),目的是为以后开展促销活动提供可供借鉴的经验与教训(provide useful experience and lessons for future promotion activities)。

实训项目 06　旅行社促销方案设计

Project 6　Design a Promotion Mix for Travel Agencies

一、实训目标（Training Objectives）：

1. 通过实训加深对旅行社促销理论知识的理解。

2. 提高对旅行社促销内容、手段及流程的实际操作能力；学会使用信息技术手段制作旅游促销文案。

3. 培养创新求异的思维方式。

二、实训学时（Training Period）：2～8 学时

三、实训地点（Training Place）：旅行社情景实训室

四、实训设备（Training Equipment）：联网计算机、移动硬盘或 U 盘、A4 绘图纸、铅笔、橡皮。

五、项目描述（Project Description）：

促销方案的好坏决定了旅行社产品的销售前景，促销方案的内容可包括旅游市场情况、促销活动目标、对象、主题、时间、步骤、销售手段、地点、费用预算、效果预估等。根据需要，在特定促销目标和特定促销预算指导下，对不同促销技巧的组合运用，并制定方案，用 PPT 汇报方案成果。

六、实训任务及要求（Tasks and Requirements）：

实训任务一览表

序号	实训任务名称	实训内容	实训学时	实训地点
01	旅游市场基本情况	市场规模，旅游消费观念和需求，近几年旅游产品的设计、销售、价格、利润等方面的情况，未来变化趋势等	2	旅行社情景实训室
02	产品促销的目标和任务	包括游客数量、组团数量、销售额、利润、市场占有率、品牌知名度等	2	
03	促销行动方案的设计	促销对象、主题、产品、时间步骤、销售手段的组合、具体活动的安排等，促销手段包括媒体广告、张贴海报、发宣传单、发放纪念品、电话促销、公关活动、产品发布会、上门设点直销、网络销售等	2	
04	促销的费用预算	分项列出活动费用，并计算总额	2	

注：教师可根据需要选用实训项目和学时。

（一）旅游市场基本情况（市场规模，旅游消费观念和需求，近几年旅游产品的设计、销售、价格、利润等方面的情况，未来变化趋势等）。

（二）旅行社产品促销的目标和任务（完成任务的要求，包括游客数量、组团数量、销售额、利润、市场占有率、品牌知名度等）

☆（三）促销行动方案的设计（促销对象、主题、产品、时间、步骤、销售手段的组合、具体活动的安排等，促销手段包括媒体广告、张贴海报、发宣传单、发放纪念品、电话、公关活动、产品发布会、上门设点直销、网络销售等）。

（四）促销的费用预算（分项列出活动费用，并计算总额）。

（五）根据班级人数，每组可适当编制 2~6 人规模。通过组内讨论，进行相关促销要素的组合搭配，并设计制作旅行社促销方案用于课堂展示。

七、实训成果（Practical Results）：

1. 每组完成旅行社促销方案 WORD 电子文档 1 份和方案展示 PPT 电子档 1 份。

2. 将上述两个文件放入文件夹，命名为："班级名称＋小组编号＋旅行社促销方案实训作业"。

八、考核标准（Assessment Criterion）：

项目	考核内容和要求	分值	得分
表现	按时完成任务，工作积极主动，具有合作精神	20	
内容	内容全面、真实、精确	40	
格式	格式规范、语言简洁、样式美观	20	
创新	有创意，有市场潜力	20	
小计		100	

☆为实训重点。

第七章 旅行社接待业务管理
Chapter Seven　Management of Reception in Travel Agencies

【学习目标】　Learning Objectives

1. 了解旅行社接待业务的性质和作用（nature and role）；
2. 熟悉旅行社接待业务（reception）的工作任务、工作程序；
3. 掌握旅行社各类接待业务的特点；
4. 了解旅行社接待业务的最新发展趋势（development trend）。

> 为民造福是立党为公、执政为民的本质要求。必须坚持在发展中保障和改善民生，鼓励共同奋斗创造美好生活，不断实现人民对美好生活的向往。
>
> ——党的二十大报告摘录

✓ 本章课程视频讲解　　　✓ 实训指导书
✓ 线上课堂链接　　　　　✓ 优秀学生作品精选
✓ 本章训练题库　　　　　✓ 时政新闻
✓ 本章拓展资源

第一节　旅行社接待概述
Section One　An Overview of Travel Agency Reception

旅行社提供接待服务的过程与旅游者的消费过程是同步进行的(synchronous with consumption process),因此旅行社的接待服务对旅游者评价旅游产品及旅行社的服务质量起着决定性作用(play a decisive role in evaluating service quality)。

一、接待工作概述

1　An Overview of Reception

(一) 接待工作概念

1.1　Definition of Reception

狭义(in a narrow sense)的旅行社接待工作是指根据旅行社的接待计划,组织安排实施(organize, arrange and implement)计划,负责(responsible for)旅行团在旅游过程中的导游讲解服务(explanation service)和旅行生活服务(travel service)。广义泛指旅行社为游客提供的所有的接待工作,如咨询(consultation)、门市、导游等。

(二) 接待人员的分类

1.2　Types of Receptionists

按照导游人员的业务范围(business scope),导游人员大致可以分为海外领队(tour leader)、全程陪同导游人员(national guide)、地方陪同导游人员(local guide)和景点景区导游人员(fixed-point guide)四个类别。

海外领队(tour leader):经国家有关行政主管部门批准(with the approval of),受可经营出境业务(operate an outbound business)的旅行社的委派,全权代表(on behalf of)旅行社带领旅游团从事旅游活动的人员。

全程陪同导游人员(national guide):受组团社委派(appointed by),作为组团社的代表(as the representative),提供全程陪同服务(provide full escort services),负责中间环节的衔接(connect the intermediate links),监督接待计划的实施(supervise the implementation of reception plans),协调领队、地陪、司机等人员关系的导游服务人员。

Chapter Seven Management of Reception in Travel Agencies

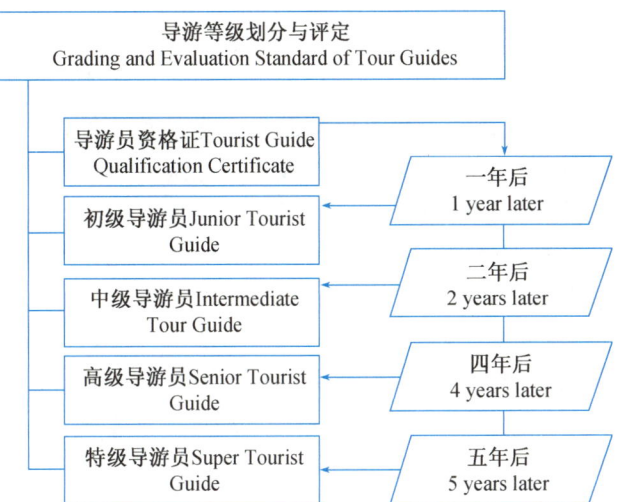

图 7－1 导游人员的等级划分与晋级年限
Tourist Guide Classification and Promotion Timeline

地方陪同导游人员(local guide):受接待社委派,代表接待社实施(carry out)接待计划,提供活动安排、讲解、翻译工作(explanations and translations)的人员。

景点景区导游人员:又称讲解员或定点导游,在景点景区如博物馆(museum)、自然保护区(nature reserves)进行导游讲解的人员。

二、接待工作的阶段管理

(一) 准备接待阶段的管理

(1) 委派适当的接待人员(Appoint appropriate receptionists)。

接待部门负责人(manager of the reception department)应在平时对该部门导游员的性格(personality)、能力、知识水平、身体条件(physical condition)、家庭情况(family situation)、思想状况(ideological status)等进行全面了解,做到心中有数。当接待任务下来时,接待部门经理便能够根据旅游团的特点,比较顺利地选择适当的导游员承担接待任务(undertake the reception task)。

(2) 检查接待工作的准备情况(Check the preparation of reception work)。

(3) 必要的提示和指导(Necessary tips and guidance)。

2 Management of Reception

2.1 Management of Preparatory Reception

2.2 Management of Reception

2.2.1 Establish a reporting system for instructions

2.2.2 Spot check and supervise reception site

2.3 Management in Summary Stage

2.3.1 Establish a reception summary system

2.3.2 Deal with praise and complaints from tourists

Handling tourists' praise and complaints is another important part of the travel agency reception summary.

（二）接待阶段的管理

1. 建立请示汇报制度

旅游团队接待工作是一项既有很强的独立性（strong independence）又需要由旅行社加以严格控制的业务工作。为了加强对旅游团接待过程的管理，旅行社应根据本旅行社和本地区的具体情况（the specific conditions），制定出适当的请示汇报制度（formulate appropriate reporting system）。

2. 抽查与监督接待现场

旅行社还应建立旅游团接待现场抽查（spot check）和监督制度（supervision system），由接待部经理或总经理等人在事先未打招呼（without prior notice）的情况下，亲自到旅游景点、饭店/旅馆、餐馆等旅游团活动的场所，以获取有关接待方面的各种信息（obtain all kinds of information）。通过现场抽查和监督（supervision），可以迅速、直接地（quickly and directly）了解接待服务质量和旅游者的评价，为旅行社改进服务质量提供信息。

（三）总结阶段的管理

1. 建立接待总结制度

为达到提高接待工作效率（improve efficiency）和服务质量的目的，旅行社应建立总结制度（establish a summary system），要求每一名接待人员（receptionist）在接待工作完成后对接待过程中发生的各种问题和事故（problems and accidents）、处理的方法及其结果、旅游者的反馈（feedback from tourists）等进行认真总结（make a summary），必要时应写出书面总结报告，交给接待部经理。

2. 处理旅游者的表扬和投诉

处理旅游者的表扬和投诉是旅行社接待总结阶段的另一项重要内容。一方面，旅行社通过对优秀工作人员（excellent staff）及其事迹（their deeds）的宣扬，可以在接待人员中树立良好的榜样（set a good example）。另一方面，管理人员通过处理投诉，既教育了受批评的导游员本人，也对其他接待人员进行了鞭策，使大家在今后的接待工作中不再犯类似的错误（not to make similar mistakes）。

第二节　团队旅游接待业务
Section Two　Reception of Group Tour

一、入境旅游接待

1　Inbound Tour Reception

（一）入境旅游的概念

1.1　Definition of Inbound Tour

入境旅游，是指旅行社招徕、组织、接待（attract, organize and receive）外国旅游者来中国旅游，香港特别行政区（Hong Kong Special Administrative Region）、澳门特别行政区（Macao Special Administrative Region）旅游者来内地旅游，中国台湾地区（Taiwan province）居民来大陆（mainland）旅游，以及招徕、组织、接待在中国内地的外国人，在内地的香港特别行政区、澳门特别行政区居民和在中国大陆的台湾地区居民在境内旅游的业务。入境旅游具有停留时间长（long stay）、外籍人员多（large number of foreigners）、预订期长（long booking period）、落实环节多（many implementation links）等特点。

（二）入境旅游接待程序

1.2　Reception Procedure of Inbound Tour

1. 接待前期准备

1.2.1　Pre-reception preparation

由国内组团旅行社的计调部门（Operations department）或与相关部门（relevant departments）共同完成，包括做好计划（make plans）、落实吃住行游购娱的行程安排（implement the travel arrangements）、安排接待人员（arrange reception personnel）、准备机动经费（prepare flexible funds）、整理提供团队的完整信息（provide complete information）等前期准备工作，并向全陪导游详细交代任务和注意事项。

（1）制订接待计划。接待计划的内容由团队基本情况和要求、日程安排（schedule）、团队成员名单（list of group members）（最好附有每个成员的照片）三部分组成。

（2）配备合适的全陪导游。国内组团社应根据旅游团的特点和具体要求，选择配备合适的导游作为全陪人员。同时，也要对地陪导游（local guide）的选择提出要求。

（3）与境外组团社保持联系。国内接待旅行社必须随时与境外（overseas）组团社保持联系（keep in touch with），尽可

— 127 —

National and local guides must be fully familiar with the reception plan.

1.1.2 Implement reception

能详细掌握该团队的情况及变化情况(keep detailed information of group members as much as possible)。

(4) 全陪和地陪必须全面熟悉接待计划,掌握所接待团队的全部信息。

2. 实施接待工作

全陪负责协调并监督(coordinate and supervise)各地导游实施接待计划,各地的地陪导游负责(responsible for)操作当地的接待计划。国内组团社及各地接待社负责全程跟踪支持、监控(track, support and monitor the whole process)。主要环节(main links)有:① 入境接团;② 入住饭店;③ 核对计划日程;④ 参观游览;⑤ 餐饮(food and beverage);⑥ 购物;⑦ 文娱活动(recreational activities);⑧ 出境送站(see off the tourists)。

二、出境旅游接待

(一) 出境旅游的概念与特点

2 Reception of Outbound Tour

2.1 Definition and Characteristics of Outbound Tour

出境旅游,是指旅行社招徕、组织、接待中国内地居民(mainland residents)出国旅游,赴香港特别行政区、澳门特别行政区和中国台湾地区旅游,以及招徕、组织、接待在中国内地的外国人,在内地的香港特别行政区、澳门特别行政区居民和在大陆的中国台湾地区居民出境旅游(travel abroad)的业务。

Tour leader is mainly responsible for the contact with overseas travel agencies, in order to command and coordinate the whole process of reception.

根据《中国公民出国旅游管理办法》,中国公民自费出国旅游(travel abroad at their own expense),遵循"有计划,有组织,有控制"(planned, organized and controlled)发展的指导方针(guidelines),目前主要以团体方式(in groups)进行,3人以上即为团队。出境旅游的接待,主要是由领队负责与境外接待旅行社接洽,担任全过程接待的指挥、协调工作。同时,国内组团旅行社应全程跟踪协助、支持。

(二) 出境旅游接待程序

2.2 Procedures for the Reception of Outbound Tour

1. 前期准备工作

2.2.1 Preparatory work

Make a detailed overseas reception plan.

(1) 制订接待计划。国内组团社根据与旅游团的协议,制订详尽的境外接待计划,内容由团队基本情况和要求、日程安排、团队成员名单(最好附有每个成员的照片)三部分组成。

(2) 办理出境手续。按照国际惯例(international practice),凡进入任何国家旅行的游客,必须持有三种基本证明(basic

certificates),即护照(passport)、签证(visa)和预防接种证明(vaccination certificate)。

（3）准备具体交通票证、单据、证明及资料。落实出境机票(车、船票)，及境外各站之间的交通票据。准备各国出入境卡、海关申报单(customs declaration forms)、必要的外币(foreign currency)机动经费等。

（4）配备合格的领队。旅行社应选派精通业务、外语熟练的全陪导游直接担任领队，也可由组团社从游客中挑选威信高（或职务高）(with high prestige or high position)、负责任、有一定出国旅游经验者(have certain overseas traveling experience)，充任领队。如果是一个单位单独组团，则一般由单位的领导担任领队。领队最好懂外语，或者整个旅游团队应至少有一人懂外语。

It is better to assign a tour leader who is proficient in foreign languages.

2. 接待工作的实施

出境旅游接待工作，实际上是组团社在与旅游团队签订旅游合同的基础上，与境外接待社商定的全程接待计划的具体实施。在操作上，境外接待社负责具体执行，而领队或组团社选派的全陪则主要负责全程监督(supervise)、协助各项事宜的落实(assist the implementation)，并维护旅游团队(tour group)全体成员的正当合法权益(safeguard legitimate rights of all members)。

2.2.2 Implement the reception

（1）出发预备会(preliminary meeting)。会议内容包括：宣布领队(announce the tour leader)，详细通报行程安排(inform the itinerary in details)，检查每位成员随身携带的旅行证件是否办理完备且有效(complete and valid)，说明办理出入境手续的程序，介绍旅游目的地国家(destination countries)概况，提出旅游纪律要求(rules for the travel)等。

（2）出发。按规定的时间、地点，集中全体成员(gather all the members)，清点(count)人数，前往出境口岸(port of exit)。再次提醒每位参加出境旅游的成员检查其随身携带的出境所必需的证件，随身行李(carry-on luggage)是否带齐，强调出境纪律和注意事项(emphasize the rules and precautions)。

（3）出境。包括以下手续：① 办理登机手续；② 办理我国的出境手续；③ 按要求办理好行李托运，保管好行李卡；④ 进行我国的边防安全检查。

（4）途中。出境旅游往往在飞机上有很长的旅途(long journey)，需要领队提醒并带领全体团员按照机上的要求，礼貌乘坐。

（5）进行境外的入境边防检查。

(6) 入住饭店。在前往饭店的途中(on the way to the hotel),领队应当与导游交代团队所需的房间数量及种类(number and types)。到达饭店(upon arrival at the hotel),在协助导游进行入住登记后,将导游办好的住房卡分发给全体团员,宣布用餐、叫早(morning call)、出发游览等时间和集合地点(announce the time and gathering place),然后安排大家进房间休息。

(7) 核对旅游安排计划(check the travel schedule)。领队应及时与当地导游核对旅游计划日程及游览项目(tour items)等,要严格按双方达成的旅游合同办事(strictly follow the contract),原定的游览项目不能少(the original tour items shall not be less);但超计划的(beyond the plan)自费项目(self-funded items),应充分征求全体团员的意见后再定,游客自愿参加。如接待计划与原定合同有出入(there is any discrepancy between the reception plan and the original contract),经协商仍不能达成一致的情况下,可以向国内组团旅行社汇报请示再定(report to domestic agency for instructions)。

(8) 组织参观游览。领队要监督游览计划项目的完整实施(complete implementation),切实保障游客的正当权益(ensure tourists' legitimate rights)。游览期间,领队负有对全体游客的召集责任,有义务(have the obligation)带领大家按照预定的时间、地点进行游览,防止人员丢失,杜绝出现意外事故(prevent the loss of personnel and prevent accidents)。

(9) 在国外的出境。大体同我国出境手续(roughly the same as China's exit procedures),主要包括:① 办理登机手续;② 办理国外的出境手续;③ 按要求办理好行李托运,保管好行李卡(luggage card);④ 通过外国的边防安全检查(foreign border security inspection)。然后,登机踏上返程(board the plane and head back)。

(10) 回国的入境。从飞机下来直接进行入境的边防安全检查(border security inspection),一般比较简单,如果是我国航空公司运送的游客,往往不做边防安检,游客可直接去领取行李,办理我国的海关(customs)入境手续。通过海关检查(customs inspection)后,领队须集中(gather)全团人员,收拾好所携带的全部行李,与国内组团旅行社安排的接待导游联络,组织全体人员和行李上车,返回出发城市,最后解散旅游团队(dissolve the tour group),完成整个旅程(complete the whole journey)。

3. 接待后续完善工作

（1）撰写"领队工作小结"(summary of the tour leader's work)。内容有团队人员基本情况、旅游行程安排及实施情况，团队成员对本次旅游活动的反映和建议(reflections and suggestions)，改进旅行社接待工作的建议等。

（2）协助旅行社办理(deal with)团员们委托的遗留问题(remaining problems)。如果旅游途中发生了事故，还要协助旅行社做好善后工作(deal with the aftermath)，或协助游客向保险公司索赔(claim compensation from the insurance company)等。

（3）应尽早(as soon as possible)去旅行社办理结账手续和归还出国时借出的物品。

（三）旅游接待中领队与导游的关系

旅游接待中，领队与导游处理好关系是接待工作圆满完成的重要保证。

1. 领队、全陪、地陪的各自职责

领队的职责(duty of the tour leader)，是代表境外的组团旅行社，全权负责(in charge of)旅游团队在旅游目的地国家的旅游活动。全陪的职责，是代表国内组团旅行社，负责协调各地、监督实施入境旅游团队在国内的全部接待活动(coordinate and supervise all reception activities)。地陪的职责，是代表国内各地接待旅行社负责当地所有接待活动的圆满完成。

2. 领队、全陪、地陪的相互关系

领队在整个旅游活动中，负责沟通派出方旅行社和接待方旅行社、导游以及与游客之间关系，监督接待方旅行社执行旅游计划，协助各地导游落实各项服务，维护游客旅游消费的正当合法权益。全陪则作为国内组团旅行社的代表，协调以领队为首的入境旅游团队与国内各地的接待旅行社的协作关系，保证入境旅游团队在各地旅游中各个环节的正常衔接，监督整个接待计划的顺利实施。地陪应与领队、全陪友善合作，全面提供在当地的所有旅游接待服务项目并保证质量。

三、国内旅游接待

（一）国内旅游的概念及特点

国内旅游是指旅行社招徕、组织和接待中国内地居民在境

2.2.3 Follow-up improvement work

2.3 The Relationship Between Tour Leaders and Tour Guides

Good relationship between the tour leader and the tour guide is important.

2.3.1 The roles and responsibilities of tour leaders, national guides and local guides

2.3.2 Relationship among tour leaders, national and local guides

The tour leader shall be responsible for communicating with different parties, the relationship between the tour guide and tourists, supervising the implementation of the tourism plan, assisting the tour guide to implement various services, and safeguarding the legitimate rights of tourists.

3 Domestic Tourism Reception

3.1 Definition and Characteristics of Domestic Tour

内旅游的业务。国内旅游一般具有准备时间短(short preparation time)、日程变化小(few schedule changes)、消费水平差别大(big difference in consumption level)等特点。

3.2 Group Reception of Domestic Tour

(二) 国内旅游的团队接待

The specific reception procedures of domestic tour are basically the same as those of international tour, consisting of three parts: preliminary preparation, implementation and follow-up improvement.

国内旅游的团队接待,与国际旅游的入境接待(inbound tour reception)基本相同(basically the same),只是少了入境和出境的手续,对领队和导游的外语也没有要求。除非有些在我国工作的外国人组团在国内旅游,当然还是要求懂外语的导游。国内旅游的具体接待工作程序(reception procedures)与国际旅游基本一致,都有接待的前期准备、实施接待工作、接待后续完善工作三个部分。

第三节 散客及特殊旅游接待
Section Three Reception Services for Individual and Special Tourists

1 Definition and Characteristics of Individual Tour

一、散客旅游的概念与特点

1.1 Definition of Individual Tourist

(一) 散客旅游的概念

散客旅游,又称自助或半自助旅游(self-service or semi-self-service tour),在国外称为自主旅游(independent tour),是由游客自行安排旅游行程,零星现付各项旅游费用(pay sporadic travel expenses)的旅游形式。相比于团队旅游,散客旅游具有批量小(small number)、批次多(many batches)、预定期短(short schedules)、要求多、变化多等特点。

The number of individual tour in China is often less than nine.

散客旅游也并不意味着只是单个游客,它可以是单个游客,也可以是一个家庭或几个亲朋好友,还可以是临时组织起来的散客旅游团,人数通常少于旅游团队,我国现行规定在9人以下。

Individual tourists often rely on travel agencies.

散客并不意味着完全不依靠旅行社,其全部旅游事务都由游客自己办理,实际上不少散客旅游活动都借助旅行社的帮助,其旅游日程、线路等由旅游者自己选定,然后再由旅行社作某些安排,如机票、旅馆、导游等。

(二) 国内散客旅游的分类

散客旅游又分为三类。一般按计价方式,主要分为:

(1) 包价旅游,接待方式、程序同团队旅游一样,只是人数为 9 人以下。

(2) 小包价旅游(small package tour),又叫部分包价旅游(partial package tour)。人数也是 9 人以下,只安排部分的行程,或食宿,或景点游览等。

(3) 自助游(self-help tour)。自助游是指我国公民在国内自助式旅游,包括借助航空、铁路等交通工具的自助游和自己驾驶汽车外出旅游的自驾游。但自助游的游客在旅游期间,通常也要求旅行社提供部分服务,主要是单项的服务,如预订住宿、机车船票、餐饮、景点门票、娱乐门票等接待服务。旅行社提供了这些代为订购的消费,一方面可以收取手续费;另一方面还可以从建立了业务往来关系的单位拿到协议价格(get the agreed price),并有一定的折扣或折返比率(discount or discount rate)。这种接待方式,既方便了游客,也创造了经济收益。

由于自助式旅游具有行程和景点自己选择,时间自主安排等诸多满足个性化需求的优点,受到越来越多的中等以上收入(tourists with medium income or above)的游客和中青年的喜爱,成为一种旅游业务的发展趋势。自助游的游客量越来越大,正成为更多旅行社的主要业务之一。

二、散客旅游的接待工作

(一) 散客旅游接待的分类

(1) 从接待途径来分,主要是两种,即门市接待(outlet reception)和网站接待(website reception)。门市接待是传统的接待方式。而网站接待是新兴的方式,等同于电子商务,由于其便利、高效,越来越受到游客的欢迎,正在成为旅行社散客接待的重要途径。

(2) 从接待对象来分,主要是三类,即本地游客在本地的单项或多项服务(single or multiple services),外地游客在本地的单项或多项服务,本地游客赴外地的单项或多项服务。

(3) 从接待方式来分,又可分为现场接待(on-site reception)、电话接待(telephone reception)和信函接待(letter re-

---

1.2 Classification of Domestic Individual Travel

Individual tourism can be divided into three categories according to the valuation method.

2 Reception of Individual Tourists

2.1 Classification of Reception of Individual Tourists

Website reception is a new way, which is equivalent to e-commerce.

There are mainly three kinds of services from the reception objects.

ception)三种方式。无论是门市接待还是网站接待,大体都有这三种接待方式。

2.2 Allocation of Receptionists for Individual Tourists

The receptionists should be skilled in business, informative, knowledgeable, dedicated and familiar with all the business of travel agencies.

(二)散客旅游接待人员配备

散客旅游的接待工作难度相对大,往往各种单项或几项服务都要求接待人员来完成。因此,旅行社安排的散客旅游接待人员,应该是由业务精熟、信息丰富、知识面广、敬业精神强、熟悉旅行社全部业务的人员来担任,或者由有经验的导游来兼职,或者是做过导游的人员来做工作。

(三)散客旅游接待的主要工作程序

2.3 Main Procedures for the Reception of Individual Tourists

Optimize and establish market sites, and establish modern websites.

Establish an efficient booking implementation mechanism.

Provide timely, high-quality and efficient reception services.

Summarize feedback regularly.

(1)建点建站。优选并建立门市点,建立现代化的网站。

(2)广泛收集旅游产品相关信息。包括:餐饮、饭店住宿、交通、景点(scenic spots)。

(3)采购旅游产品。根据旅游市场需求,与饭店客房、餐饮、景点等旅游企业建立广泛的业务往来协议(establish extensive business agreements),代为单项销售其客房、门票,代为推荐餐饮,代购机、车、船票等,作为本旅行社提供给散客的旅游产品。

(4)建立高效的预订落实机制。应在接收到游客消费要求的信息后,第一时间向各相关部门传达(convey consumption requirements to the relevant departments),迅速落实接待服务项目,及时向游客反馈信息,并建立跟踪询问制度(establish a system of follow-up and inquiry),及时了解、督促其落实状况。

(5)组织提供适时、优质、高效的接待服务,让游客满意。

(6)定期总结反馈信息。通过门市接待和网站接待,对一个时期内获取的游客具体要求进行整理和分析,反馈给采购部门。同时,不断探求新的旅游产品及相关产品的信息,以供旅行社快速调整产品结构(adjust the product structure)、不断增加新的旅游品种(continuously increase new tourism varieties)。

3 Reception of Specific Tourist Activities

三、特殊旅游接待

3.1 The Definition and Characteristics of Special Tourism

(一)特殊旅游的概念及特点

3.1.1 The definition of specific tourist activities

1. 特殊旅游的概念

特殊旅游,指为了满足游客的个性愿望(satisfy the

individual wishes),以兴趣、爱好(interests,hobbies)等专门目的,前往特定的地域、地点,进行一些特定的旅游性活动(specific tourist activities)。特殊旅游被认为是自助旅游的一种特殊形式。我国目前的特殊旅游大致有以下几种类型。

(1) 考古类旅游(Archaeological tour),前往探访古墓(ancient tombs)、古老原始地带(primitive areas);

(2) 探险类旅游(Adventure tour),前往悬崖进行攀岩(climbing cliffs),或前往山洞探险(exploring caves);

(3) 文化类旅游(Cultural tour),前往专门欣赏古老建筑(ancient buildings)、古代书法(ancient calligraphy)、碑刻(stone inscriptions)等;

(4) 科考类旅游(Science tour),前往探寻科学发现(explore scientific discoveries),如探寻神农架野人(Shennongjia savages)、喜马拉雅山雪人足迹(Himalayas snowman footprints)等;

(5) 体育类旅游(Sports tour),为体验驾车乐趣(experience driving pleasure),驾汽车或骑自行车长途旅行(long-distance travel);到特定滑雪场(ski resorts)的滑雪旅游(skiing tour);去海边潜水的潜水旅游(diving tour)等。

2. 特殊旅游接待的特点

(1) 有特定的旅游目的地(specific tourist destination)。已经有特定的人群经常或定期前往,一般预订时间较长。但游客总量较小。游客一般需具有较高的收入、较好的身体素质和心理素质。

(2) 计划性非常强(much planned)。一般要求条件较好的吃、住、行等,对其他如游、购、娱等不感兴趣。往往需要提供特殊的工具、向导、设施等,故消费层次较高,有时消费的费用相当大,接待的经济效益颇佳。

(3) 对接待工作要求比较高。为使接待工作便于沟通,要求接待人员应具备相应的专业知识(professional knowledge),或者对游客特殊的兴趣、爱好(special interests and hobbies)有一定的了解。

(二) 特殊旅游接待程序

特殊旅游接待,同样分为三个阶段,即接待的前期准备、实施接待工作、接待后续完善工作(follow-up improvement work)三个部分。

3.1.2 The characteristics of special tourism

Tourists generally need to have higher income, better physical and psychological quality.

The level of consumption is relatively high.

3.2 Special Tourist Reception Procedures

Special tourism reception can also be divided into three stages.

3.2.1 Pre-reception preparation

1. 接待前准备

无论其人数多少,特殊旅游接待程序基本与国内团队旅游一致,但必须有针对性地进行特殊准备,有些还需要提前(in advance)进行特别的准备事项(special preparations)。除了上述一般性的安排(general arrangements)计划,挑选导游,准备吃、住、行(food, accommodation and transportation)的条件外,还要求有以下特定的准备工作:

(1) 可能要求旅行社提前探寻特定路线或特定地点(explore specific routes or locations)。

(2) 要求领队或导游掌握较丰富的相关知识(master more abundant relevant knowledge)。

(3) 要求旅行社准备特殊目的所需要的专用设施、工具、装备(prepare special facilities, tools and equipment)等。

(4) 极有可能建立较长期的、定期的游客群体,为在接待中满足其个性需求(individual needs),特别强调旅行社应建立详尽的游客档案(establish detailed tourist archives),准备充分的游客相关信息(adequate information)。

3.2.2 Implementing reception work

2. 实施接待工作

大体与国内旅游团队相同。需要注意的是,特殊旅游接待往往比通常观光性质的旅游接待的危险性要大,因此,必须制定对付危险发生(deal with dangerous occurrences)的应急预案(formulate emergency plans),准备相应的救生设备(prepare corresponding life-saving equipment)、营救运输车辆(rescue transport vehicles)、紧急联络设备(emergency liaison equipment)等。接待人员应熟练掌握(be proficient in)这些设备的使用。同时,旅行社应该建立后续支持的预备队伍(establish a reserve team for follow-up support),坚持值班制度(adhere to the duty system),保证联络和支持的畅通(ensure smooth communication and support),随时应付紧急情况(cope with emergencies)的发生。

3.2.3 Follow-up improvement after reception

3. 接待后续完善工作

旅行社应该做出比一般的旅游团队更为详尽的总结,并专门建立档案(special archives)。

第四节　旅行社同业批发业务管理
Section Four　Management of Inter-industry Wholesale Business in Travel Agencies

一、同业批发业务简介

1　Brief Introduction of Inter-industry Wholesale Business

同业批发业务（wholesale business）是一种新型旅游业务，近几年在国内兴起。所谓同业批发业务，是指一系列（a series of）针对旅游同业客户的旅游产品批发业务，其中包括同业产品（inter-industry products）的开发、区划客户网络的建设与管理、同业批发业务具体操作三大阶段。

目前，我国主要有三种同业批发形态：以地接社在客源地设立的联络处或办事处（liaison office in the source area）为主导的批发商形态；以大型组团社包机（专列）为主导的客源地批发形态；组团社与地接社密切合作的客源地总代表批发商形态。从严格意义上说，这三种形态还不能算真正的批发商，但却形成了中国旅游批发商的雏形。

At present, there are three main types of wholesale business in our country, which has formed the rudiment of China's tourism wholesalers.

中国旅游批发商主要业务类型按其产品可分为：单一旅游产品批发、机票加酒店商务度假产品批发、常规观光旅游产品（conventional tourism product）批发、主题旅游产品（theme tourism product）批发四种。

二、同业批发业务流程及管理技巧

2　Business Process and Management Skills

（一）同业批发旅游产品的开发

2.1　Development of Inter-industry Wholesale Products

同业批发旅游产品的开发是在接待社产品开发基础之上，结合在客源地建立的大交通供给（large traffic supply）而组成的旅游产品。具体包括接待产品的采购、大交通的供给体系的建立、批发产品的整合（integration of wholesale products）、产品手册的编制（compilation of product manuals）四个环节。

1. 批发产品的采购

2.1.1　Procurement of Wholesale Products

接待社的批发商会优先（give priority to）批发自己公司的产品，也就不涉及批发产品的采购问题。而大型组团社设计的批发产品，会选择市场排名靠前（high market ranking）、接待质量稳定(stable reception quality)、价格相对便宜(relatively low price)的接待社作为合作伙伴(as partners)。

2. 建立稳定的大交通供给体系

以地接业务为主的旅行社,其机、车、船票的采购能力是核心能力。一般情况下,大型组团社和实力强大的旅游批发商,旺季时普遍采用包机(chartered flights)或包专列(chartered trains)的形式进行机票、车票等资源的采购。这样,一方面可以保证供应,一方面可以获得竞争优势。航空公司(airlines)一般都是根据批发商上一年度(in the previous year)的拿票量(the amount of tickets)来决定给予什么样的支持政策(support policy),有时会制定一个随销售量而不断递增的返点政策(return-point policy),所以批发商要通过自己的销售能力、公关能力(public relations ability)和资金实力(financial strength),确立自己在航空公司销售系统(sales system)的地位。

3. 批发产品的整合

接待产品和大交通采购完成后,要根据当地市场(local market)情况进行批发产品的整合(should be integrated),接待质量、价格、产品多样化是整合阶段要面对的主要问题。接待质量是基础,是批发商在游客市场立足的关键(establish a foothold in the tourist market),拥有稳定的接待质量(reception quality)才能建立在同业批发市场的地位和客户网络(customer network)。价格是关键,接待社提供的产品一般都是标准型产品(standard products),批发商会根据客源市场的调研结果,选择价格最低的产品进行组合,价格越低,利润才会越高。产品多样化(product diversification)是趋势,借助产品差异化优势开辟新的利润丰厚的市场(lucrative market),是旅行社走出价格战误区(make travel agencies out of the price war)的新的发展之路。

4. 产品手册的编制

产品整合(product integration)完成之后,根据区域市场的调研,编制(compile)具有个性特色的产品手册。

(二)区域客户的建设与管理

区域客户的建设与管理包括客户资料(customer information)的获取与分析(acquisition and analysis)、旅游产品的区域营销覆盖、区域客户的销售、客户网络(customer network)的管理与维护四个环节。

2.2.1 Acquisition and analysis of customer data

1. 客户资料的获取与分析

对于旅游批发商来说,建立目标市场的区域客户网络是业务进展的关键。获得(obtain)区域旅行社同业客户资料的方法有如下几种:通过旅游主管单位发布的各种统计资料(various statistical data),通过《中国旅行社名录》(China Travel Agency List)、报章类资料、别人的介绍等,获得有价值的客户名单(valuable customer lists)和办公地址(office addresses)。

2.2.2 Regional marketing coverage of tourism products

2. 旅游产品的区域营销覆盖

产品区域覆盖的常用手段有:传真、电子邮件、旅游同业DM媒体广告。为下一阶段的客户拜访(customer visits),达成合作意向(cooperation intentions)和实质性业务操作(substantive business operations)打下坚实的基础(solid foundation)。

2.2.3 Visiting regional customers

3. 区域客户的拜访销售

如果是批发商第一次进行整个区域市场(regional market)的拜访,首先要进行电话促销,进行电话预约(telephone appointment),以核实(verify)客户的地址,将办公地址相近的(similar addresses)客户安排在一起,尽量提高拜访效率(improve the visiting efficiency)。其次要做好相应的准备,如产品手册(product manuals)、名片、记事本(notepad);熟悉推广产品的主打卖点(main selling points of the products)、与同类产品相比的竞争优势(competitive advantages)、合作接待社的基本情况与接待优势、批发商自身的服务范围(service scope)和服务特色(service characteristics)等。

2.2.4 Management and maintenance of customer network

Customers can be divided into three types: quasi-customers, potential customers and unintentional customers.

4. 客户网络的管理与维护

第一轮拜访(first round of visits)后的客户,对其进行有效的整理,可以将客户分为:准客户、潜在客户、无意向客户三种类型。准客户(quasi-customers)最重要,是批发商打开市场(open up the market)的关键,通过准确的信息传递和优质服务,将其转化为自己的忠诚客户(loyal customers)。根据"二八原则"(Pareto principle),20%的客户会给批发商带来80%的业务和利润。

2.3 Operation Flow of Wholesale Business

(三)批发业务的操作流程

批发业务的操作流程可以分为业务询价电话(inquiry telephone)、报价及确认(quotation and confirmation)、业务操作(business operation)、后续服务与改进(follow-up service and improvement)四个环节。

2.3.1 Inquiry telephone

1. 业务询价电话

如果是批发商向市场推出的散客成团产品,应该问清游客的人数、姓名、身份证号码、具体出行时间(specific travel time)等。团队的电话询价要注意报价准确(accurate quotation),对方往往采取一团多询,给对方一个讨价还价的空间(give them a bargaining space),还应该注意问客户需求,如:团队人数、团队特征、有无特殊需求,根据需求进行特殊接待。接听组团社团队业务咨询来电时,应该与组团社确定产品内容、发团日期、出票时间、首付款比例、哪里接团、多少人、有无儿童、有无特殊要求、返程方式等,并注意将团队相关信息及时传给接待社。

Send the relevant information of the group to the reception agency.

2.3.2 Quotation and confirmation

2. 报价及确认

接听组团社的团队询价电话(answer the group inquiry telephone)后,应该根据客户要求打印产品行程单(print the itinerary)及报价单(quotation sheet),并做好产品的分项报价(make the sub-quotation),如果达成合作意向(reach the intention of cooperation),双方可以传真确认相关接待事宜。确认内容包括价格、行程、时间、人数、住宿标准、餐饮标准、有无少数民族特殊饮食安排(special dietary arrangements for ethnic minorities)、车型、区间交通票、返程交通票、全陪姓名、联系电话等。

2.3.3 Business operation

3. 业务操作

业务确认完成后,要将确认单发给接待社,由接待社开始进行产品要素(product elements)的相关确认工作。按照与组团社的约定(in accordance with the agreement with organizing travel agency),安排送票时间和送团时间,如果有必要,安排行前说明会(the pre-trip presentation)。旅游团出发时,批发商最好安排自己的管理人员到机场和火车站送团,完成业务操作全部环节。

Keep in close contact with the operator and the organizing travel agency to understand the reception quality and customer satisfaction.

旅游过程中要与接待社的计调人员、组团社的全陪密切联系,了解接待质量和客户满意度。旅游结束后,批发商可以安排专人接团,根据与组团社达成的结账协议,把团款结清(settle the tour payment),并及时处理旅游目的地的投诉与相关问题(deal with the complaints and related problems)。

2.3.4 Follow-up service and improvement

4. 后续服务与改进

旅游团业务结束后,完成结账、回访等工作,根据反馈进行产品改进和新产品研发。

实训项目 07　旅行社接待计划的制订

Project 7　Make a Reception Plan for Travel Agencies

一、实训目标(Training Objectives)：

1. 通过实训加深对旅行社接待工作相关理论知识的理解。

2. 通过旅行社模拟接待服务,使学生熟悉旅行社接待工作的基本操作流程与规范,掌握对客销售与服务技巧,学会基本的旅行社接待常识,能够从事接待普通上门咨询顾客并能促进业务成交。

3. 培养与客人沟通交流的能力。

二、实训学时(Training Period)：2～8 学时

三、实训地点(Training Place)：旅行社情景实训室

四、实训设备(Training Equipment)：联网计算机、移动硬盘或 U 盘、A4 绘图纸、铅笔、橡皮。

五、项目描述(Project Description)：

实训教师提供模拟旅行社资料及各组客户的相关资料并进行分析,学生分组进行模拟训练,各组轮流演练与客户交流、与计调人员商定线路产品细节、与客户签订合同的流程。完成接待回访工作。处理客户投诉与表扬事宜。总结与资料归档。并用 PPT 汇报成果。

六、实训任务及要求(Tasks and Requirements)：

实训任务一览表

序号	实训任务名称	实训内容	实训学时	实训地点
01	组团社接待操作基本流程设计	通过讨论,查阅资料,完成接待流程设计	2	旅行社情景实训室
02	接待表格的制作	查阅资料并讨论,掌握预报计划、书面确认、计划变更、正式计划与再确认的撰写	2	
03	填报导游任务单、团款收支明细表等,制作旅游接待计划方案	查阅资料并讨论,熟悉全程导游任务单的格式及应用,掌握团队款项收支明细表的应用	2	

注:教师可根据需要选用实训项目和学时。

根据班级人数,每组可适当编制2~6人规模。通过组内讨论,进行相关旅游接待计划表格的填写。组内分工,制作并完成旅行社接待计划,并在课堂上展示。

七、实训成果(Practical Results):

1. 每组完成旅行社接待计划WORD电子文档1份和展示PPT电子档1份。

2. 将上述两个文件放入文件夹,命名为:"班级名称+小组编号+旅行社接待计划实训作业"。

八、考核标准(Assessment Criterion):

项目	考核内容和要求	分值	得分
表现	按时完成任务,工作积极主动,具有合作精神	20	
内容	内容全面、真实、精确	40	
格式	格式规范、语言简洁、样式美观	20	
创新	有创意,有市场潜力	20	
小计		**100**	

第八章　旅行社服务质量管理
Chapter Eight　Service Quality Management in Travel Agencies

【学习目标】　Learning Objectives

1. 了解旅行社服务质量的内涵(connotation)与产生机理；
2. 理解旅行社服务质量评估的方法(assessment method)和服务质量差距模型(service quality gap model)；
3. 掌握旅行社服务质量的改进方法(improvement method)。

> 坚持以推动高质量发展为主题，把实施扩大内需战略同深化供给侧结构性改革有机结合起来，增强国内大循环内生动力和可靠性，提升国际循环质量和水平。
>
> ——党的二十大报告摘录

✓ 本章课程视频讲解　　✓ 实训指导书
✓ 线上课堂链接　　　　✓ 优秀学生作品精选
✓ 本章训练题库　　　　✓ 时政新闻
✓ 本章拓展资源

第一节 旅行社服务质量概述
Section One An Overview of Service Quality in Travel Agencies

旅行社服务质量好坏不仅决定了企业的竞争能力,甚至决定了区域旅游业的生命力。

The service quality of travel agencies not only determines the competitiveness of the enterprises, but also determines the vitality of regional tourism industry.

一、旅行社服务质量的概念

(一)产品和服务的特征比较

1 Definition of Service Quality in Travel Agencies

1.1 The Comparison of Characteristics Between Products and Services

服务是个人或社会组织(social organization)为消费者直接或凭借某种工具、设备、设施和媒体等所做的工作或进行的一种经济活动(economic activity),是向消费者个人或企业提供的(provide to consumers),旨在满足对方某种特定需求(aim to meet their specific needs)的一种活动和好处。服务主要以活动形式表现使用价值或效用,是一种特殊形式的劳动产品,即通过提供必要的手段和方法,满足接受服务的对象的需求的"过程"。服务的特征通常表现为:服务是无形的(不可感知性)(intangible, imperceptible)、不可分离的(生产消费同时性)(inseparability, simultaneous production and consumption),具有异质性(heterogeneity)和不可储藏性(non-storage)。

服务与商品的另一感性差别(perceptual difference)是服务具有较强的经验特征(strong experience feature)和信任特征(credence feature):购买服务获得的品质和效果难以事先预期(can't predict in advance)。1970 年,美国经济学家尼尔森(Nielsen)将包含货物商品和服务商品在内的产品品质(product quality)分为两类:寻找品质(seeking quality)和经验品质(experiential quality)。寻找品质指顾客在购买之前就能够确认的产品属性(product attributes)(如颜色、款式、手感、气味等)及产品的价格。经验品质指那些只有在购买之后或在消费过程中才能体会到的产品属性,包括耐用程度(durability)、满足程度等。

Experience quality refers to those attributes that can only be perceived after purchasing or during consumption.

1973 年,达比和卡内(Darby and Canet)两人在商品品质二分法(commodity quality dichotomy)的基础上增加了信任品质。信任品质:指那些顾客即使在购买和消费之后也很难做出评价的属性。

Trust quality refers to the attributes that are difficult to evaluate even after purchase and consumption.

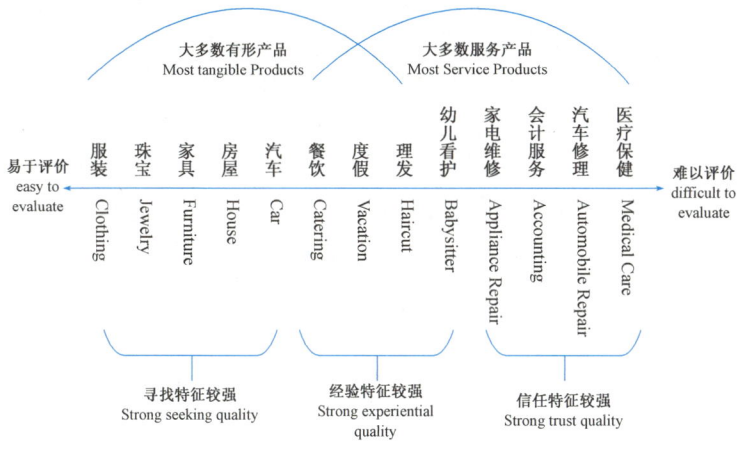

图 8-1 三大类产品/服务的特征比较

A Comparison of the Characteristics of Three Categories of Products/Services

(二) 旅行社服务质量的概念与内涵

服务质量是指服务能够满足规定和潜在需求(meet the requirements and potential needs)的特征和特性的总和,是指服务工作能够满足被服务者需求的程度,是企业为使目标顾客满意而提供的最低服务水平(minimum level of service),也是企业保持这一预定服务水平的连贯性程度(the consistency degree)。服务质量管理是指为保证某一产品、过程或服务质量满足规定的质量要求所必需的有计划、有系统的全部活动(all planned and systematic activities)。

旅行社产品具有综合性强(strong comprehensiveness)的特点,与提供单一服务的企业相比,其产品质量更加不易被控制(more difficult to control)。旅行社服务质量是指旅行社满足旅游者需要和期望的程度,是旅游者对旅行社提供服务的期望(expectations of service)和其实际经历该旅游项目所形成的感知(perceptions of the actual experience)之间的比较,在这里,旅游者是评价旅游服务质量高低的主体。

(三) 服务质量差距模型

服务质量差距模型是 20 世纪 80 年代中期到 90 年代初美国营销学家帕拉休拉曼(A. Parasuraman)、赞瑟姆(Valarie A.

1.2 Connotation of Service Quality in Travel Agencies

Tourists are the main body to evaluate the quality of tourism service.

1.3 Service Quality Gap Model

Zeithamal)和贝利(Leonard L. Berry)等人提出的,又称 PZB 模型、5GAP 模型。5GAP 模型是专门用来分析质量问题的根源。感知服务质量差距(差距 5)即顾客期望与顾客感知的服务之间的差距,这是差距模型的核心。要弥合这一差距(to bridge this gap),就要对以下四个差距进行弥合(to bridge the following four gaps):差距 1,管理者认识的差距(managers' understanding gap);差距 2,质量标准差距(quality standard gap);差距 3,服务交易差距(service transaction gap);差距 4,营销沟通的差距(marketing communication gap)。

Service quality is a function of service quality gap. Measuring various gaps within an enterprise is an effective way to measure service quality.

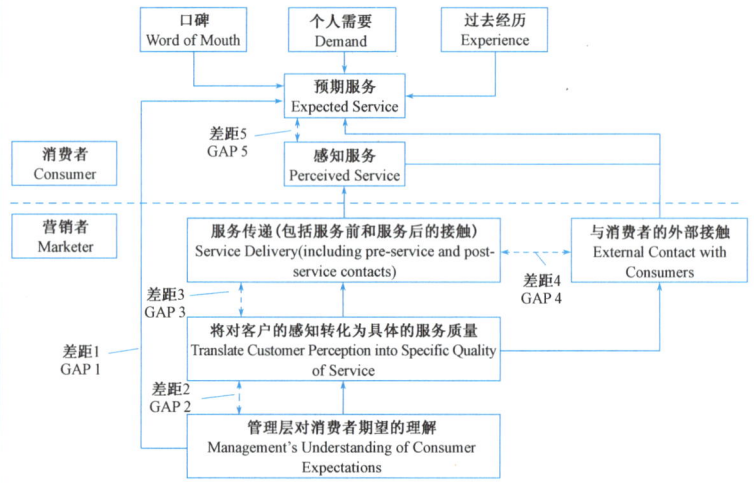

差距 1(Gap 1);管理者理解的差距 Gap of managers' understanding;
差距 2(Gap 2);质量标准差距 Gap of quality standard;
差距 3(Gap 3);服务交易差距 Gap of service transaction;
差距 4(Gap 4);营销沟通的差距 Gap of marketing communication;
差距 5(Gap 5);感知服务质量差距 Gap of perceived service quality。

图 8-2 旅行社服务质量产生的原因
Causes of Service Quality in Travel Agencies

服务质量是服务质量差距的函数,测量企业内部存在的各种差距是有效测量服务质量的手段,差距越大,顾客对企业的服务质量就越不满意。因此,差距分析(gap analysis)可以作为复杂的服务过程控制的起点,为改善服务质量提供依据。因此,近 20 年来,服务质量差距研究便成了学者们关注的焦点(the focus of scholars' attention)。自从 PZB 模型提出至今,该模型在旅游服务质量研究领域(in the field of tourism service quality research)不断地(continuously)被完善和扩展。这些扩展研究(extended studies)基本上都是围绕着顾客、各级管理者和一线员工三个层面,采用定性或定量两种研究方法展开的。

The studies are basically carried out around the three levels of customers, managers at all levels and front-line employees, using qualitative or quantitative research methods.

二、旅行社服务质量的实现

2 The Implementation of Service Quality in Travel Agencies

(一)预期质量与感知质量的定义

2.1 Definition of Expected Quality and Perceived Quality

顾客对服务质量的预期称为"预期质量"。顾客对服务企业所提供服务的预期主要受到以下因素的影响:企业形象(corporate image)、顾客口碑(customer reputation)、市场沟通(market communication)、个人经验及需求(personal experience and demand)等。

顾客实际感知的服务水平称为"感知质量"。顾客对服务企业提供的服务实际感知的水平取决于旅行社的实体环境(depend on the physical environment)、服务人员及服务流程(service personnel and service process)等方面。

(二)预期质量与感知质量之间的差距

2.2 The Gap Between Expected Quality and Perceived Quality

当旅游者对旅行社的服务质量表示不满时,通常是旅游者对旅行社服务的感知质量水平低于(lower than)预期质量水平(差距5),对二者之间的差距进行分析有助于找到质量问题的根源(find the root of the quality problem),否则会导致以下后果(lead to the following consequences):① 消极的质量评价(劣质)和质量问题(negative quality evaluation or inferior quality and quality problems);② 口碑不佳(bad reputation);③ 对公司形象的消极影响(negative impact on corporate image);④ 丧失业务(loss of business)。

图 8-3 旅行社服务质量的实现

The Implementation of the Service Quality in Travel Agencies

第二节 旅行社服务质量的评估
Section Two　Evaluation of Service Quality in Travel Agencies

1　Evaluation of Service Quality in Travel Agencies

Five service quality levels: tangible facilities, reliability, responsiveness, assurance and emotional engagement.

一、旅行社服务质量的评估

SERVQUAL 理论是依据全面质量管理（Total Quality Management，TQM）理论在服务行业中提出的一种新的服务质量评价体系（quality evaluation system），其理论核心是"服务质量差距模型"（service quality gap model）。SERVQUAL 将服务质量分为五个层面：有形设施、可靠性、响应性、保障性、情感投入，每一层面又被细分为若干个问题。SERVQUAL 通过调查问卷的方式，让用户对每个问题的期望值、实际感受值及最低可接受值（the minimum acceptable value）进行评分（rate the expected value），并由其确立相关的 22 个具体因素来说明它。然后通过问卷调查（questionnaire survey）、顾客打分（customer rating）和综合计算（comprehensive calculation）得出服务质量的分数。

图 8-4　SERVQUAL 概念性模型
SERVQUAL Conceptual Model

This model has been widely accepted and adopted by managers and scholars.

近年来，该模型已被管理者和学者广泛接受和采用。模型以差别理论为基础，即顾客对服务质量的期望，与顾客从服务组织实际得到的服务之间的差别。模型分别用五个尺度（five scales）评价顾客所接受的不同服务的服务质量。研究表明，

The tangibility of travel agency service refers to the tangible part of travel agency products.

SERVQUAL 是一个评价服务质量和用来决定提高服务质量行动的有效工具(effective tool)。

(一) 服务的有形性

1.1 Tangibility of Services

旅行社服务的有形性指旅行社产品中的有形部分,包括旅行社和相关部门的硬件设施设备、服务设施的外观、宣传品的摆放(placement of publicity materials)和员工的仪容仪表(appearance)等方面。其组成项目(components)有:

Q1. 现代化的服务设施(modern service facilities);

Q2. 服务设施具有吸引力;

Q3. 员工有整洁的服装和外套(employees' neat clothes and coats);

Q4. 公司的设施与他们所提供的服务相匹配(company's facilities match the services they provide)。

(二) 服务的可靠性

1.2 Reliability of Services

旅行社服务的可靠性是指旅行社可靠而准确地履行服务承诺的能力(fulfill their service commitments reliably and accurately)。旅行社的产品涉及交通、餐饮、住宿、娱乐等多个相关部门,具有很高的不确定性(highly uncertain),因此旅游者在评价旅行社的服务质量时最看重可靠性因素。其组成项目有以下几点。

Q5. 公司向顾客承诺的事情都能及时完成(company's commitment to customers can be accomplished in time);

Q6. 顾客遇到困难时,能表现出关心并帮助(When customers encounter difficulties, they can show concern and help);

Q7. 公司是可靠的(The company is reliable);

Q8. 能准时提供所承诺的服务(Provide the promised services on time);

Q9. 正确记录相关的记录(correctly record relevant records)。

(三) 服务的反应性

1.3 Service Responsiveness

旅行社服务的反应性(responsiveness)是指旅行社随时帮助旅游者并提供快捷有效的服务的意愿(willingness)。旅行社是否能够及时地满足旅游者的各种要求,表明旅行社是否具备了以服务为导向的经营观念(have a service-oriented business concept),即是否将旅游者的利益放在第一位(put the interests of tourists first)。其组成项目有以下几点。

　　Q10. 不能指望他们告诉顾客提供服务的准确时间（You can't expect them to tell customers when to provide services on time）；

　　Q11. 期望他们提供及时的服务是不现实的（It is unrealistic to expect them to provide timely service）；

　　Q12. 员工并不总是愿意帮助顾客（Employees are not always willing to help customers）；

　　Q13. 员工因为太忙一直无法立即提供服务，以满足顾客的需求（Employees are too busy to provide services immediately to meet customer needs）。

1.4　Guarantee Ability of Services

（四）服务的保证性

　　旅行社服务的保证性是指旅行社服务人员具有友好的态度和胜任工作的能力，包括：服务人员完成任务（accomplish tasks）的能力，对顾客的礼貌和尊敬，与顾客有效的沟通，将顾客最关心的事放在心上的态度。其组成项目有以下几种。

　　Q14. 员工是值得信赖的（Employees are trustworthy）；

　　Q15. 在从事交易时，顾客会感到放心（Customers will feel at ease when they engage in transactions）；

　　Q16. 员工是礼貌的（Employees are polite）；

　　Q17. 员工可以从公司得到适当的支持，以提供更好的服务（Employees can get appropriate support from the company to provide better service）。

1.5　Empathy of Service

（五）服务的移情性

　　旅行社服务的移情性是指旅行社的服务人员设身处地地为旅游者着想和对旅游者给予特别的关注并为旅游者提供个性服务。要求服务人员具有接近旅游者的能力和敏锐的洞察力（keen insight to effectively understand the needs of tourists），能够有效地理解旅游者的需要。其组成项目有以下几点。

　　Q18. 公司不会针对顾客提供个别服务（The company will not provide individual services to customers）；

　　Q19. 员工不会给予顾客个别关心（Employees will not give individual care to customers）；

　　Q20. 不能期望员工了解顾客的需求（Employees cannot be expected to understand customers' needs）；

　　Q21. 公司没有优先考虑顾客的利益（The company does

not give priority to the interests of customers);

Q22. 公司提供的服务时间不能符合所有顾客的需求(The service time provided by the company cannot meet the needs of all customers)。

二、旅行社服务质量的评估方法

SERVQUAL 问卷的题目根据服务的有形性、可靠性、反应性、保证性和移情性五个标准进行设计,每个标准具体化为 4~5 个问题(concretized into 4~5 questions)。被调查的旅游者对每个问题进行判断(judge each question),给出相应的分数(give corresponding scores)。从而测量得到旅游者对旅行社服务质量的预期水平,以及测量旅游者对旅行社服务质量的实际感知水平。SERVQUAL 计算公式:

$$SQ = \sum_{i=1}^{22}(P_i - E_i) \quad (i = 1、2、3、\cdots n, n = 22)$$

式中:SQ 为感知服务质量;P_i 为第 i 个因素在顾客感受方面的分数;E_i 为第 i 个因素在顾客期望方面的分数。由此公式获得的 SQ 是在五大属性(five attributes)同等重要条件下的单个顾客的总感知质量。

但是在现实生活中顾客对决定服务质量的每个属性的重要性的看法是不同的(hold different views on the importance of each attribute)。因此,推而广之(by extension),测量旅行社的整体服务质量实际上就是计算 SERVQUAL 分数的加权平均数(weighted average),权数表示每个标准在服务质量中的重要性。通过顾客调查后应确定每个服务质量属性的权重,然后加权平均就得出了更为合理的 SERVQUAL 分数。公式为:

$$SQ = \sum_{j=1}^{5} W_j \sum_{i=1}^{22}(P_i - E_i) \quad (i = 1、2、3、\cdots 22; j = 1、2、3、4、5)$$

W_j 为第 j 个属性的权重;i 表示每个属性或维度下评价项目的数目,在此公式中,假设每个维度中评价项目权重一致,即评价项目不再考虑项目权重,得到单个顾客平均的 SERVQUAL 分数。最后将调查中所有顾客的 SERVQUAL 分数加总再除以顾客数目 m 就得到某企业该项服务产品平均的 SERVQUAL 分数,即

$$SERVQUAL = (\sum_{i=1}^{m} SQ)/m$$

2 Evaluation Methods of Tourism Service Quality

The SERVQUAL questionnaire is designed according to five criteria of service tangibility, reliability, responsiveness, assurance and empathy.

SQ is the perceived service quality; ***P_i*** is the score of the *i*th factor in customer perception; ***E_i*** is the score of the *i*th factor in customer expectation.

W_j is the weight of the *j*th attribute. *i* represents the number of evaluation items under each attribute or dimension. In this formula, it is assumed that the evaluation item weights in each dimension are the same, that is, the evaluation item will no longer consider the item weights, then get the average SERVQUAL score for a single customer. Finally, add up the ***SERVQUAL*** scores of all customers in the survey and divide by the number of customers' ***m*** to get the average ***SERVQUAL*** score of the service product.

第三节 旅行社服务质量的控制与改进
Section Three Strategies for Controlling and Improving Service Quality in Travel Agencies

Whether the tourists are satisfied with the service depends on the comparison between the actual perceived quality of the customer and the expected service quality.

根据事先制定的(early-made service standards)服务规范对服务质量进行控制,可以保证服务质量达到旅行社的预期服务水平(expected service level),但是旅游者对服务是否满意取决于顾客实际感受到的质量与预期的服务质量之间的比较,即旅游者对服务的感受与预期不一致(差距5)。当旅行社发现企业的服务水平与顾客的预期之间存在偏差(inconsistent with customers' expectation)时,应该寻找差距存在的原因,并设法予以改进。

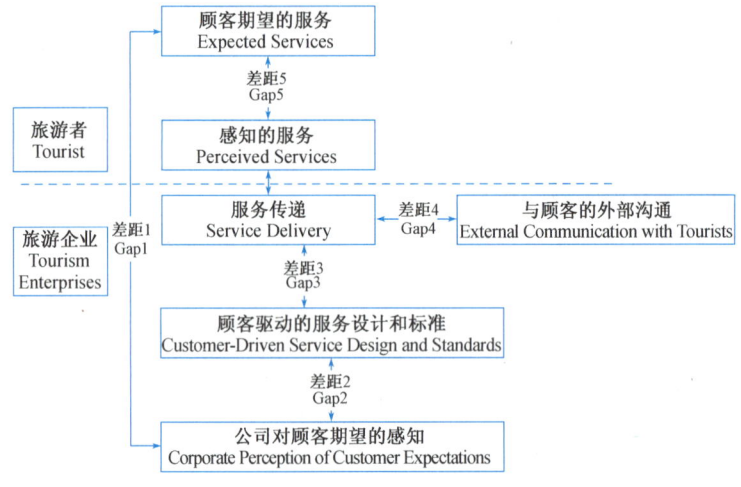

图8-5 基于服务质量差距模型的质量改进
Quality Improvement Based on Service Quality Gap Model

从"服务质量差距模型"可知,差距5的存在是旅游者对旅行社的服务表示不满(dissatisfied with the service)的原因,而差距5的形成是前面4个差距的结果,只有针对模型中的5个差距进行分析,才能找到服务差距存在的真正原因(find the real reason for the existence of service gap)。

1 Gap 1

一、差距1

差距1是顾客对服务的预期与管理者对顾客预期的认知

之间的差距,即管理者对顾客的服务预期感觉不准确。

产生的原因有:① 对市场研究和需求分析的信息不准确;② 缺乏向上沟通(lack of upward communication),管理者与顾客之间缺乏交互(lack of interaction);一线员工(front-line employees)与管理者之间沟通不充分(inadequate communication),臃肿的组织层次(bloated organizational hierarchy)阻碍或改变(hinder or change)了在顾客联系中所产生的信息;③ 对关系的关注不够充分:缺乏市场细分(market segmentation),关注交易(concern about transactions)而非关系;④ 服务补救不充分(inadequate service remedy):缺乏倾听顾客抱怨;没有有效应对服务失败的机制(lack of effective mechanism to deal with service failure)。

二、差距 2

2　Gap 2

差距 2 是管理者对顾客预期的认知与根据其制定的服务质量标准之间的差距,即管理者虽然了解了旅游者的预期,但没有建立有效的操作规范(establish effective operational norms)来保证员工提供顾客预期的服务。

原因如下:① 服务设计不良(poor service design);② 没有顾客驱动的服务标准(no customer-driven service standards);③ 有形展示和服务场景不当(inappropriate physical presentation and service scenarios)。

三、差距 3

3　Gap 3

差距 3 是服务质量标准与实际服务表现(actual service performance)之间的差距,即旅行社的员工提供的服务不符合质量标准的规定(meet the requirements of the quality standards)。

这一差距指在服务生产和交易过程中(in the process of service production and transaction)员工的行为不符合质量标准,由以下几点原因造成。① 人力资源政策的缺乏:无效招聘(ineffective recruitment)、角色模糊(ambiguous roles)、员工技术工作不匹配(mismatches between employees' technical work)、内部营销不充分(inadequate internal marketing);② 顾客没有履行其角色(fail to fulfill their roles):顾客忽略了自身的角色和责任(customers neglect their roles and respon-

sibilities)、顾客相互间的负面影响;③ 服务中介的问题(intermediate problems);④ 供给与需求不匹配(supply and demand do not match):没有平衡需求的高峰和低谷、不恰当的顾客组合(inappropriate customer mix)。

4 Gap 4

Gap 4 is the gap between the actual service and the promised service.

四、差距 4

差距 4 是实际服务表现与旅行社对外沟通之间的差距,即旅行社提供的服务与对外的承诺(external commitments)不一致。

这一差距指营销沟通行为所做出的承诺与实际提供的服务不一致。产生的原因是:① 营销沟通计划与服务生产没统一(no unification between marketing communication plan and service production);② 对顾客期望的无效管理(ineffective management of customers' expectations);③ 过度承诺(excessive commitment);④ 组织内部水平沟通不充分(inadequate communication):销售和运营之间、各分支机构之间。

此外,"标准跟进"(standard follow-up)或"标杆瞄准"(benchmarking)也是服务企业提高服务质量的一种方法。采用这种方法的旅行社将自己的产品、服务和市场营销过程同市场上的竞争对手,尤其是水平最高的竞争对手的标准进行对比,在比较和检验中逐步提高自身的水平(gradually improve service quality in comparison)。

实训项目 08　旅行社服务质量方案

Project 8　Design a Service Quality Scheme for Travel Agencies

一、实训目标(Training Objectives)：

1. 通过实训加深对旅行社服务质量相关理论知识的理解。

2. 提高对服务质量的关注程度；掌握服务质量的评价维度；学会制作服务质量调查问卷；掌握改进旅行社服务质量的方法。

3. 培养以人为本的服务意识、严谨求实的工作作风、科学管理的思维方式。

二、实训学时(Training Period)：2～8学时

三、实训地点(Training Place)：旅行社情景实训室

四、实训设备(Training Equipment)：联网计算机、移动硬盘或U盘、A4绘图纸、铅笔、橡皮。

五、项目描述(Project Description)：

利用服务质量差距模型，制作调查问卷，收集调查结果并进行计算分析，掌握服务质量改进的方法。并制作成PPT汇报成果。

六、实训任务及要求(Tasks and Requirements)：

实训任务一览表

序号	实训任务名称	实训内容	实训学时	实训地点
01	旅行社服务质量的评估	采用SERVQUAL方法来评估服务质量。这种方法主要应用问卷调查工具。测量旅游者对旅行社服务质量的预期水平，以及测量旅游者对旅行社服务质量的实际感知水平。	2	旅行社情景实训室
02	旅行社服务质量的改进	发现企业的服务水平与顾客的预期之间存在偏差时，应该寻找差距存在的原因，并设法予以改进。	2	

注：教师可根据需要选用实训项目和学时。

根据班级人数，每组可适当编制2～6人规模。通过组内讨论，进行相关旅行社服务质量评估与改进工作，进行组内分工，制作并完成旅行社服务质量方案，并在课堂上展示。

七、实训成果(Practical Results)：

1. 每组完成旅行社服务质量方案WORD电子文档1份

和展示 PPT 电子档 1 份。

2. 将上述两个文件放入文件夹,命名为:"班级名称+小组编号+旅行社服务质量方案实训作业"。

八、考核标准(Assessment Criterion):

项目	考核内容和要求	分值	得分
表现	按时完成任务,工作积极主动,具有合作精神	20	
内容	内容全面、真实、精确	40	
格式	格式规范、语言简洁、样式美观	20	
创新	有创意,有市场潜力	20	
小计		**100**	

第九章 旅行社财务管理
Chapter Nine Financial Management in Travel Agencies

【学习目标】 Learning Objectives

1. 了解旅行社资产(travel agency assets)的构成(composition)及其管理的基本内容(basic content)。

2. 了解旅行社成本费用(costs)的构成及基本核算方法(basic accounting methods)。

3. 理解旅行社营业收入及利润(income and profit)的界定办法及来源构成。

4. 掌握财务分析(financial analysis)的内容和日常三大报表(three major report forms)的对比分析。

合理缩减外资准入负面清单,依法保护外商投资权益,营造市场化、法治化、国际化一流营商环境。

——党的二十大报告摘录

✓本章课程视频讲解
✓线上课堂链接
✓本章训练题库
✓本章拓展资源

✓实训指导书
✓优秀学生作品精选
✓时政新闻

Financial management of tourism enterprises is based on the financial activities and financial relations in the process of production and operation of tourism enterprises.

旅游企业财务管理是基于旅游企业生产经营过程中客观存在的财务活动和财务关系而产生的,它是利用价值形式(by means of value form)对旅游企业生产经营过程进行的管理,是旅游企业组织财务活动、处理财务关系的一项综合性管理工作(comprehensive management work)。旅游企业财务活动是指资金的筹集、投放、使用、收回及分配(such as raising, putting in, using, recovering and distributing funds)等一系列行为。旅游企业财务关系(financial relationship)就是旅游企业组织财务活动过程中与有关各方所发生的经济利益关系(economic interest relationship)。

旅行社财务管理就是利用货币形式(in the form of currency)对旅行社资金运动(fund movement)和业务收支(business income and expenditure)进行综合管理,通过预测、计划、核算、分析、监督与控制(through forecasting, planning, accounting, analysis, supervision and control),使旅行社依法改善经营管理,加强经济核算,提高旅行社的经济效益。旅行社财务管理的对象是资金的循环和周转(circulation and turnover),主要内容是通过对资金、成本、收入管理及财务分析(by means of capital, cost, income management and financial analysis),处理各种经济关系,推动企业有效决策(decision-making)、计划和控制,实现利润的最大化(maximize profits)。

第一节 旅行社资产管理
Section One Asset Management in Travel Agencies

1 Travel Agency Assets and Their Composition

一、旅行社资产及其构成

资产管理是旅行社财务管理的一项重要内容。资产是旅行社所拥有的全部资本的具体化(concretization of all capital)。旅行社凭借其所拥有的资产经营各种旅游产品,并获得预期的经济收益(achieve the expected economic benefits)。虽然旅行社的资产构成与饭店、车船公司等其他旅游企业基本相同,主要包括流动资产(current assets)、固定资产(fixed assets)、无形资产(intangible assets)和其他资产,但是各种资产所占的比例(the proportion of various assets)却与其他旅游企业相去甚远,具有一定特殊性(certain particularity)。因此,旅行社的资产管理方式也有别于其他旅游企业。目前,我国多数旅行社资产管理的重点是流动资产管理(current assets management)和固定资产管理(fixed assets management)。

二、旅行社流动资产的管理

流动资产,是指旅行社可以在一个营业周期(within a business cycle)(通常为年)内将其转变成为现金(convert into cash)或者耗用的资产。流动资产是旅行社进行业务经营活动所必备的重要条件(essential conditions),其数额大小及其构成情况在一定程度上制约着旅行社的财务状况,反映着旅行社的支付能力和短期偿债能力(reflect the payment ability and short-term debt-paying ability)。旅行社流动资产主要包括四部分:货币资产、生息资产、债权资产和存货资产。

2　Management of Travel Agency's Current Assets

Travel agency's current assets mainly include four parts: currency assets, interest-bearing assets, creditor's assets and inventory assets.

(一) 货币资产

旅行社的货币资产,主要包括现金和银行存款(cash and deposits)。它是旅行社所有资产中最具有流动性(most liquid assets)的一种资产。现金经常用于向旅游供应部门(tourism supply departments)和企业采购各种旅游服务、支付旅行社各类劳务费用(labor costs)及其他各种费用,偿还到期的债务等。银行存款主要用于旅行社的各种经济往来与结算(economic transactions and settlement)、发放工资和补充旅行社的库存现金等。

2.1　Currency Assets

(二) 生息资产

生息资产亦称短期有价证券或者金融资产,主要包括期限在一年以下(含一年)的国库券、商业票据、银行承兑汇票和可转让定期存单等。生息资产一般具有三个特点:第一,能够在短期内变成现金(can be converted into cash in the short term);第二,能够产生较多的利息(can generate more interest);第三,市场风险小(have less market risk)。由于具有以上各种优点,生息资产又常被看成"准现金"(quasi-cash)。

为了减少因旅行社保存超出日常开支所需要的货币资金而蒙受利润损失,旅行社应把暂时闲置的货币资金投资于生息资产。但生息资产也会因为货币市场上供求关系的变化而出

2.2　Interest-bearing Assets

现价格波动,在个别情况下某些票据也存在违约风险。

（三）债权资产

2.3 Creditor's Assets

旅行社的债权资产主要指应收账款。应收账款在旅行社的流动资产中占有较大的比例（account for a large proportion）。加强债权资产的管理对于旅行社具有重要意义。旅行社对债权资产的管理主要采取以下措施：首先,制定和执行正确的信用政策（credit policies）,旅行社的债权资产状况取决于旅行社制定的信用政策及其执行情况；其次做好应收账款的催收工作；最后是建立坏账准备金。

（四）存货资产

2.4 Inventory Assets

存货是企业的储备物资（reserve materials）；占流动资产的比重很少（account for a small proportion of current assets）,主要是一些低值易耗品（low-value consumables）（如办公耗材、纯净水票等）；计入成本费用中；通过各期的营业收入回笼。对存货资产（inventory assets）的管理主要体现于：第一,改进和完善物资的采购环节（procurement link）,尽量在保证物资质量的前提下,降低存货购进成本；第二,加强存货的实物管理,建立存货管理责任制度,实行定额控制,避免损失,减少浪费；第三,对存货要定期清查,对盘盈、盘亏要及时查明原因,区别不同情况（distinguish different situations）,妥善处理（handle them properly）。

Establish the responsibility system of inventory management, implement quota control, avoid loss and reduce waste.

三、旅行社固定资产的管理

3 Management of Fixed Assets in Travel Agencies

固定资产,是指使用年限在一年以上的（with a service life of more than one year）房屋、建筑物、机器（machines）、机械、运输工具和其他与生产经营有关的设备、器具、工具（equipment, instruments and tools related to production and operation）等。不属于生产经营主要设备但单位价值在2 000元以上（with unit value of more than 2000 RMB）,并且使用年限超过两年的物品（service life of more than two years）,也应当作为固定资产。旅行社对固定资产的管理,主要应从以下几个方面入手。

(一) 固定资产折旧的计提

1. 固定资产计提折旧的范围

计提折旧的固定资产(depreciated fixed assets),包括房屋和建筑物;在用的机器设备(machinery and equipment)、运输车辆(vehicles);季节性停用、修理停用的设备;融资租入的设备;以经营租赁方式租出的固定资产。

不准计提折旧的固定资产(fixed assets excluding depreciation),包括房屋、建筑物以外的未使用、不需用的机器设备(unused and unnecessary machinery and equipment);以经营租赁方式租入的固定资产(fixed assets rented by operating lease);已提足折旧仍继续使用的固定资产(have been fully depreciated but still continue to be used)和未提足折旧提前报废的固定资产;国家规定不计提折旧的其他固定资产(如土地等)(such as land)。

2. 固定资产计提折旧的方法

旅行社计提折旧的方法一般分为两种:平均年限法(直线法)(the average time method or straight line method)和工作量法(the workload method)。

(1) 平均年限法

平均年限法又称为直线法,是我国目前最常用的计提折旧方法(the most commonly used depreciation method in China)。旅行社采用平均年限法计提固定资产的折旧(calculate the depreciation of fixed assets)时,先以固定资产的原始成本扣除净残值(first deduct the net residual value from the original cost of fixed assets),然后按照固定资产的预计使用年限进行平均分摊(make an average apportionment according to the expected useful life),计算每年或每月的折旧额和折旧率。平均年限法的计算公式为:

$$年折旧率 = \frac{1-预计净残值率}{固定资产预计使用年限} \times 100\%$$

$$月折旧率 = \frac{年折旧率}{12}$$

$$月折旧额 = 固定资产原值 \times 月折旧率$$

固定资产净残值率(net salvage value ratio of fixed assets),一般按照固定资产原值的(the original value)3%~5%确定。对不同的固定资产,旅行社应按其类别规定具体的折旧年限(specify depreciation periods)。我国对于不同类别

3.1 Depreciation of Fixed Assets

3.1.1 Scope of depreciation of fixed assets

3.1.2 Method of depreciation of fixed assets

固定资产折旧年限的规定(regulations on the depreciation years of different types of fixed assets)为:营业用房 20~40 年,非营业用房(non-business premises)35~45 年,简易房 5~10 年,建筑物 10~25 年;大型客车(33 座以上)30 万公里或 5~10 年,中型客车(32 座以下)30 万公里或 7~8 年,小轿车 20 万公里或 5~7 年,行李车 30 万公里或 7~8 年,货车(trucks)50 万公里或 12 年,摩托车 15 万公里或 5 年。

(2) 工作量法

工作量法是一种以固定资产的具体使用时间或使用量(use time or usage amount)为自变量(independent variable),且与年限无绝对直接依存关系(have no absolute direct dependency relationship with the number of years)的折旧方法。这种折旧计提方法适用于不同经营期间(in different periods of operation)使用程度不均衡、发生磨损程度也相差较大,以具体使用时间或使用量为自变量的一些固定资产,如旅游汽车。工作量法的计算公式(calculation formula)为:

$$单位工作量折旧额 = \frac{原值 \times (1 - 预计净残值率)}{预计使用年限内可以完成的工作量}$$

(二) 固定资产的处理

1. 修理费用的提取

旅行社发生的固定资产修理费用(repair expenses incurred),计入当期成本费用。对数额较大、发生不均衡的修理费用,可以分期摊入(be amortized by stages)成本费用,也可以根据修理计划分期从成本中预提。

2. 固定资产盘亏、盘盈及报废的处理

对盘亏及毁损的固定资产,应按原价扣除累计折旧、过失人及保险公司赔款后的差额计入营业外支出(out-of-business expenses)。对盘盈的固定资产应按其原价减去估计折旧后的差额(original price minus the estimated difference after depreciation)计入营业外收入。对出售或清理报废固定资产变价净收入(变价收入、残料价值减去清理费用后的净额)与固定资产净值(原价减累计折旧)(the original price minus the accumulated depreciation)的差额,计入营业外收入(non-operating income)或营业外支出(out-of-business expenditure)。

3.2 Management of Fixed Assets

3.2.1 Extraction of repair expenses

3.2.2 Management of loss, earnings and abandonment of fixed assets

第二节 成本费用管理
Section Two Management of Costs and Expenses

成本是制定价格的经济依据。商品出售价格的最低界限(floor price),是由商品的成本价格(cost)决定的,旅行社成本费用是补偿生产经营耗费的尺度,是企业维持简单再生产(simple reproduction)的起码条件和进行扩大再生产(expanding reproduction)的出发点。成本费用是一项综合指标(comprehensive index),其管理效率也是衡量企业管理水平的重要标志(important symbol)。通过同类企业成本费用指标(cost and expense indicator)的对比与分析,可以揭露企业业务经营中的问题,从而积极推动企业充分挖掘内部潜力(internal potential),努力(strive to)提高经营管理水平。

一、旅行社成本费用概述

旅行社成本费用指旅行社在一定时期内的经营活动过程中发生的以货币表现的各种耗费,包括旅游服务(吃、住、行、游、保险)采购成本和期间费用(营业费用、管理费用、财务费用)(operating expenses, management expenses, financial expenses),其比例往往占旅行社全部销售收入的80%~90%。

(一) 营业成本

旅行社的营业成本,又称变动成本(variable costs),是指在经营过程中发生的(incurred in the course of operation)各项直接支出(direct expenditures),包括房费、餐费、交通费、文娱费、行李托运费(baggage consignment charges)、票务费、门票费、专业活动费、签证费、陪同费、劳务费(labor charges)、宣传费、保险费、机场建设费(airport construction charges)等代收、代付费用。

(二) 营业费用

营业费用,是指旅行社各营业部门在经营中发生的各项费

---

1 An Overview of Travel Agency Costs and Expenses

It refers to all kinds of expenditures that occur in the course of business activities of travel agencies in a certain period of time.

1.1 Operating Costs

1.2 Operating Expenses

用,可称为半变动成本(semi-variable costs),包括运输费、装卸费、包装费、保管费、保险费、燃料费、水电费、展览费、广告宣传费、邮电费(posts and telecommunications)、差旅费、洗涤费、清洁卫生费、低值易耗品摊销(amortization of low-value consumables)、物料消耗(material consumption)、经营人员的工资(含奖金、津贴和补贴)、职工福利费(employee welfare)、服装费及其他营业费用。

1.3 Management Expenses

(三) 管理费用

管理费用,是指旅行社组织和管理经营活动所发生的费用,以及由旅行社统一负担的费用(expenses uniformly paid by travel agencies),包括公司经费、工会经费、职工教育经费、劳动保险费(labor insurance premium)、待业保险费(unemployment insurance premium)、劳动保护费(labor protection fee)、董事会费、外事费、租赁费、咨询费、审计费、诉讼费、排污费(sewage discharge fee)、绿化费、土地使用费(land use fee)、土地损失补偿费(land loss compensation fee)、技术转让费(technology transfer fee)、研究开发费、税金、燃料费、水电费、折旧费(depreciation fee)、修理费、无形资产摊销(amortization of tangible assets)、低值易耗品摊销、开办费摊销、交际应酬费、坏账损失、存货盘亏和毁损、上级管理费及其他管理费用。

1.4 Financial Expenses

(四) 财务费用

财务费用,是指旅行社筹集资金而发生的费用。财务费用是指旅行社为筹集资金(raise funds)而发生的费用,包括旅行社在经营期间发生的利息净支出(net interest expenditure)、汇兑净损失(net exchange loss)、金融机构手续费(handling fees of financial institutions)及筹资发生的其他费用。旅行社发生的下列支出,不得计入成本和费用:

(1) 为购置和建造固定资产、购入无形资产和其他资产发生的支出(Expenditures paid for the purchase and construction of fixed assets, intangible assets and other assets);

(2) 对外投资支出和分配给投资者的利润(Expenditure on foreign investment and profits allocated to investors);

(3) 被没收财物的损失(Loss of confiscated property);

(4) 支付的各项赔偿金、违约金、滞纳金、罚款以及赞助、捐赠支出等(Payment of various damages, liquidated damages, late fees, fines, as well as sponsorship, loss and donation expenses);

(5) 国家规定不得列入成本、费用的其他开支(Other expenditures of costs and expenses that shall not be included according to state regulations)。

二、旅行社的成本费用核算

2 Cost Accounting in Travel Agencies

旅行社成本费用核算可以根据旅行社的经营规模和范围分别实行单团核算和部门批量核算。相对应地(correspondingly),对成本的分析也可以按核算的要求实行单团成本分析(single group cost analysis)和部门批量成本分析(department batch cost analysis)。

(一) 单团核算与成本分析

2.1 Single Group Accounting and Cost Analysis

单团核算,是指旅行社以接待的每一个旅游团(者)为核算对象进行经营盈亏的核算。单团核算有利于(conducive to)考核每个团队的经济效益,有利于各项费用的清算和考核,有利于降低成本(reduce costs)。为了达到控制成本,提高旅行社经济效益的目的,应采取以下几个步骤。

Single group accounting refers to the accounting of operating profits and loss for each tour group.

(1) 在综合分析市场状况和旅行社自身经营状况(operating conditions)的基础上编制成本计划,制定出一套分等级的计划成本(a set of hierarchical planning costs),并以此作为衡量(measure)旅行社经济效益的标准。

(2) 将单团的实际成本与计划成本进行对比,找出(find out)差异。对于差异较大的旅游团要逐项进行分析(analyze item by item),找出导致成本上升或下降(increase or decrease of costs)的原因并加以改进。

(3) 加强信息反馈(strengthen information feedback),把在成本分析中发现的差异及其原因及时送到有关领导和部门,以便加强对成本的控制(cost control)。

(二) 部门批量核算与成本分析

2.2 Department Batch Accounting and Cost Analysis

部门批量核算,是指旅行社的业务部门在规定期限内,以接待的旅游团(者)的批量(the batch of tourist groups)为核算对象进行的核算。这种核算方法适用于业务量较大的旅行社(with large business volume)。

接待业务量较大的旅行社应实行部门批量成本分析(carry out cost analysis and accounting)和核算,将不同部门接待的旅游团,作为成本核算的对象进行成本的归集和分配

（collect and distribute），核算出各个部门接待一定批量旅游者的成本水平和经济效益。旅行社在进行成本分析和核算时应采取以下几个步骤：

（1）编制各部门接待一定批量旅游者的计划成本及计划成本降低额（率）（planned cost reduction），核算出实际成本及实际降低额。

（2）按照部门接待旅游者的数量变动、产品结构变动、成本变动三方面进行因素替代分析（substitution analysis），找出各因素的影响程度（find out the influence degree of each factor）。

（3）将信息反馈给有关部门（feedback to relevant departments），采取措施（take measures），扭转不利因素的影响（reverse the impact of adverse factors）。

3 Cost Control in Travel Agencies

三、旅行社成本费用的控制

（一）制定成本费用标准

3.1 Establishing Cost and Cost Standards

旅行社制定成本费用标准的方法主要有分解法（decomposition method）、定额法（quota method）和预算法（budget method）。

3.1.1 Decomposition method

1. 分解法

分解法，是指将目标成本费用和成本费用降低目标，按成本费用项目进行分解，明确（clarify）各成本费用项目应达到的目标和降低的幅度。在此基础上，把各成本费用项目指标按部门进行归口分解（cost project indicators are decomposed according to departments）。然后，各部门再把成本费用指标落实到各个岗位或个人（implement the cost indicators to each post or individual），再由各个岗位或个人分别制定各项成本费用支出的目标和措施（each post or individual will formulate the objectives and measures of each cost expenditure separately），对分解指标进行修订（revise the decomposition indicators）。各项修订后的指标要以实现目标成本费用为标准，进行综合平衡，经过综合平衡（be balanced comprehensively）以后，即可形成各项成本费用开支的标准。

3.1.2 Quota method

2. 定额法

定额法，是指旅行社首先确定各种经营成本或费用（various operating costs or expenses）的合理定额（reasonable quotas),并以此为依据制定成本费用标准。凡是能够直接确定定额的成本或费用,都应制定标准成本或费用(standard costs or fees)。不能直接确定定额的成本费用,也要比照本行业平均水平确定成本费用开支标准限额,用以控制盲目的成本费用开支(control the blind cost and expenditure)。

3. 预算法

预算法,是指旅行社在把经营费用划分为同销售收入成比例增加(increase proportionally with sales revenue)的变动费用(variable expenses)、不成比例增加的半固定成本(semi-fixed costs)费用或半变动成本(semi-variable costs)费用,以及与销售收入增减无关(have nothing to do with the increase or decrease of sales revenue)的固定费用(fixed expenses)的基础上,按照各部门的业务量分别制定预算,并以此作为费用控制的标准。各部门的业务量不同,其费用预算也不一样。旅行社可据此对业务量不同的各个部门制定弹性费用预算。

(二) 日常控制

旅行社成本费用的日常控制,主要包括建立成本控制信息系统(establish cost control information system)、实行责任成本制(implement responsibility cost system)和进行重点控制(carry out key control)三项措施,并通过这些措施对旅行社经营管理的成本费用实行全过程、全面(comprehensively)和全员的(wholly)控制。

3.1.3　Budget method

3.2　Daily Control

Departments have different business volumes and cost budgets. Travel agencies can then make flexible cost budgets for different departments with different business volumes.

第三节　营业收入与利润的管理
Section Three　Revenue and Profits Management

在市场经济条件下,每一个企业都是独立核算、自负盈亏的基本经济单位(basic economic unit),都要求以自己的营业收入来抵偿生产或业务经营中的耗费(compensate for the expenditure in production or business operation)。因此,企业只有取得营业收入,才能收回耗费的资金(recover the expended funds),为新的经营过程创造条件(create conditions for new business process)。另外,企业的营业收入减去营业成本后的余额近似(similar to)企业的毛利(gross profit)。只有增加营业收入,才能履行上交国家税收的义务(fulfill the tax obligation),同时,保障投资者分红逐年增加,才能提高职工的工资待遇。

一、旅行社营业收入的构成

1 Composition of Travel Agency Revenue

指旅行社在一定时期内,包括向旅游者提供服务而获得的全部收入,还包括营业外收入(non-operating income)。旅行社的营业收入主要由以下几个部分构成。

(一) 综合服务费收入

1.1 Revenue from Travel Services

指为旅游团(者)提供综合服务所收取的收入,包括导游费、餐饮费、市内交通费、全程陪同费、组团费和接团手续费。

(二) 房费收入

1.2 Revenue from Accommodation

指旅行社为旅游者代订饭店的住房后,按照旅游者实际住房等级和过夜天数(overnight days)收取的住宿费用(accommodation fee)。

(三) 城市间交通费收入

1.3 Revenue from Traffic

指旅游者为旅游期间在旅游客源地与旅游目的地(tourist origin and destination)之间,及在旅游目的地的各城市或地区之间乘坐各种交通工具(various means of transportation)所付出的费用而形成的收入。

(四) 专项附加费收入

1.4 Revenue from Special Services

主要指旅行社向旅游者收取(collect)的汽车超公里费(extra-mile charge)、风味餐费、游江(湖)费、特殊游览门票费、文娱费、专业活动费、保险费、不可预见费(unforeseen fee)等项收入。

(五) 单项服务收入

1.5 Revenue from Individual Services

主要指旅行社接待零散旅游者和代办委托(entrusted)事项所取得的服务收入、代理代售国际联运客票(international intermodal passenger tickets)、国内客票的手续费收入,以及代办签证收费等收入。

（六）营业外收入

主要指利息、债券、股票净收益等（mainly refers to interest, bonds, stock net income and so on）。

1.6 Revenue of Out-of-Business

二、旅行社营业收入的管理

旅行社营业收入实现的确认原则与时间界定主要遵循下列原则。

2 Management of Travel Agency Revenue

（一）确认营业收入的原则

按照国家的有关规定（relevant provisions），旅行社在确认营业收入（confirm business income）时应实行权责发生制。根据权责发生制，旅行社在符合以下两种条件（meet the following two conditions）时，可确认其获得了营业收入：一是旅行社已经向旅游者提供了合同上所规定的服务；二是旅行社已经从旅游者或者组团旅行社处收到价款或取得了收取价款权利的证据。

2.1 The Principle of Revenue Recognition

（二）界定营业收入实现时间的原则

由于旅行社经营的旅游产品不同，其营业收入实现的时间也各异。根据有关规定（relevant provisions），对旅行社营业收入实现时间的界定原则有如下几种。

2.2 The Principle of Defining the Realization Time of Business Revenue

1. 入境旅游

旅行社组织境外旅游者到境内旅游，以旅游者离境或离开本地时作为确认其营业收入实现的时间（take the time when the tourists leave or leave the country as the time to confirm the realization of their business income）。

2.2.1 Inbound tourism

2. 国内旅游

旅行社组织国内旅游者在国内旅游，接团旅行社应以旅游者离开本地时、组团旅行社应以旅游者旅行结束返回原出发地时作为确认其营业收入实现的时间（take the time when tourists leave the destination or they return to their original place as the time to confirm the realization of their business income）。

2.2.2 Domestic tourism

3. 出境旅游

旅行社组织中国公民到境外旅游（travel abroad），以旅游者旅行结束返回原出发地时作为确认其营业收入实现的时间

2.2.3 Outbound tourism

(take the time when tourists return to their original place after their travel as the time to confirm the realization of their business income)。

但是旅行社出售的是无形产品(intangible products),一般又采用远期销售方式,因此不可能是"一手交货,一手交钱"(one-hand delivery, one-hand payment)的现款交易(cash transaction),而只能采取预付或后付款两种方式(two ways of prepayment or post-payment)。旅行社的销售原则上应采取预付款办法以保证自己的合法收入(legitimate income)。

三、旅行社利润管理

3 Management of Travel Agency's Profits

(一) 旅行社利润的概念及构成

3.1 Definition and Components of Travel Agency's Profits

The profit is the balance of business income after deducting costs, business taxes and other expenditures in a certain period.

旅行社利润是其经营活动的财务结果(financial result),是一定时期内营业收入扣除成本、营业税及其他支出后的余额。旅行社的利润由营业利润(operating profit)、投资净收益(net investment income)和营业外收支净额构成(net out-of-business income and expenditure)。它是旅行社在一定时期内经营活动的最终财务成果(ultimate financial result),是旅行社经营活动的效率和效益的最终体现。旅行社的利润分为利润总额和营业利润。

利润总额＝营业利润＋投资净收益＋营业外收支净额

旅行社营业利润＝营业收入－营业成本－营业费用－营业税金－管理费用－财务费用。

旅行社的投资净收益＝投资收益－投资损失

旅行社营业外收支净额＝营业外收入－营业外支出

3.1.1 Operating profits

1. 营业利润

旅行社营业利润,是指营业收入扣除营业成本、营业费用、营业税金、管理费用和财务费用(deduct operating costs, operating expenses, operating taxes, management expenses and financial expenses)后的净额。

3.1.2 Net return on investment

2. 投资净收益

旅行社投资净收益,是指投资收益扣除投资损失后的数额。投资收益包括对外投资分得的利润、取得的股利(dividends)、债券利息(bond interest)、投资到期收回或中途转让取得的款项高于投出资产账面净值的差额。投资损失是投资不当(improper investment)而产生的投资亏损额或指投资到期

(at maturity)收回或中途转让取得的款项低于投出资产的账面净值的差额。

3. 营业外收支净额

旅行社营业外收支净额,是指营业外收入减营业外支出后的差额(difference)。营业外收入包括固定资产盘盈(net income from the inventory)和变卖的净收益、罚款(fines)净收入、确实无法支付而按规定程序批准后转做营业外收入的应付账款(accounts payable)、礼品折价(gift discounts)和其他收入等。营业外支出包括固定资产盘亏和毁损、报废的净损失、非常损失、技工学校经费、赔偿费、违约金、罚息和公益性捐赠(public welfare donation)等。

3.1.3 Net out-of-business income and expenditure

(二)旅行社的利润分析

利润分析是指旅行社根据期初的利润计划,对本期内所实现的利润进行的评价,主要包括利润总额分析、利润总额构成因素分析和营业利润分析三个方面的内容。

3.2 Profit Analysis of Travel Agencies

Profit analysis mainly includes three aspects: total profit analysis, total profit component analysis and operating profit analysis.

1. 利润总额分析

利润总额分析,是旅行社运用比较分析法(comparative analysis method)将本期(current period)的利润总额同上期(previous period)的利润总额或本期的计划利润指标进行对比,分析其增、减变动的情况。计算本期利润比上期的利润增长(减少)的情况(calculate the increase or decrease of profits),可以使用下面的公式:

3.2.1 Total profit analysis

$$本期利润上期增长(减少)额 = 本期利润总额 - 上期利润总额$$

$$利润增长(减少)率 = \frac{利润增长(减少)额}{上一期利润总额} \times 100\%$$

计算本期计划利润完成情况可以使用下面的公式:

$$完成计划百分比 = \frac{本期实际利润总额}{本期计划利润总额} \times 100\%$$

$$超额或未完成计划百分比 = 完成计划百分比 - 100\%$$

2. 利润总额构成因素分析

旅行社在分析其利润总额增长情况后,还应对利润的构成因素进行分析,以便发现导致本期利润变化的主要因素,并采取相应的措施(take corresponding measures)。如果发现某项因素的增长比例(growth ratio)或绝对额(absolute amount)与上一期相差较大(quite different from),则应对其发生的原因进行深入的分析(analyze seriously)。

3.2.2 Analysis of components of total profits

3.2.3 Analysis of operating profits

3. 营业利润分析

营业利润分析,是指旅行社通过将利润计划指标与实际结果对比,运用因素分析法(factor analysis method),找出影响营业利润实现的因素,以便采取措施、加强管理,为进一步增加营业利润指明方向(point out the direction)。

在营业收入一定的情况下,影响营业利润高低的因素是营业成本(business costs)、营业费用(business expenses)、营业税金(business tax)、管理费用(management expenses)和财务费用(financial expenses)。

3.3 Profit Management of Travel Agencies

(三)旅行社利润的管理

利润管理主要内容是确定目标利润和进行利润分配(the main content of profit management is to determine target profits and to distribute profits)。

3.3.1 Determining target profit

1. 确定目标利润

旅行社确定了目标利润后,还应在营业期结束时(at the end of the business period)将实际完成的利润同目标利润进行对比,以加强对利润的管理(strengthen the management of the profits)。旅行社计算目标利润的公式为:

$$目标利润=预计营业收入-目标营业成本-预计营业税金-预计费用$$

旅行社在确定了目标利润(target profit)之后,可以运用各种方法来测算出为实现目标利润所应完成的销售量及所产生的各种成本和费用(various costs and expenses)。其中量本利法(Cost-Volume-Profit Analysis,CVP)是进行这种测算(calculation)的一种有效的方法。

3.3.2 Profit distribution

2. 利润分配

目前,我国旅行社大致可以分为股份制(joint-stock)旅行社和非股份制(non-joint-stock)旅行社两类,其利润分配办法(profit distribution methods)各不相同。根据国家有关规定,股份制旅行社在依法向国家缴纳所得税(income tax)后,应首先提取(withdraw)公益金(public welfare funds),然后按照以下顺序分配所剩余的利润(distribute the remaining profits):

(1)支付优先股(preferred stock)股利(dividends);

(2)按公司章程(articles of association)或股东会议决议提取盈余公积金;

(3)支付普通股(common stock)股利。

非股份制旅行社应在依法向国家缴纳所得税后,按照下列程序分配税后利润(distribute after-tax profits):

(1) 支付被没收的(confiscated)财务损失(financial losses)和各项税收的滞纳金、罚款(fines)。

(2) 弥补旅行社过去年度的亏损(make up for the losses)。根据国家有关规定,旅行社发生亏损,可用下一年度的利润弥补(be compensated by the profits of the next year),延续5年未弥补的亏损,可用所得税后的利润(profits after income tax)弥补。

(3) 提取法定盈余公积金。

(4) 提取公益金(extract public welfare funds)。

(5) 向投资者分配利润(distribute profits to investors)。旅行社过去年度未分配的利润(undistributed profits),可以并入本年度(the current year)利润一并分配(distributed together)。

根据国家有关规定,旅行社提取的法定盈余公积金应为税后利润的10%;法定盈余公积金已达旅行社注册资金的50%后,可不再提取。旅行社提取的盈余公积金用于弥补亏损或按规定转增资本金(make up for losses or to increase capital as required)。旅行社提取的公益金主要用于职工集体福利设施(welfare facilities)支出。

The statutory surplus reserve fund drawn by travel agencies should be 10% of after-tax profits.

第四节 旅行社的财务分析
Section Four Financial Analysis of Travel Agencies

1　Financial Statements of Travel Agencies

The financial statements mainly includes balance sheets, income and loss statements, cash flow statements and related schedules.

1.1　Balance Sheet

Balance sheet is based on the basic accounting equation of "assets＝liabilities＋owner's equity".

1.2　Travel Agency Profit and Loss Statements

profit（loss）＝revenue－cost（cost）

一、旅行社的财务报表

旅行社的财务报表是反映旅行社财务状况和经营成果（reflect the financial status and operating results）的书面文件（written documents），主要包括资产负债表、损益表和现金流量表及有关附表。

（一）资产负债表

资产负债表，是反映旅行社在某一特定日期财务状况的报表。它以"资产＝负债＋所有者权益"这一会计基本等式为依据，按照一定的分类标准（certain classification criteria）和次序反映旅行社在某一个时间点上资产、负债和所有者权益的基本状况（basic status）。资产负债表包括三大类项目：资产、负债和所有者权益（assets, liabilities and owner's equity）。

报表左方：资产类、流动资产、长期投资、固定资产、无形及递延资产（intangible and deferred assets）、其他长期投资。

报表右方：负债类（liability category）（流动负债＋长期负债＋递延税项）、所有者权益类（owner's equity category）。

资产负债表揭示了旅行社资产结构、流动性、资金来源、负债水平（level of liabilities）、负债结构（structure of liabilities）等方面的状况，反映了旅行社的变现能力、偿债能力和资产管理水平，为旅行社的投资者和管理者提供了重要的决策依据（important decision-making basis）。

（二）旅行社损益表

损益表又称收益表，是反映旅行社在一定期间的经营成果及其分配情况（operating results and their distribution）的报表。其基本等式（equation）为：利润（亏损）＝收入－费用（成本）。损益表分为五个主要部分：营业收入、经营利润、营业利润、利润总额和净利润（total profit and net profit）。

（1）收入按其重要性进行列示(list according to its importance)，主要包括主营业业务收入(main business income)、其他业务收入、投资收益、补贴收入(subsidy income)、营业外收入；

（2）费用按其性质进行列示(list according to their nature)，主要包括主营业务成本、主营业务税金及附加(taxes and surcharges)、营业费用、管理费用、财务费用、其他业务支出、营业外支出、所得税(income tax)等；

（3）利润按营业利润、利润总额(gross profits)和净利润(net profits)等利润的构成分类分项列示。

（三）旅行社现金流量表

1.3 Travel Agency Cash Flow Statements

通过对现金流量的分析可大致判断(roughly judge)其经营周转(operation turnover)是否顺畅；向管理者和其他有关单位(部门)提供在一定时期内现金和现金等价物(cash and cash equivalent)流入和流出(in-flow and out-flow)信息；其结构包括：① 经营活动产生的现金流量(cash flow generated by business activities)；② 投资活动产生的现金流量(cash flow generated by investment activities)；③ 筹资活动产生的现金流量(cash flow from financing activities)；④ 汇率变动对资金的影响额(impact of exchange rate changes on funds)；⑤ 现金及现金等价物净增加额(net increase of cash and cash equivalents)。

二、旅行社的财务分析

2 Financial Analysis of Travel Agencies

财务分析以财务报表为主要依据(mainly based on)，采取一定方法进行计量分析(adopt certain methods to conduct quantitative analysis)以反映和评价旅行社的财务状况和经营成果。旅行社常用的财务分析方法有增减分析(increase-decrease analysis)和比率分析(ratio analysis)。财务分析可以帮助旅行社管理者了解旅行社资产流动性(assets liquidity)、负债水平(debt level)、资金周转(capital turnover)情况、偿还债务能力(debt repayment ability)、获利能力(profitability)及未来发展趋势，从而对旅行社财务状况和经营风险(operational risk)做出较合乎实际的评价。

2.1 Analysis of Increase and Decrease

(一) 增减分析

将两个期间的财务报表数字加以对比计算出两个期间的增减变动差额(calculate the difference between the increase and decrease of the two periods)并编制成比较对照表(compile a comparative table),比较旅行社连续两个期间(two consecutive periods)财务报表的历史数据,分析其增减变化的幅度及其变化原因,判断旅行社财务状况发展的趋势。如资产负债表增减分析(the balance sheet increase or decrease analysis)、损益表增减分析(the income statement increase or decrease analysis)。

2.2 Ratio Analysis Method

Ratio analysis reflects the relationship between items by calculating the ratio.

(二) 比率分析法

比率分析,是指在同一财务报表的不同项目之间,或在不同报表的有关项目之间进行对比,以计算出来的比率反映各项目之间的相互关系,据以评价旅行社财务状况和经营成果的一种方法。旅行社分析和评价本企业财务状况和经营成果的主要财务指标(main financial indicators)包括:流动比率、速动比率、应收账款周转率、资产负债率、资本金利润率、营业利润率和成本费用利润率。

2.2.1 Current ratio

It reflects the ability of travel agencies to repay current liabilities in the shortest possible time.

1. 流动比率

流动比率,是反映旅行社短期偿债能力(short-term debt paying ability)的一项指标。它表明旅行社偿还(repay)流动负债的保障程度。其计算公式为:

$$流动比率 = \frac{流动资产}{流动负债} \times 100\%$$

2.2.2 Current ratio

2. 速动比率

速动比率是速动资产(流动资产-存货资产)和流动负债之间的比率,反映旅行社在最短时间内偿还流动负债的能力。速动比率的计算公式为:

$$速动比率 = \frac{速动资产}{流动负债} \times 100\%$$
$$= \frac{流动资产 - 存货资产}{流动负债} \times 100\%$$

2.2.3 Accounts receivable turnover rate

3. 应收账款周转率

应收账款周转率,是旅行社赊销收入净额与应收账款平均额的比率,反映应收账款的周转速度。应收账款周转率的计算公式为：

$$应收账款周转率 = \frac{赊销收入净额}{应收账款平均余额}$$

$$= \frac{营业收入 - 现金销售收入}{(期初应收账款余额 + 期末应收账款余额)/2}$$

4. 成本费用利润率

成本费用利润率反映的是旅行社在营业过程中为取得利润而消耗的成本和费用情况，是利润总额与成本费用总额之间的比率。该比率可以用下列公式表示：

$$成本费用利润率 = \frac{利润总额}{成本费用总额} \times 100\%$$

5. 资产负债率

资产负债率又称举债经营比率，是旅行社负债总额（短期负债＋长期负债）与其资产总额之间的比例关系。资产负债率是反映旅行社偿债能力大小的一个标志，揭示（reveal）出负债在全部资产中所占的比重（the proportion of liabilities in all assets），及资产对负债的保障程度。其计算公式为：

$$旅行社资产负债率 = \frac{负债总额（短期负债＋长期负债）}{资产总额} \times 100\%$$

6. 资本金利润率

资本金利润率是指旅行社利润总额与资本金总额的比率，用以衡量投资者投入旅行社资本金的获利能力。其计算公式为：

$$资本金利润率 = \frac{利润总额}{资本总额} \times 100\%$$

7. 营业利润率

营业利润率是旅行社利润总额与营业收入净额之间的比率。它是衡量旅行社盈利水平的重要指标，表明（indicate）在一定时期内旅行社每100元的营业净收入能够产生多少利润。其计算公式为：

$$营业利润率 = \frac{利润总额}{营业净收入额} \times 100\%$$

$$= \frac{利润总额}{营业收入 - 营业成本} \times 100\%$$

2.2.4 Ratio of profits to cost

Ratio of profits to cost reflects the cost and expenses consumed in order to make profits in the business process.

2.2.5 Asset-liability ratio

Also known as debt operation ratio, reflects the solvency of travel agencies.

2.2.6 Net income to equity ratio

The ratio is used to measure the profitability of investors investing in travel agency capital.

2.2.7 Operating profit margin

The ratio is an important indicator to measure the profitability of travel agencies.

Project 9 Conduct a Financial Performance Analysis for Travel Agencies

实训项目09 旅行社财务报表分析

一、实训目标(Training Objectives):
1. 通过实训加深对旅行社相关财务知识的理解。
2. 加深对理论知识的了解,培养学生的动手分析能力,初步具备阅读公司财务报表,计算相关财务指标,并独立运用所学知识撰写财务分析报告的能力。
3. 培养严谨求实的工作作风。
二、实训学时(Training Period):2~4学时
三、实训地点(Training Place):旅行社情景实训室
四、实训设备(Training Equipment):联网计算机、移动硬盘或U盘、EXCEL报表软件、铅笔、橡皮。
五、项目描述(Project Description):
针对一家特定的旅行社公开数据,通过对EXCEL财务报表分析系统模块的上机操作,熟悉财务报表软件,掌握利用财务软件进行财务报表分析,为报表使用者提供决策有用的信息,实现理论与实践的有机融合。用PPT汇报成果。
六、实训任务及要求(Tasks and Requirements):

实训任务一览表

序号	实训任务名称	实训内容	实训学时	实训地点
01	了解财务软件和EXCEL软件的使用	了解各财务软件的安装及运行环境、EXCEL软件的功能模块和其在财务数据处理方面的广泛运用;熟悉财务软件的安装及运行环境、与财务报表分析相关的功能模块、数据处理基本流程等实务操作	1	旅行社情景实训室
02	了解三大财务报表基础分析系统	对于给定的上市旅游公司案例,能够运用EXCEL独立完成资产负债表、利润表、现金流量表的水平分析和结构分析	1	
03	财务指标分析系统	熟悉系统,能够理解一些财务指标的经济含义	1	
04	杜邦综合分析系统	熟悉杜邦分析系统的日常应用场景和具体案例分析	1	
注:教师可根据需要选用实训项目和学时。				

  根据班级人数,每组可适当编制2~6人规模。通过上机实训,每个小组完成一份简单的财务报表分析报告,字数不少于800字,要求指标计算准确,文字分析部分逻辑清楚。内容应包括企业概况、财务报告基础分析、相关财务指标数据分析和杜邦综合分析等,并在课堂上展示汇报。

  七、实训成果（Practical Results）：

  1. 每组完成旅行社财务分析报告WORD电子文档1份和展示PPT电子档1份。

  2. 将上述两个文件放入文件夹,命名为:"班级名称＋小组编号＋旅行社财务分析报告实训作业"。

  八、考核标准（Assessment Criterion）：

项目	考核内容和要求	分值	得分
表现	按时完成任务,工作积极主动,具有合作精神	20	
内容	内容全面、真实、精确	40	
格式	格式规范、语言简洁、样式美观	20	
创新	有创意,有市场潜力	20	
小计		100	

参考文献

[1] 蔡芳,李淑娟,陈延亭.旅游市场学[M].成都:电子科技大学出版社,2007.
[2] 戴斌,杜江.旅行社管理[M].北京:高等教育出版社,2005.
[3] 杜江.旅行社经营与管理[M].天津:南开大学出版社,2001.
[4] 国家旅游局人教司.旅行社财务部的业务与管理[M].北京:中国旅游出版社,1992.
[5] 郭鲁芳.旅行社经营管理[M].大连:东北财经大学出版社,2002.
[6] 韩勇,丛庆.旅游市场营销学[M].北京:北京大学出版社,2006.
[7] 李宝明.旅行社经营管理[M].北京:经济科学出版社,2004.
[8] 李胜芬,侯志强.旅行社经营与管理:理论、方法与案例[M].北京:中国科学技术出版社,2008.
[9] 李晓标,解程姬.旅行社经营与管理[M].北京:北京理工大学出版社,2015.
[10] 梁智.旅行社运行与管理[M].大连:东北财经大学出版社,2014.
[11] 廖建华.旅行社经营与管理[M].广州:广东高等教育出版社,2013.
[12] 刘晓杰,常永翔.旅行社经营与管理[M].北京:旅游教育出版社,2018.
[13] 朴松爱,吴铭岐.旅行社管理[M].北京:中国旅游出版社,2007.
[14] 帕特·耶尔.旅行社经营业务[M].北京:旅游教育出版社,2004.
[15] 宋子千.旅行社经济分析[M].北京:中国旅游出版社,2008.
[16] 苏英,陈书星.旅行社经营与管理[M].北京:化学工业出版社,2011.
[17] 孙宗虎,肖书民.旅行社管理流程设计与工作标准[M].北京:人民邮电出版社,2008.
[18] 万剑敏.旅行社产品设计[M].北京:旅游教育出版社,2008.
[19] 王坚.旅行社企业管理[M].北京:北京大学出版社,2006.
[20] 王健民.旅行社产品经营智慧[M].北京:旅游教育出版社,2008.
[21] 王缇萦.旅行社经营与管理[M].上海:上海人民出版社,2006.
[22] 王永强.旅行社经营与管理[M].北京:对外经济贸易大学出版社,2008.
[23] 吴江洲.我国旅行社分工体系调整研究[D].桂林:广西大学,2004.
[24] 徐东文.旅行社经营与管理[M].北京:高等教育出版社,2001.
[25] 徐云松.旅行社经营管理[M].杭州:浙江大学出版社,2005.
[26] 余志勇.旅行社经营管理[M].北京:北京大学出版社,2015.
[27] 杨富斌.旅行社法律责任制度研究[M].北京:中国法制出版社,2014.
[28] 姚延波.旅行社管理[M].北京:高等教育出版社,2012.
[29] 中华人民共和国国家旅游局.旅行社安全管理实务[M].北京:中国旅游出版社,2012.
[30] 朱智等.旅行社经营与管理[M].北京:清华大学出版社,2018.